International Business Law Practice Series

International Employment Law: The Multinational Employer and the Global Workforce

Dennis Campbell-General Editor
Director, Center for International Legal Studies
Salzburg, Austria

Editors
Christian T. Campbell
Center for International Legal Studies
Salzburg, Austria

Donald C. Dowling, Jr.
Hewitt Associates
Lincolnshire, Illinois, United States

PUBLISHED UNDER THE AUSPICES OF THE CENTER FOR INTERNATIONAL LEGAL STUDIES

Transnational Publishers, Inc.
Ardsley, New York

International Employment Law: The Multinational Employer and the Global Workforce

Dennis Campbell-General Editor
Director, Center for International Legal Studies
Salzburg, Austria

Editors
Christian T. Campbell
Center for International Legal Studies
Salzburg, Austria

Donald C. Dowling, Jr.
Hewitt Associates
Lincolnshire, Illinois, United States

Published under the auspices of the Center for International Legal Studies in cooperation with the Section of International Law and Practice of the American Bar Association and Franklin Pierce Law Center

Transnational Publishers, Inc.
Ardsley, New York

Library of Congress Cataloging-in-Publication Data

International employment law : the multinational employer and the global workforce / general editor, Dennis Campbell ; editors, Christian T. Campbell, Donald C. Dowling, Jr.
p. cm.-- (International business law practice series)
Includes bibliographical references.
ISBN 1-57105-105-8
1. Labor laws and legislation, International. 2. International business enterprises--Employees--Legal status, laws, etc. I. Campbell, Dennis. II. Campbell, Christian T. III. Dowling, Donald C. IV. Series.

K1705 .I45 2000
341.7'63--dc21

99-057991

Manufactured in the United States of America

TABLE OF CONTENTS

THE AUTHORS

Carole Basri
Deloitte & Touche LLP
Two World Financial Center, 15th Floor
New York, New York, United States 10281
Telephone: (212) 4366514
Telefax: (212) 4365989

Consultant, Deloitte & Touche. Executive Director of the Greater New York Chapter of the American Corporate Counsel Association. Educated: New York University School of Law. Co-chair, International Law Section of the New York State Bar Association on Corporate Law. Director, International Advertising Association for the United States Chapter. Member, PLI Corporate General Counsel Advisory Committee and Professional Ethics Committee of the Association of the Bar of the City of New York. Co-author, *Corporate Legal Departments* (3rd ed.).

Carl Bevernage
De Bandt, van Hecke & Lagae
Rue Brēderode 13
B1000 Brussels, Belgium
Telephone: (322) 5019411
Telefax: (322) 5019494

Partner, De Bandt, van Hecke, Lagae & Loesch. Admitted: 1970, Kortrijk; 1971, Brussels. Chairman, Ad Hoc Committee of the CCBE on liberalization of the legal profession. Educated: University of Louvain (Dr. Jur., 1967); Tulane University Law School (LL.M., 1968). Practice Areas: Employment, Pensions, Employee Benefits, Health Care. Author, "Handling Crises in International Employment Operations. Lessons from Renault, Levi Strauss and Clark Bum Reorganizations", *Institute for International Law* (1999).

Andrew J. Boling
Baker & McKenzie
One Prudential Plaza
130 East Randolph Drive
Chicago, Illinois, United States 60601
Telephone: (312) 8618000
Telefax: (312) 8612899

Partner, Baker & McKenzie. Educated: Augustana College (B.A., 1980); Illinois University (J.D., 1984). Member: American Bar Association. Admitted: 1984, Illinois. Practice Areas: Labor and Employment Law, Litigation, Arbitration, Alternative Dispute Resolution, Franchise Law.

Susanne Borch
Advokat
Jægerborg Alle 39
DK2920 Charlottenlund, Denmark
Telephone: (4539) 632383
Telefax: (4539) 632384

Susanne Borch passed the Danish Bar in 1980 and has had her own private practice since 1985, specializing national and international employment law, national and international insurance and finance, and construction law. Member, Employment and Industrial Relations Law Committee, International Bar Association. Fellow, Oxford University. Delegate, International Labor Organization, Geneva, Switzerland. Editor, *Employment and Industrial Relations Law Journal*, International Bar Association. Educated: London University (LL.M.).

Donald C. Dowling, Jr.
Hewitt Associates LCC
100 Half Day Road
Lincolnshire, Illinois, United States 60069
Telephone: (847) 2955000
Telefax: (847) 2959689

Legal Consultant, Hewitt Associates LLC. Educated: University of Chicago (A.B., 1982); University of Florida (J.D., 1985). Member, Order of Coif. Chair, American Bar Association International Employment Law Committee. Member, Board of Advisors, *Euro-Watch Newsletter*. Member, Editorial Board, *Journal of Alternative Dispute Resolution in Employment*. Co-chair, American Bar Association Section of International Law and Practice Annual Meeting, Toronto, Ontario, Canada, August 1998. Senior Editor, *International Labor and Employment Laws* (BNA/ABA, 1997).

Isabel C. Franco
Demarest & Almeida
509 Madison Avenue, Suite 509
New York, New York, United States 10022
Telephone: (212) 3719191
Telefax: (212) 3715551

Resident Partner, New York office of the Brazilian law firm of Demarest & Almeida. Educated: Universidade de Sao Paulo, School of Law (LL.B., 1978); Fordham University Law School LL.M., 1996). Admitted to the Brazilian Bar and is licensed in New York as Foreign Legal Consultant. Co-chair, Inter-American Law Committee of the American Bar Association (International Section of Law and Practice). Executive Vice-chair, New York State Bar Association (International Section of Law and Practice). Editor, New York State Bar Association International Chapter Newsletter. Member, Task Force on International Legal Services of the Association of the Bar of the City of New York. Director, Brazilian-American Chamber of Commerce in New York.

Janet M. Gaymer
Simmons & Simmons
21 Wilson Street
London EC2M 2TX, England
Telephone: 76282020
Telefax: 76282070

Partner, Simmons & Simmons and Head, Employment Law Department. Educated: Oxford University and London University (LL.M.). Past-chair, Law Society's Committee on Employment Law. Past-chair, Employment Law Sub-Committee of the City of London Solicitors Company. Founder, Chair, and Vice-President of the United Kingdom Employment Lawyers Association. Founder and Chair, European Employment Lawyers Association. Member, Council of the Advisory Conciliation and Arbitration Service. Honorary Fellow, Society for Advanced Legal Studies. Visiting Law Fellow, St. Hilda's College, Oxford.

David Greene
Edwin Coe Solicitors
2 Stone Building
Lincoln's Inn
London WC2A 3TH, England
Telephone: 6914000
Telefax: 6914050

Partner, Edwin Coe Solicitors and Head, Dispute Resolution Department. Qualified, Solicitor of the Supreme Court of England and Wales, 1980. Member, United Kingdom Government Committee on rules for procedure of civil court actions. Practice specializes in contentious employment disputes.

Sergio Karas
Karas & Associates
212 King St. W.
Toronto, Ontario M5H 1K5, Canada
Telephone: (416) 5061800
Telefax: (416) 5995582

Educated: York University (B.A.); Osgoode Hall (LL.B.). Admitted: 1988. Member, Canadian Bar Association and International Bar Association. Member, Board of Directors of Jewish Immigrant Aid Services. Member, Law Society of Upper Canada, Canadian Bar Association, International Bar Association, and Inter-Pacific Bar Association. Practice Area: Immigration Law.

Esther Kauffmann
Demarest & Almeida
509 Madison Avenue, Suite 509
New York, New York, United States 10022
Telephone: (212) 3719191
Telefax: (212) 3715551

Associate, New York office of the Brazilian law firm of Demarest & Almeida. Educated: Universidade de Sao Paulo, School of Law (1988).Member: Brazilian Bar, Sao Paulo Section. Practice areas: Corporate Law and Labor Law.

Edmund M. Kneisel
Kilpatrick Stockton LLP
Suite 2800, 1100 Peachtree Street
Atlanta, Georgia, United States 30309
Telephone: (404) 8156500
Telefax: (404) 8156555

Partner, Kilpatrick Stockton LLP. Admitted: 1974, Georgia. Educated: Duke University (A.B., 1968); University of Georgia (J.D., *cum laude*, 1974).Member, State Bar of Georgia and American Bar Association. Practice Areas: Litigation, Employment Law, and Insurance. Managing Editor, *Georgia Law Review*, 1973-1974.

Jessica Learmond-Criqui
Fladgate Fielder
25 North Row London W1R 1DJ, England
Telephone: 3234747
Telefax: 6294414

Member, Fladgate Fielder. Admitted: 1991. Educated: Kings College London (LL.B. and LL.M.). Practice Areas: Employment Law, Employee Benefits, Pensions, and Immigration Law. Co-author, *Profit-related Pay* (1995).

Fiona McLaren
Clyde & Co.
51 Eastcheap
London EC3M 1JP, England
Telephone: 6231244
Telefax: 6235427

Partner, Clyde & Co. Admitted: 1990. Practice Areas: Employment Law, including the drafting of contracts of employment, service agreements, handbooks, and policies to directors' duties and liabilities, restrictive covenants of confidential information, employment tribunal cases for unfair dismissal and discrimination cases, business transfers, and redundancy programs.

Tiziano Membri
Studio Legale
Corso Di Porta Vittoria 8
20122 Milan, Italy
Telephone: (541) 18940
Telefax: (541) 17643

Admitted: Italian Bar, 1991. Educated: Law School of the Catholic University of Milan (1988). Practice Areas: Acquisitions, Contracts, Labor Law. Author, "Italy", *International Employment Law.*

Robert J. Mignin
Seyfarth, Shaw, Fairweather & Geraldson
55 E. Monroe Street, Suite 4200
Chicago, Illinois, United States 60603-5803
Telephone: (312) 3468000
Telefax: (312) 2698869

Partner, Seyfarth, Shaw, Fairweather & Geraldson. Admitted: 1973, Illinois. Educated: Knox College (B.A., *cum laude*, 1970); University of Illinois (J.D., 1973). Practice Areas: Labor and Employment Law and Employment Litigation. Member, *University of Illinois Law Review*, 1971-1973. Member, Chicago, Illinois State Association and American Bar Association. Editor, *Federal Employment Laws and Regulations: How to Comply*, 1995; *Employment Discrimination*, 1998; *Chicagoland Employment Law Manual*, 1995.

Steven A. Miller
Seyfarth, Shaw, Fairweather & Geraldson
55 E. Monroe Street, Suite 4200
Chicago, Illinois, United States 60603-5803
Telephone: (312) 3468000
Telefax: (312) 2698869

Associate, Seyfarth, Shaw, Fairweather & Geraldson. Admitted: 1997, Illinois. Educated: University of Northern Iowa (B.A., 1992; M.A., 1993) University of Michigan (J.D., 1997). Member, Chicago Bar Association and Illinois State Bar Association. Practice Areas: Labor, Employment, and Discrimination Law. Executive Production Editor, *Michigan Journal of International Law*.

Douglas M. Nabhan
Williams, Mullen, Christian & Dobbins
Two James Center
1021 East Cary Street
P.O. Box 1320
Richmond, Virginia, United States 23218-1320
Telephone: (804) 6431991
Telefax: (804) 7836507

Partner, Williams, Mullen, Christian & Dobbins. Admitted: 1984, Virginia; 1997, United States Court of Appeals, Sixth Circuit. Educated: Purdue University (B.S., 1977); Cumberland Law School; University of Richmond (M.B.A., 1981; J.D., 1984). Member, American Bar Association, *Omicron Delta Kappa*, Order of Barristers, *Cumberland Law Review* National Moot Court Team. Recipient, Emerson G. Spies Award, 1991. Author, "The Jencks Rule", *Labor Law Journal*, 1994. Practice Areas: Labor and Employment Law.

Octavio Novaro H.
Barrera, Siqueiros y Torres-Landa, S.C.
Montes Urales 470 - Piso 1
Lomas de Chapultepec
11000 Mexico, D.F., Mexico
Telephone: (525) 5408000
Telefax: (525) 5205115

Senior Associate, Barrera, Siqueiros y Torres-Landa. Educated: National Autonomous University of Mexico (1992); Universidad Panamericana (Labor Law, 1993).

Jack A. Raisner
Outten & Golden LLP
1740 Broadway, 25th Floor
New York, New York, United States 10019
Telephone: (212) 2451000
Telefax: (212) 9774005

Associate, Outten & Golden LLP. Associate Professor, St. John's University. Admitted: 1984, New York; 1985, United States District Court, Southern District of New York. Educated: Boston University (B.S., 1978); Benjamin N. Cardozo School of Law (J.D., 1983). Practice Areas: Labor and Employment Law, and Civil Litigation. Member, American Bar Association (Co-chair, Drug and Alcohol in the Workplace Subcommittee) and National Employment Lawyers Association. Co-author, *Employee Rights Litigation: Pleading and PracticeD (1992); Disability Discrimination in the Workplace* (1992); "Cross Examining a Defense Psychologist in a Sexual Harassment Case", *The Practical Litigator*, 1993; "Off Duty Conduct," *New York University 47th National Conference on Labor* (1994); "Employment Litigation in the Second Circuit District Courts," 14 *Quinn. L. Rev.* 707, 1994; *New York Employment Complaints and Answers/FAST* (1995); *Employment Litigation in New York* (1996); "EEOC Resolves 'Untenable Choice' for Disabled Employees, or Does It?", *N.Y.L.J.*, 1997; and *Employment Law, General Practice in New York* (1998). Author, 4th Supplement, *New York Employment Law* (1995); "Employees Face Danger Under New York's Whistleblower Statute", *N.Y.L.J.*, 1996.

Charles M. Rice
Kilpatrick Stockton LLP
Suite 2800, 1100 Peachtree Street
Atlanta, Georgia, United States 30309-4530
Telephone: (404) 8156500
Telefax: (404) 8156555

Associate, Kilpatrick Stockton LLP. Admitted: 1979, Georgia; 1980, South Carolina. Educated: Georgia State University (B.A., *summa cum laude*, 1976); University of Georgia (J.D., *cum laude*, 1979). Practice Areas: Employment Disability Discrimination, Personnel Policies, and Family and Medical Leave Act. Member, Editorial Board, *Georgia Law Review*, 1977-1978. Author, "Give Me A Break! State Laws On Meal Periods, Rest Breaks, and Maximum Working Hours," 24 *Employment Relations Today*, 113 (Autumn 1997); "State As Well As Federal Red Tape Ties Up Employment-Related Consumer Reports," 25 *Employment Relations Today*, 85 (Spring 1998); "A Primer for Foreign Investors in Mexico-Hiring, Firing and Mandated Benefits," 5 *Latin American Law and Business Report*, 2 (July 31, 1997).

Mario E. Castro Sammartino
Attorney and Counselor at Law
Talcahuano 768, Piso 7 (1013)
Buenos Aires, Argentina
Telephone: (5411) 43719990
Telefax: (5411) 43719990

Professor of Law, Universidad Argentina de la Empresa) and Universidad Catolica Argentina. Admitted: 1987, Argentina. Educated: Universidad de Buenos Aires (Law) and Universidad Católic Argentina (Law). Member, Public Bar Association of Buenos Aires and Bar Association of Buenos Aires. Honorary Fellow, Center for International Legal Studies. Practice Areas: Corporate Law and Commercial Law. Author, *Commercial Law Handbook*; *Commercial Companies Law*; *Insurance Law*.

Christopher Seaton
Burges Salmon
Narrow Quay House
Narrow Quay
Bristol BS1 4AH, England
Telephone: (44117) 9392000
Telefax: (44117) 9024400

Partner, Burges Salmon. Admitted as Solicitor, 1993. Educated: B.Sc. (Hons.). Member, Employment Lawyers' Association and South West Employment Tribunal Users Committee.

Nancy J. Sedmak
Bureau of National Affairs Inc.
1231 25th Street, N.W.
Washington, D.C., United States 200037
Telephone: (202) 4524200
Telefax: (202) 4524610

Managing Editor, *Labor Relations Reporter*. Educated: Chatham College (B.A.), Columbus School of Law of Catholic University of America (J.D.), and University of Leicester (LL.M.). Past-president, District of Columbia Chapter, Industrial Relations Research Association. Member, Pennsylvania Bar, American Bar Association Section of Labor and Employment Law, Section of International Law and Practice, and Section on Individual Rights and Responsibilities and the International Society for Labor Law and Social Security. Co-author, *Primer On Equal Employment Opportunity*. Contributor, *Labor Arbitration. A Practical Guide For Advocates* and *International Labor and Employment Laws*.

D. Bruce Shine
Shine & Mason
Suite 201, 433 East Center Street
Kingsport, Tennessee, United States 37660
Telephone: (423) 2468433
Telefax: (423) 2467464

Partner, Shine & Mason. Admitted: 1964. Educated: Tusculum College (B.S., 1960), Vanderbilt University (J.D., 1964); Columbia University Graduate School of Law (1965); University of Leicester, United Kingdom (LL.M., European Management and Employment Law, 1999). Fellow, American Bar Foundation. Member, American Bar Association and District of Columbia Bar. Practice Areas: Employment Law, Administrative Law, Education Law, Construction Law, and Employee Stock Ownership Plans. Certified Mediator, United States District Court, Eastern District of Tennessee, 1996; Commissioner, Alternative Dispute Resolution Commission of the Tennessee Supreme Court, 1996-. Certified Mediator, State of Tennessee, 1997. Author, "The European Union's Efforts To Allow Professionals To Cross Borders To Practice Their Calling", 49 *Labor Law Journal*, No, 2 (February 1998); "Can the NLRB Help Cinderella and Little Orphan Annie?", 47 *Labor Law Journal*, No. 11 (November 1996); "A Primer on Unemployment Insurance Law for the General Practitioner," 23 *Tennessee Bar Journal*, No. 2, 1987; "The Employment-at-Will Doctrine - Time to Terminate, But How?", 18 *Tennessee Bar Journal*, No. 4, 1982; "A Survey of Tennessee Labor Cases Since 1954", 47 Tennessee Law Review, No. 2, Winter 1980; "Finally, A Federal Remedy for Discharged Workmen's Compensation Claimants in Tennessee", 16 *Tennessee Bar Journal*, No. l, February 1980; "The Psychology of Faculty Unions in the Seventies", 16 *International Journal Instructional Media*, No. 1, 1979-1980; "The October '76 Term Revolution - End of an Era? New Trends in Race and Religious Employment Discrimination", 13 *Tennessee Bar Journal*, No. 4, 1977. Co-Author, "ESOP: The American Workers' Leveraged Buyout", 95 *Case & Comment*, No. 1, 1990.

Patrick Thiebart
Caubet Chouchana Meyer
49 Champs Elysees
75008 Paris, France
Telephone: (331) 40754075
Telefax: (331) 40754040

Partner, Caubet Chouchana Meyer. Admitted, 1992, Paris Bar. Educated: University of Paris (Maitrise en Droit Prive, 1985; DEN in European Law, 1988). Diploma, Centre Universitaire d'Etudes des Communautés Européennes, 1987. Member: International Bar Association (Section on Business Law); Association of European Employment Lawyers; French Competition Law Association; Franco-British Lawyers Society; Association Française des Avocats Conseils d 'Entreprises. Author, "L'Avanée de la Construction Communautaire en Matière de Politique des Transports", *Gazette du Palais*, February 9-10, 1994; "France", in "Unfair Trade Practices", *Comparative Law Yearbook of International Business* (1996). Practice Areas: Employment and Labor Law, Commercial Law, Litigation, and Arbitration.

Juan Francisco Torres-Landa R.
Barrera, Siqueiros y Torres-Landa, S.C.
Montes Urales 470 - Piso 1
Lomas de Chapultepec
11000 Mexico, D.F., Mexico
Telephone: (525) 5408000
Telefax: (525) 5205115

Partner, Barrera, Siqueiros y Torres Landa, S.C. Admitted: 1988. Educated: National Autonomous University of Mexico (Lic. en Derecho, 1988); Harvard University (LL.M., 1990). Practice Areas: Corporate Law, Foreign Investment, International Trade, Environmental, Antitrust, and Mining and Minerals. Member: International Bar Association.

Miguel A. Zaldivar
Steel Hector & Davis LLP
200 South Biscayne Boulevard
Miami, Florida, United States 33131-2398
Telephone: (305) 5777000
Telefax: (305) 5777001

Partner, Steel Hector & Davis LLP. Admitted: 1986, Venezuela; 1995, Florida; 1997, District of Columbia. Educated: Universidad Católica Andrés Bello, Venezuela (LL.B., 1986); University of Illinois (LL.M., 1988); University of Miami (J.D., *cum laude*, 1995). Practice Areas: International Law, Corporate Law, Employment Law, Project Finance, and Privatization. Fulbright Scholar, 1987-1988. Professor of Law, Universidad Católica Andrés Bello, Labor Law, 1991-1993. Visiting Professor, IESA, Caracas, Management for Lawyers, 1990. Director, Venezuelan-American Chamber of Commerce of Florida, 1994.

PREFACE

This book documents a breakthrough in how practitioners address international employment law problems – a breakthrough that happened when "multinational" companies recognized the need to become "global".

Previous works on international employment law have focused on comparative employment laws; that is, earlier books collected up summaries of various countries' internal domestic employment doctrines, explaining *seriatim* the main employment rules in selected countries.

Many of these books proved to be a useful resource. They are the tools a practitioner picks up first in helping a client with a quick, specific question on foreign employment law – a one-off inquiry, such as: "Does South Africa really have a new affirmative action law?" Or, "Can we still impose a mandatory retirement age in Europe?" Or, "Why is our Mexican plant manager insisting we pay everyone a Christmas bonus and 10 per cent profit-sharing?" While useful, however, such publications do not substitute for the local counsel needed for more sticky overseas employment problems.

Until the very recent push among multinational employers to become truly "global" corporations, a set of good books summarizing the world's local employment laws and a comprehensive rolodex of employment lawyers around the world were all one needed to solve international employment law problems.

In those days, multinational employers were content operating as networks of discrete local (or regional) business units. This meant the "international" employment law questions that came up involved some foreign country's law. For example, a multinational headquartered in Country "A" might have confronted an employment issue arising in its operations in Country "B" or Country "C". Lawyers at headquarters would look into the local laws of the affected countries, engaging local counsel as necessary.

This process worked fine as long as multinationals' employment operations remained collections of largely autonomous local (or regional) operations. But this model fell apart with the emergence of the truly global corporation. The change came when technology (e.g., e-commerce, telecommunications, transportation) and global free trade (under the World Trade Organization) pushed the business world to recognize that the third millennium will be the first era of genuinely global commence.

Multinationals fearing they can no longer operate as collections of localized business units are now scrambling to "go global". They are re-engineering their entire business structures — starting with marketing, production, and sourcing — to take advantage of the new technologies, new trade rules, and new global efficiencies that are evolving into the new global market.

Consumer-products giant Procter & Gamble provides an example. Procter & Gamble unveiled a program called "Organization 2005" in which the formerly Cincinnati-based multinational is reshuffling the headquarters of its various business lines, dealing them out to cities around the planet. Procter & Gamble "home care" goes off to Brussels, Belgium, "food and beverage" moves to Caracas, Venezuela, and "feminine protection" lands in Kobe, Japan. World headquarters for the Procter & Gamble "baby care" line stays in Cincinnati, Ohio.

When multinationals like Procter & Gamble talk about "going global", they are quick to discuss outward-focused aspects of their business (i.e., marketing, production, and sourcing). But eventually any serious multinational realizes a truly global company is, first and most importantly, internally global. By definition, a global company's talent – the people who make up the company – must operate as a global team (or a network of global teams), not as a network of autonomous business units organized by country or region.

In a real global company, decision-making is decentralized. Superior/subordinate relationships span national borders. Project teams include members in various nations. Co-workers work together across oceans, linked not by proximity of offices, but by technology. No company can operate this way under the old model of localized employee relations.

Co-workers, team members, and superior/subordinate relationships simply will not function globally if all the players are operating out of different local playbooks (that is, if each has different work policies, different incentives, different motivators, different rules). Truly global teams emerge only after an employer structures talent-management from a global perspective.

It is easy for any company to decide to globalize its talent. But many major legal questions block the road.

How can a multinational motivate an integrated global "team" when only certain team members (depending on their home countries) get stock options and the protection of harassment policies, while others get profit-sharing and generous annual bonuses, and still others receive lengthy vacations, paid leave, and short workweeks?

How can a multinational be global when its approach to collective bargaining is national and the collective agreements governing its workforce therefore differ radically from location to location, blocking efforts to globalize production?

How can an employer be global when its code of conduct and policies all spring full-blown from the home office, and overseas employees see these documents as "headquarters imperialism"?

Unfortunately for lawyers and consultants, global employment questions like these do not lend themselves to the old model. The answers are not to be found in a compendium of the world's local employment laws; nor can the more difficult issues be shifted to a local labor lawyer abroad. Rather, thee global employment questions require big-picture, crossborder advice which simultaneously accounts for employment laws and practices everywhere that an employer operates.

Components of these questions might be referred out for local input. However, a global corporation needs a global employment practitioner to oversee global employment projects, synthesizing various local-law responses into a single global solution. The legal questions which arise in addressing global talent management are complex matters spanning all the countries in play, and headquarters, too.

The problems do not get resolved by looking up summaries of local employment laws in some comparative employment law treatise.

Which leads to the purpose of this book, i.e., to serve as a starting-point for a multinational company addressing all the crossborder legal issues inherent in globalizing its talent.

Apart from the final section of this book (a quick, traditional comparative-law tour of selected local employment laws around the world), this publication speaks to the advisor needing context to help a multinational company deal with the talent issues inherent in integrating human resources globally.

Chapters in this book touch on the most pressing employment matters which are inherently crossborder, such as managing employee loyalty worldwide; choice-of-law issues in crossborder employment disputes; global talent management; harmonizing policies, work conditions, and incentives worldwide; employment issues in international acquisitions; global business ethics issues in employment, including codes of conduct and crisis management; and collective-representation issues in the global workplace.

Incidentally, while the discussion here has taken the point of view of a global employer, much of this book addresses practitioners who represent individual employees and labor unions caught up in crossborder employment. As the workplace becomes truly global, the crossborder employment issues that emerge equally affect employers and employees and their representatives.

Unfortunately, this book by itself is not going to answer every crossborder employment law question that arises as a multinational transforms itself into a global corporation. However, as the first work dedicated to inherently crossborder employment issues, it is a start. The hope is that, as the multinational companies of the new millennium become the global employers they strive to be, solutions will emerge for the many problems in this area still unresolved.

Donald C. Dowling, Jr.

Global Legal Consultant, Hewitt Associates

Lincolnshire, Illinois, United States

Part I

The Practice of International Employment Law

CHAPTER 1

INTERNATIONAL LABOR AND EMPLOYMENT LAW — PRACTICE AND CONSULTING

Donald C. Dowling, Jr.
Hewitt Associates LCC
Lincolnshire, Illinois, United States

A. INTRODUCTION

When lawyers and clients think of private international law, they usually think of international business transactions. On further reflection, many realize that tax, securities, and litigation all can also have international components — such as when a client company earns profits, sells shares, and gets into disputes in a number of countries.

However, every single area of private law practice has its international counterpart. International criminal law can mean representing clients charged with crimes, such as drug dealing, committed across national boundaries. International estate law can mean representing estates with assets in more than one country. International environmental law can mean representing alleged polluters whose emissions drift across national boundaries.

Most lawyers would see employment law as a purely local area of law practice — any one country's employment laws will apply at the situs of employment. Even if a multinational company is based, say, in Canada, and has a factory, say, in France, Canadian employment law would seem to cover the company's Canadian employees, and French employment law would cover the French. Such a company might therefore need a Canadian employment lawyer and a French employment lawyer. However, there would not seem to be any role for an international employment lawyer.

This view has served well over the years. However, it ignores the global realities of business in the new millennium. As business becomes more global, as expatriate employment becomes more common, as worldwide communications become more fluid, and as labor unions become more internationally savvy, there is increasing pressure on multinational companies to harmonize employment, compensation, and benefit practices. Why are companies' managers subject to mandatory retirement except in the United States, where age discrimination is illegal? Why does eligibility for stock options turn on an employee's country of residence and not his performance? Why does an ombudsman exist to address sex harassment complaints, but only those coming from certain of a company's facilities? How can a United States company draft effective harassment policies when United States discrimination laws apply abroad, but only to United States citizen employees? How can a multinational human resources staff centralize personnel data without running afoul of data privacy laws? Why do expatriates from Europe insist on long vacations when they are assigned to the United States? How can a company's single code of conduct against sweatshop labor apply in its operations (and its suppliers' operations) around the world? How can a company that is globalizing its sourcing, production, and distribution get its local unions to cooperate? How does a company shutting down facilities in a number of countries explain why certain employees get generous severance pay, others get generous notice, and others get almost nothing? How does an acquirer in an acquisition do due diligence when the target company has employment operations in a handful of countries? And, how does an employer integrate its culture after a deal, when radical differences exist in employment conditions, work rules, and pay?

Although the vast majority of employment lawyers still have purely local practices, clients, i.e., multinational companies, expatriate employees, and aggressive unions, have very real needs for crossborder employment law advice which are not yet being met. There is an emerging market for counselors who can speak to crossborder employment law.

This chapter examines what it means to practice "international employment law". The starting point here is the monumental distinction between the "employment-at-will" doctrine of the United States and the "indefinite employment" concept of Civil Law countries. Although, of course, international employment law practice arises in contexts not linked to the United States, the distinction between employment-at-will and indefinite employment points up a key contrast which touches on critical aspects of international employment law practice in many contexts. After exploring this distinction, this chapter looks briefly at what international employment law is and discusses what it is not. It then focuses on two key trade blocs, i.e., NAFTA and the EU, and their effect on international employment law practice.

B. WHY UNITED STATES LAWYERS ARE AT A DISADVANTAGE IN INTERNATIONAL EMPLOYMENT ISSUES

In the United States, employment lawyers and international[1] transactional lawyers (corporate lawyers who work on crossborder deals) tend not to work any closer together than do, say, divorce lawyers and environmental lawyers, or securities lawyers and patent lawyers. In fact — even though almost all United States

---

1 As used in this chapter, "international" means crossborder; that is, an issue involving two countries — usually the country where an employer corporation is based, and another country where it is employing workers. "International" is distinct from "foreign" or "comparative" employment law issues, which are issues relating to a nation other than that of the speaker.

employers are organized as some form of corporation — in the United States, employment law is a completely separate practice area from corporate (transactional) law. In the United States, the practice or legal concentration of "employment law" on crossborder employment law matters and that of "international law" are worlds apart, and this distance causes problems.[2] As compared to lawyers from other countries, United States lawyers are at an unfortunate disadvantage.

This situation contrasts sharply with many other countries, where lawyers and clients see employment law as a sub-category of corporate law. "Corporate law" in these countries involves all the laws relating to corporations — necessarily including the rules governing a corporation's relationships with its employees. Accordingly, much of the world outside the United States fashions a substantially closer link between employment law practice and corporate practice (including corporate international law practice). In many other countries, employment law is to corporate law as in the United States, for example, environmental law is to real estate law, or personal tax law is to estate planning: The practice areas are distinct yet interrelated. Any competent specialist in one must be more than vaguely familiar with the doctrines of the other.

In this specific regard, corporations outside the United States tend to be better represented on the employment law effects of their crossborder transactions than do clients of United States international lawyers. Outside the United States, transactional lawyers are trained to spot, for example, issues of:

(1) Early works council and labor ministry notification of mergers;

(2) Vesting of benefits granted to employees of start-up units such as joint venture companies;

(3) Transfers of employees' acquired rights in mergers and acquisitions;

(4) Severance pay liabilities in corporate restructurings; and

(5) Unionizations or applications of multi-employer collective agreements in new employer entities without formal representation elections.

---

2 In the United States, the phrase "employment law" means law related to non-union employees, while "labor law" means law related to union-member employees in an employer collective bargaining unit. However, as used in this chapter, "employment law" speaks generally to both labor and employment law.

United States companies represented by United States international lawyers have, in the past, lost considerably because their United States-trained international counsel failed to advise them on these issues during the early stages of a deal.[3]

In crossborder transactions, United States international lawyers tend not to miss issues of, for example, foreign environmental law, tax law, or securities law. This is because these foreign laws tend to arise abroad in the same contexts as they arise in the United States. Even without the answers, United States international lawyers know when to ask the right foreign environmental, tax, and securities law questions. This unfortunately is not the case regarding foreign employment laws, for three reasons: The confusing influence of the United States employment-at-will doctrine, the lulling influence of the low United States union representation rate, and the distracting influence of United States discrimination law.

1. Confusing Influence of the United States Employment-at-Will Doctrine

The reason employment issues in the United States often do not arise in the same context as they do abroad has a lot to do with the employment-at-will doctrine,[4] which is the starting point for United States employment relationships. Even though United States employment lawyers will say exceptions have eroded the common law employment-at-will doctrine, the doctrine remains the starting point of United States employment relationships. This is not the case in much of the rest of the world, including the birthplace of employment-at-will, England.[5]

---

[3] For examples by this author, see "International Labor and Employment Law", chapter 23 in Low, Norton, and Drory (eds.), *The International Lawyer's Deskbook,* at pp. 347–353 (1996); "Labor and Employment Law in the International Context", chapter 22, in Nanda (ed.), *The Law of Transnational Business Transactions* (1996 & supp.) at pp. 17–18, reprinted in 9 *International Quarterly* 585 (1997); "Preparing for the Internationalization of United States Employment Law Practice", 43 *Labor Law Journal,* at pp. 350, 355 and 360 (1992); with Honig, "How to Handle Employment Issues in International Deals, 13 *Preventive Law Rep.*, Number 1, at pp. 3, 3–4 and 6–7 (Spring 1994).

[4] The United States employment-at-will doctrine dates at least to the English case of Lumely v. Gye, 118 Eng. Rep. 749 (QB 1853). The doctrine holds that the standard employment relationship is a contract which either party is free to terminate at any time — to quit or fire — without liability for damages relating to the future. A terminable-at-will employment contract is every bit as binding as any other contract; for example, an employee-at-will has an enforceable contractual right to wages for any period already worked. A terminable-at-will contract simply does not contain any term by which either party commits to future performance. Dowling, "A Contract Theory for a Complex Tort: Limiting Interference with Contract Beyond the Unlawful Means Test", 40 *University of Miami Law Review* 487, at pp. 502–504 (1986), reprinted in 35 *Defense Law Journal* 503, at pp. 520–523 (1986).

[5] Current English law generally requires employers to pay severance to fired employees (fired other than for cause) who have two or more years' tenure on the job. (The two-year requirement is being reduced to one year.) Also, consistent with a European Union Directive, current English law requires employers to provide workers with a contractual document which sets out all the important terms and conditions of employment which the employer will grant to the employee during the employment relationship, including what constitutes cause for termination. As a result, British employment law solicitors do not see the United Kingdom as an employment-at-will jurisdiction.

United States international lawyers have a hard time spotting foreign employment issues because, outside of the United States, corporations' employment relationships tend not to be primarily governed by private arrangements which corporations voluntarily enter with their employees. Rather, in most industrialized countries outside the United States, once someone becomes an employee of an employer, a comprehensive and paternalistic set of legal rules automatically governs the relationship.

The most significant such rule that generally applies abroad is the so-called doctrine of "indefinite employment" (often claimed to be more accurately called the doctrine of "infinite employment"). Outside the United States, generally, the employment relationship is not freely terminable at an employer's will. Although employees everywhere are free to quit when they want, employers outside the United States who fire workers without cause often must pay hefty severance amounts which — such as workers' compensation awards — are easily calculable in many countries.[6] Outside the United States and Canada, severance liability is rarely linked to discrimination. To get severance pay, fired workers do not need to claim that the real reason for the discharge was membership in a protected group. Severance awards in Europe can amount to hundreds of thousands of dollars (several years' pay). Severance liabilities even in less developed areas, such as Latin America, reach levels that often surprise United States lawyers and employers.

Countries outside the United States go beyond the "indefinite" employment doctrine and regulate other areas that, stateside, are left to the generosity of the employer. Because legal systems outside the United States view the employer-employee relationship as a creature of state-imposed rules and not as a private contract, foreign jurisdictions tend to regulate the employment relationship far more intrusively than does the United States. Vacation leave and maternity leave are two illustrative examples.

a. *Vacation and Holidays*

The United States is virtually alone among major countries, both industrialized and not industrialized, in not requiring employers to grant vacation and holidays, paid or unpaid. United States employers can legally refuse to give employees even one day off per year for vacations and holidays. Indeed, the number of annual vacation days which United States employers tend to give voluntarily is substantially lower than the legally-mandated vacation periods in much of the rest of the world, both industrialized and not industrialized.

---

[6] In the case of severance pay, often as a mathematical function of the workers' age, job tenure, and pay rate.

According to a press release of June 11, 1999, by Hewitt Associates L.L.C. of Lincolnshire, Illinois, United States:

> Typically, United States companies determine vacation time based on length of service, while vacation time in other countries is often mandated by law, regardless of length of time on the job. Typically, United States employees reaching 15 or more years of service are granted vacation allowances comparable to those mandated by government in other countries [for recent hires]. . . .

Indeed, a survey found that "paid vacation" is the most frequently granted employee benefit at small and mid-sized United States businesses, being granted by 72 per cent of those firms, meaning that 28 per cent of small and mid-sized United States employers fail to provide paid vacation.[7]

b. *Maternity Leave*

Until 1993, the United States had no law requiring employers to give women time off to bear children. Also, the law which the United States ultimately did pass[8] (trumpeted as a key achievement of President Clinton's first term) is not too significant by non-United States standards, because it does not even require United States employers to pay anything to women on leave. By contrast, laws in other countries, both industrialized and not industrialized, require employers to:

(1) Grant leave before and after giving birth;

(2) Pay women all or most of their regular pay during the leave[9]; and

(3) In some countries, require employers to provide on-site childcare.[10]

Europe and countries elsewhere are even now requiring that employers grant paternity leave to fathers.

Indeed, even the legal systems of less industrialized countries require employers to grant employees terms of employment that are decades ahead of United States law. For example, Mexico's constitution requires employers to set aside 10 per cent of annual profits for employee profit sharing, and the Mexican constitution prohibits enforcing most non-compete agreements. Mexican law even requires hefty year-end bonuses (*aguïnaldo*), so Mexican workers end up with at least 54 or 56 weeks' pay

---

7 Crain's Chicago Business, July 5, 1999, p. F16.

8 United States Family and Medical Leave Act, 29 United States Code, sections 2601 *et seq.*

9 See European Union Council Directive Concerning the Protection at Work of Pregnant Women, or Women Who Have Recently Given Birth, Directive 92/85, *Official Journal* (Number L348) (October 1, 1992) (harmonizing maternity pay laws which had existed previously, for decades, in most of the European Union member states).

10 Venezuela Labor Law, *Venezuelan Official Gazette*, December 20, 1990.

per year. As another example, Venezuelan law contains a far-reaching concept of constructive discharge under which even employees who quit make claims for severance pay.

2. Lulling Influence of the Low United States Union Representation Rate

Putting aside the effect of the difference in legal systems, another reason United States lawyers tend not to spot foreign employment law issues involves an unfortunate tendency to overlook issues involving foreign labor unions and worker representative bodies. This problem arises from the very low rate of union representation in the United States non-government workforce: Although nearly omnipresent abroad, unions are not on the radar screen of many United States lawyers.

In addition, the United States law that prevents employer-dominated unions effectively makes illegal in the United States the in-house worker representative groups, such as works councils, which are so common abroad. Most United States lawyers never think about worker consultation, worker participation, works councils, and laws requiring employers to notify worker representatives (and government officials) of business changes. When these United States lawyers do crossborder deals, they tend to neglect these issues — sometimes at their clients' substantial expense.

Indeed, United States lawyers in sectors like service industries and the computer industry (which stateside are not broadly unionized) have been known to negotiate foreign acquisitions without asking anything about the collective bargaining agreement their United States client would inherit. Other United States companies have opened up foreign factories without realizing a union could (and often does) come to represent the new workforce without advance notice or even an election.[11] Also, United States companies doing foreign deals often neglect to ask for the multi-employer collective bargaining agreement in the target industry — which sets out terms and conditions of employment, including pay rates, even for non-signatory companies.

3. Distracting Influence of United States Discrimination Law

Yet another reason United States lawyers tend to miss employment issues in the international context relates to the distracting influence of United States

---

[11] "International Labor and Employment Law", chapter 23 in Low, Norton, and Drory (eds.), *The International Lawyer's Deskbook,* at pp. 347–353 (1996); Dowling, "Labor and Employment Law in the International Context", chapter 22 in Nanda (ed.), *The Law of Transnational Business Transactions* (1996 and supplement) at pp. 17 and 18, reprinted in 9 *International Quarterly* 585 (1997); Dowling, "Preparing for the Internationalization of United States Employment Law Practice", 43 *Labor Law Journal*, pp. 350, 355, 360 (1992); Dowling and Honig, "How to Handle Employment Issues in International Deals", 13 *Preventive Law Rep.* Number 1, at pp. 3, and 4, and 6 and 7 (Spring 1994).Venezuela Labor Law, *Venezuelan Official Gazette*, December 20, 1990.

discrimination law. As the United States employment law system evolved in its employment-at-will context, the perceived unfairness of certain employer behaviors naturally led to calls to legislate protections for employees.

However, because the employment-at-will doctrine was antithetical to legislation paralleling that in other countries requiring "indefinite" length employment, severance pay, and paid vacations, holidays, and maternity leaves, United States legislatures ended up prohibiting only discrimination on the grounds of membership in certain protected groups. United States employees who are not members of these groups often have no remedy for grossly unfair firings, and members of protected groups are often forced to articulate valid objections as discrimination even when the employer may have acted more inhumanely than discriminatorily.

The result is that United States discrimination law has become the most far-reaching body of discrimination law on the planet, and it has come almost to swallow up United States non-union sector employment law. When United States employers complain about the high costs that United States employment law imposes on their businesses, they generally refer only to the unpredictable and often astronomical costs of specific discrimination claims brought by specific women and minorities. They are not talking about across-the-board costs such as those imposed in other countries.

United States employment lawyers are so alert to the nuances of discrimination law that they are quick to express shock at the shortage overseas of comprehensive equal employment, affirmative action, and harassment policies. However, before criticizing foreign legal systems as inadequate in protecting victims of discrimination, a lawyer needs to factor in the many protections abroad which apply to all employees, not merely those in specially protected groups. Many foreign countries do not need heavy-handed discrimination laws, not only because these countries do not bear the legacy of Indian massacres, slavery and segregation that the United States bears, but also because these countries' across-the-board employment protections by definition apply to members of special groups.

The larger point is that United States employment lawyers steeped in discrimination law are often totally unprepared even to ask the right questions regarding employment laws of other countries. The employment-at-will doctrine, the unique status of unions in the United States, and the paramount role of United States discrimination law all combine to create a gulf between the practice of law in the United States (and parts of Canada), and the rest of the world.

C. WHAT "INTERNATIONAL LABOR AND EMPLOYMENT LAW" IS NOT — AND WHAT IT IS

United States lawyers need to know what international employment law is because it is the home base for so many giant multinational companies, which in total employ millions of workers abroad, because it hosts so many foreign-owned employment operations, and because it is home to so many professionals who at one time or another in their career work abroad as expatriates.

However, too often, United States lawyers lack even knowledge of what issues are at play in the international employment law universe. An example of this ignorance occured at an important conference of United States lawyers, held in August 1998. One program was titled "Employment Issues for Multinational Employers and Employees". However, the program failed to address even one of the core issues relevant to multinationals that make up international employment law practice:

(1) Hiring and firing abroad;

(2) Complying with foreign employment laws;

(3) Addressing conflicts of employment laws applied to expatriates and third country nationals;

(4) Harmonizing compensation and employee benefits among international operations;

(5) Designing expatriate employment policies;

(6) Applying and ensuring compliance of human resources policies in the international context;

(7) Accounting for employment liabilities which arise in international business transactions;

(8) Ensuring employment operations comply with laws having extraterritorial effect (such as the United States Foreign Corrupt Practices Act and Europe's data privacy laws);

(9) Drafting corporate codes of conduct and confronting the "sweatshop" labor dilemma;

(10) Coordinating collective bargaining regionally and addressing labor unions' crossborder boycotts and appeals regarding overseas labor standards; and

(11) Complying with the employment requirements of international trade treaties.

Rather than touch on even one of these topics, the August 1998 "Employment Issues for Multinational Employers and Employees" conference addressed one subject which is not really part of international employment at all (domestic United States immigration law, which is chiefly relevant to United States employers employing immigrants domestically within the United States), and two subjects which have only marginal application to the full scope of international employment law, namely:

(1) The reach of United States domestic discrimination statutes to employers not based in the United States; and

(2) The extraterritorial effect of United States employment law.

Both areas are infrequently litigated and rarely arise in the course of most United States employment lawyers' careers.

The mistake that the August 1998 conference organizers made was that they addressed nothing more than United States federal statutes (albeit statutes which sometimes affect multinational employers). While the conference did offer excellent coverage of "United States Federal Statutes Affecting Multinational Employers", it did not address the core topics affecting multinational employers and employees. Any lawyer who wants to represent clients on "Employment Issues for Multinational Employers and Employees" must venture far beyond the familiar waters of home-country statutes and learn at least something about foreign legal systems, conflicts of laws, treaties, human rights, and international business transactions.

The practice of international employment law looks less to any one country's domestic employment statutes having extraterritorial effect, and more to the sum of all the domestic employment laws of all the affected countries in the world. If an employer wants to roll out a stock option plan for employees in all the countries in which it does business, it will need to study the employment, benefits, securities, and tax laws of each country in which it wants to issue options. Any employer wishing to implement a viable sweatshop/child labor code of conduct must learn the minimum labor standards laws of all countries in which the code will apply.

Any employer planning to implement a new quality and sourcing process in its factories around the world will have to study its individual, collective, and works council agreements around the world. Any company planning to buy the assets of a global competitor and then consolidate operations can do nothing until it accounts for laws, practices, labor agreements, and the employment culture of every affected country. The August 1998 conference addressed none of these issues.

It is unfortunate for employment lawyers — who are licensed and expert in the laws of only one country — that private international employment law arises out of the whole of all the world's employment systems. Those lawyers comfortable with only their home country's domestic employment laws are best advised to stick to the practice of their domestic home-country employment law.

D. TRADE BLOCS AND THEIR EFFECT ON CROSSBORDER EMPLOYMENT ISSUES

While international employment law is the sum of all the world's employment laws, there is yet another dimension to consider: Employment laws of multi-jurisdictional bodies. Some employment doctrines emerge from global bodies such as the World Trade Organization and its General Agreement on Trade in Services. The International Labor Organization propounds broad treaties on employment policy, and trade regions such as MERCOSUR may be developing employment doctrine.

Yet, currently, the two most significant multi-jurisdictional bodies which produce binding employment rules are the European Union and the North American Free Trade Agreement.

1. North American Free Trade Agreement

Employment lawyers from the United States, Canada, and Mexico who focus on international issues will have a particular interest in employment law practice under the North American Free Trade Agreement (NAFTA) and its labor side agreement, the North American Agreement on Labor Cooperation (NAALC). However, while the increased commerce among the three NAFTA States naturally gives rise to all the standard international employment law concerns discussed elsewhere in this chapter, virtually nothing in NAFTA or in the NAALC creates either legal issues for multinational companies or law practice/consulting opportunities for lawyers. This section explains why.

The more worker-friendly regulation of employment in countries outside the United States (specifically Mexico) had a significant effect on the genesis of the NAALC labor side agreement. Originally, United States organized labor and champions of the rights of United States workers strongly opposed ratifying NAFTA due to the fear that free trade with Mexico would "suc[k]" away United States jobs.[12]

When NAFTA was still being negotiated, United States organized labor and United States workers' rights groups argued that if the North American countries were to enjoy free trade, they first needed a playing field leveled by consistent labor laws under which one country (Mexico) did not have a competitive advantage by employing workers under lower "labor standards".[13]

---

[12] *International Labor and Employment Laws,* volume 1 (1997) (BNA), chapter 20, "NAFTA/NAALC," at pp. 20–23. While productivity in Mexico has historically been lower than in the United States — meaning that for every United States job "lost" to Mexico more than one Mexican is likely to be employed — those in the United States who opposed NAFTA on employment grounds tended not to acknowledge the probabililty that any shift in jobs from the United States to Mexico would increase total employment.

[13] *International Labor and Employment Laws,* volume 1 (1997) (BNA), chapter 20, "NAFTA/NAALC," at pp. 20–23. ("in the absence of uniform labor standards throughout the three member states, [United States] labor leaders feared that United States employers would be tempted to close many of their [United States] plants and relocate in Mexico...").

United States organized labor argued that before entering NAFTA, Mexico should have to raise its "labor standards" up to the standards of United States law. However, that, of course, appeared difficult: "Mexico had ratified many more of the ILO Conventions" than had the United States, and "Mexico overall had a far stronger legislative record — than did the United States".[14]

Faced both with the inevitability of NAFTA and the fact that Mexico's employment laws are more generous to workers than are those of the United States, organized labor in the United States ended up making a relatively modest request. Because labor in Mexico is so cheap (and also perhaps because among Anglo-Saxons, Mexicans do not have a reputation for strongly respecting the rule of law), United States organized labor assumed that Mexico must not have been enforcing its internal employment laws. What was needed, United States organized labor argued, was a requirement that each NAFTA country live up to the letter of its own employment laws.

This is why — even though requiring compliance with purely domestic laws is an atypical and arguably inappropriate topic for an international trade treaty — the NAFTA countries entered the so-called NAFTA labor side agreement, which in essence simply requires each NAFTA country to enforce its own internal employment laws, whatever there may be. The treaty does not prohibit NAFTA states from changing their own labor laws; NAFTA states simply must live up to whatever employment laws they choose to keep on their books. The NAALC side agreement establishes in each NAFTA state a new bureaucracy, the countries' "National Administrative Offices", to police the others' compliance with their own internal employment laws.[15]

Yet Mexico's record on enforcing its labor laws appears not to have been anywhere near as bad as United States organized labor originally claimed. Now, even with years of experience under the NAALC, no NAFTA country has yet been forced to undergo any significant initiative to change its employment law enforcement mechanisms.[16]

---

14 *International Labor and Employment Laws,* volume 1 (1997) (BNA), chapter 20, "NAFTA/NAALC", at pp. 20–23.

15 *International Labor and Employment Laws,* volume 1 (1997) (BNA), chapter 20, "NAFTA/NAALC", at pp. 20–28 *et seq.*

16 It is unclear why United States organized labor does not encourage the United States National Administrative Office to look into the one major area of Mexican employment law which in principle goes unenforced on a widespread, national level — the Mexican constitutional requirement of setting aside and distributing to workers 10 per cent of an employer's annual profits. While Mexico technically does enforce this requirement, a widespread practice among companies doing business in Mexico is separately to incorporate services companies to employ workers. The services companies, in turn, contract with their parent businesses for employees' services. Services companies are then able to show modest but limited annual profits from their contracts, 10 per cent of which does indeed go to the workers. However, if the parent company has a fantastic year, the workers do not realize their full share. Cannot an NAALC-level argument be made that Mexico's tolerance of services companies whose only *raison d'etre* is to control profit-sharing payments violates at least the spirit of Mexico's own constitutional labor law?

Experience under the NAALC indicates (and lawyers representing United States companies' Mexican facilities well know) that large United States companies with Mexican *maquiladoras* do not flout Mexican labor law. These companies tend to pay severance, vacation, holiday pay, year-end bonuses, social security and housing fund contributions — and even provide free lunches and transportation to work in many cases. Indeed, large United States companies operating in Mexico have compelling reasons to comply with Mexican law. United States-owned companies make big, easy, popular targets for Mexican politicians to accuse of wrongdoing. Also, if publicly accused of violating Mexicans' rights, United States companies have a lot to lose stateside, given the current environment of world-wide corporate codes of conduct to eliminate sweatshops, child labor, and other alleged abuses of workplace human rights.

Indeed, practice under the NAFTA labor side agreement has focused not on country-wide enforcement policy, but rather on minutia — claims that specific companies on specific occasions got away with specific labor law violations. For example, the United States once brought charges regarding union organization efforts at a Japanese-owned Sony factory in Tamaulipas,[17] and at last, in August 1998, Mexico — fighting back after being the target of a handful of United States complaints over the years — brought charges against the United States (Mexico's charges alleged non-enforcement of United States laws protecting migrant workers at the DeCoster Egg Farm in Maine).[18]

The NAALC side agreement has led to an engaging comparative employment law dialogue among the NAFTA states — the three National Administrative Offices study their respective countries' employment laws and practices at regular conferences, such as the NAALC "Conference on Contracting Out and Contract Labor" in Toronto on December 7 and 8, 1998. However, the side agreement's dispute resolution mechanism "is bound to be a disappointment" to anyone "who would use the NAALC as a forum for voicing the equivalent of unfair labor practice complaints".[19]

The NAALC dispute resolution mechanism has ended up keeping very few lawyers busy, outside of the National Administrative Offices and the handful of companies which have been non-party witnesses named in the few NAALC charges filed. While the NAALC establishes a dispute resolution procedure, the procedure does not give rise to any substantial international employment law practice area for lawyers in the NAFTA countries.

---

[17] *International Labor and Employment Laws,* volume 1 (1997) (BNA), chapter 20, "NAFTA/NAALC", at pp. 20–31.

[18] *BNA Daily Labor Report* (August 14, 1998), at p. A–2.

[19] *International Labor and Employment Laws,* volume 1 (1997) (BNA), chapter 20, "NAFTA/NAALC", at pp. 20–40.

The handful of NAALC cases which are filed each year are prosecuted by the National Administrative Offices, as the NAALC does not create any private right of action (and, in fact, is designed for occasional systemic complaints regarding country-wide enforcement practices rather than for resolving grievances in specific workplaces). Any United States-owned company employing large numbers in Mexico will, daily, confront important crossborder and Mexican-domestic employment law issues. Few, if any, of these issues, however, will be related to the NAALC.

2. European Union

While NAFTA itself does not give rise to any significant area of international employment law practice, this is not the case for NAFTA's older and more mature sibling — the European Union (EU) treaty. NAFTA is merely an agreement on free trade among its member states, but the EU is a true customs union. It creates a single market for goods and services within the Union's entire territory. The EU regulates its member states in many ways as a federation of states, like the United States would — making the EU treaty effectively a constitutional document.[20]

Just as the United States constitution's "interstate commerce" clause gives the United States federal government authority to regulate employment, the EU concept of a "single market for goods and services" means that the Brussels-based EU needs power to harmonize employment laws among the member states — no single European state's employment laws can be allowed to impede free movement of goods and services within Europe.[21]

The EU was founded in 1957, but in its first decades it issued only a handful of important employment instruments; the EU began to enter the employment area comprehensively only in 1989. However, because of the historical reluctance of Britain to allow Brussels to regulate social matters, because employment initiatives have for long parts of the EU's history required a unanimous vote of EU member states for approval, and because employment issues are a political "hot button", the

---

20 The European Union, though, rejects this "federal" and "constitutional" language.

21 For detailed discussions of European Union employment and social regulation, see chapter 1, "The European Union" and supplement, and see generally Dinan, *Ever Closer Union?*, at pp. 394–403 (1994); Dowling, "From the Social Charter to the Social Action Program 1995–1997", 29 *Cornell International Law Journal* 42 (1996), reprinted in 8 *International Quarterly* 507 (1996); Dowling, "Employment Matters", chapter 17 in Folsom, *et al.* (eds.), *European Union Law After Maastricht* (1996); Dowling, "EC Employment Law after Maastricht", 27 *The Int'l Lawyer* 1 (1993); Dowling, "Worker Rights in the Post-1992 EC", 11 *Northwestern Journal of International Law and Business* 564 (1991); Folsom, *et al.*, *European Union Business Law Handbook,* at pp. 245–249 (1995); Stewart, *et al.*, "Labor Law and Social Policies in the EC after 1992", 23 *Law and Policy in International Business* 507 (1992).

EU has only furthered its employment agenda in earnest since the mid-1990's.[22] Yet while the EU now has a comprehensive body of employment (or "social") law, this does not necessarily mean there is a discrete group of employment lawyers who focus on EU law matters.

Under EU political procedure there exist several types of instruments (laws), one of which is the "Directive"; most EU employment instruments are Directives. A directive is not intended to create any right in any EU citizen; rather, a Directive is a sort of uniform law blueprint directed at the member states, which must, in turn, change ("transpose") their internal laws to conform.

The result is that EU employment laws become part of national member state law. For example, one important EU Directive dealt with paid maternity leave,[23] and its requirements mandated a drastic change in British law. Britain initially challenged the maternity leave Directive, but, losing the challenge, it ultimately enacted a United Kingdom law that carried out the Directive and gave women in the United Kingdom the rights to paid leave which the Directive required.

At least one United Kingdom law firm subsequently sent out a newsletter to its clients detailing the new United Kingdom maternity law requirements — interestingly, the law firm's memorandum never once mentioned the EU Directive which had been the reason for Britain's new law. Indeed, by the time the British law had passed, the EU Directive was only of historical importance within the United Kingdom The Directive's terms and its very existence were not relevant to British employers or pregnant British women.

If the United Kingdom law complied with the Directive, all that was relevant to United Kingdom lawyers and their clients was the requirements of the United Kingdom implementing law. While on a political level Brussels has been substantially changing EU employment law since 1989, these changes have little effect on the daily practice of law in Europe — as the law firm's memorandum and its silence on the EU-law genesis of its topic graphically shows.

Nevertheless, the EU's newfound aggressive regulation of employment does indeed give rise to some practice areas for lawyers. In employment-related lobbying,

---

[22] For histories of European Union employment regulation, see Chapter 1, "The European Union" and supplement and generally Dinan, *Ever Closer Union?* (1994), at pp. 394–403; Dowling, "From the Social Charter to the Social Action Program 1995–1997", 29 *Cornell International Law Journal* 42 (1996), reprinted in 8 *International Quarterly* 507 (1996); Dowling, "Employment Matters", chapter 17 in Folsom, *et al.* (eds.), *European Union Law After Maastricht* (1996); Dowling, "EC Employment Law after Maastricht", 27 *The Int'l Lawyer* 1 (1993); Dowling, "Worker Rights in the Post-1992 EC", 11 *Northwerstern Journal of International Law and Business* 564 (1991); Folsom, *et al.*, *European Union Business Law Handbook*, at pp. 245–249 (1995); Stewart, *et al.*, "Labor Law and Social Policies in the EC after 1992," 23 Law and Policy in *International Business* 507 (1992).

[23] *International Labor and Employment Laws,* volume 1 (1997) (BNA), chapter 1, "The European Union", at section V (C)(1) (b).

particularly, the EU is the place to focus within Europe. Representatives of multinational employers doing business throughout Europe and European workers' rights advocates now lobby, sometimes furiously, in Brussels and Strasbourg for regulations favorable to them.

In addition, EU-level employment regulation is key for those who advise European multinational employers on human resources policies. For example, for any employer operating throughout Europe trying to devise a uniform maternity leave plan, the logical starting place is the EU Maternity Directive. The Directive gives latitude in certain areas for different member states to choose different implementing options, but it essentially sets out a framework that tells European employers the range of maternity leave laws in Europe. The same is true in designing European company policies in any of the other areas the EU now regulates, including work conditions, work hours, vacation, part-time employment, pension portability, vocational training, discrimination and equal pay, health and safety, and protections for children, the handicapped, and the aged.

Additionally, there are some EU social instruments which apply fairly consistently throughout Europe. Every employment lawyer representing Europeans needs to account for these. Four leading examples include:

(1) The Works Council Directive (requiring large European companies with operations in at least two Member States to create and bargain with employee representative units called "works councils");[24]

(2) The Transfer of Undertakings Directive as amended in 1998 (requiring the transferee of any business to assume the employment obligations of the transferor);[25]

(3) Immigration, free movement of workers, and "rights of residence" instruments (such as the scheduled directive setting out rights of residence for third country nationals such as United States citizens), and developing instruments on portability of pensions, retirement plans, and state retirement benefits; and[26]

(4) The Data Privacy Directive (which has an extraterritorial effect as to United States and other third country employers which send employee data to their home offices — and therefore sets out requirements for any employee record-keeping procedure to be used in Europe).[27]

---

[24] Directive 94/45, 1994 OJ (L 254), at p. 64.

[25] Directive 98/50/EC (July 17, 1998).

[26] Directive 98/50/EC (July 17, 1998) at section IX and see, e.g., "Commissioner Gradin moving forward on EU residence rights", *Eur. Law Bull.*, July 14, 1998, at p. 10.

[27] Directive 95/46/EC (October 24, 1995).

E. CONCLUSION

The practice of employment law in all countries has traditionally been seen as almost a purely local practice area, akin to real estate law and divorce law. However, the new realities of the true global multinational employer, the rise of expatriate and third-country-national employees, and the increasing tendency of labor unions to "cherry pick" best practices from foreign countries is creating a real need for international employment law practitioners.

This need becomes especially clear in light of technological developments such as the internet, PeopleSoft personnel software, and companies' intranets, all of which bring a company's employees from around the world into daily contact. Effective immediately, clients are demanding legal counselors competent to advise in an era in which employment issues constantly skip over national boundaries. Some employment lawyers will be able to meet this new demand.

CHAPTER 2
COORDINATING CROSSBORDER EMPLOYMENT LAW PROJECTS

Jessica Learmond-Criqui
Fladgate Fielder
London, England

A. INTRODUCTION

It is true that the world is becoming a global village. However, although many of the issues in relation to employees are similar in many countries and there are many laws to protect the rights of employees, they are not sufficiently similar to make the practice of international employment law seamless and predictable. There are two levels on which the practice of employment law occurs:

(1) The international arena; and

(2) The domestic arena.

Many domestic laws have extra-territorial effect and it is important to understand when they do and when they do not. Nevertheless, it is prudent to assume that the laws of each country differ to a material degree and it is difficult to keep up to date with the operation of and changes to the labor laws in any jurisdiction but one's own with which you are familiar.

Local lawyers should always be consulted when the law of a country other than that of the primary lawyer is involved in a particular project.

This chapter will consider, not so much the practice of international law, but the softer issues involved in multi-jurisdictional labor law projects and how to manage them.

B. IS THERE SUCH A THING AS INTERNATIONAL EMPLOYMENT LAW?

What is international law? Does it mean the law regulating the relations between States, or conflict of laws as academics tend to consider it? Does it mean advising on transactions or litigation involving more than one jurisdiction, as practitioners tend to consider it? Or, does it mean a uniform set of rules which apply regardless of the circumstances? While one might say that banking law is truly international because of the system of Eurobonds and international financing, a similar seamless system has not arisen for labor law. International labor law for present purposes should be understood as a uniform set of rules.

Many multi-jurisdictional projects involve countries that may not be part of the same economic union. Even those within an economic and/or political union, such as the European Union, have different systems of law. The United Kingdom's system of law, for example, is a conglomeration of statutes (or acts of parliament) and case law (or Common Law). The concepts and principles of much of the law are enshrined in judgments made in our courts in particular cases. Many of the concepts and principles of employment law are found in the acts of parliament.

The law in France and many other European Union members, on the other hand, is based on Civil Law and codes which are far more detailed about the application of the law than is the English system.

To add to the mishmash of systems, there is European Union law, which is like an amoeba, super-imposing itself over the local structures and frequently changing its shape and tone through the European Courts of Justice. This is not to be confused with the European Court of Human Rights in Strasbourg.

European Union legislation has influenced domestic United Kingdom and other European Union member states domestic legislation a great deal and much of English labor law incorporates the principles prescribed in European Union legislation.

Each domestic legal system has its own rules to decide whether the domestic law applies to a particular labor law situation or whether the law of a different country applies. When faced with an international employment law situation, one of the first issues to resolve is which law will apply to the issues.

If there were such a thing as international employment law, the answer would be simple because the principles would be consistent. However, the answer is usually far from simple when one is involved in a project which spans two countries, each of which is in a different economic or political union. So, for example, it will be difficult to apply a uniform set of principles to a project involving, say, China, Russia and the United Kingdom without knowing whether China or Russia impose a system of mandatory rules in relation to a labor law situation.

In the European Union, for example, there is a system of mandatory rules that will apply regardless of the choice of law between the parties. Therefore, even if one chooses English law to apply to a contract in which an employee works for a large part of his time in France, but where he also spends some of his time in the United Kingdom, the French mandatory rules will apply to his employment to give him certain minimum rights under French law.

International law is, therefore, not so much a uniform set of principles which can be applied to all cases but, rather, an interaction of domestic laws (including the extra-territorial effect of such laws) and "federal" law. To have such interaction, one must understand the systems and rules in each country in relation to a particular situation. This reverts to a managing exercise of different systems of law and, therefore, of lawyers in each jurisdiction which is involved in the project. Bourdieu described the situation perfectly when he wrote:

> [The large law firms] must reckon with resistance from national legal fields threatened by the new world legal order or, more exactly, with the power relations and the conflicts, generated within these fields, between the modernizers, who take the side of internationalism, and the traditionalists, who put their money on protectionist barriers and the maintenance of national tradition . . . .[1]

C. THE FUTURE

Many trade unions, non-governmental organizations (NGOs) and consumers are campaigning for international action against labor rights violations and are putting companies under pressure to ensure that their sub-contractors, primarily in developing countries, properly pay attention to and apply labor standards.

There are a number of key and exciting initiatives that have taken some time to develop and try to secure fundamental labor standards internationally. While it is clear that there are a number of initiatives, none provide an overall umbrella to make it easier for the purchaser of labor law advice or the practitioner. Ultimately, a framework of regulation may begin to emerge.

1. International Institutional Action

The European Union and the United States have each developed trade regulations to deter breaches of standards and reward compliance. The World Trade Organization (WTO) has been discussing enshrining labor rights to trading agreements and treaties, and the World Bank is proposing to tie loans to compliance with minimum standards.

In addition, there are fresh initiatives from the International Labor Organization (ILO) and the Organization for Economic Cooperation and Development (OECD).

2. Corporate and Sectoral Initiatives

There has been the growth of "voluntary" corporate and sectoral codes of conduct which have become quite developed in the United States.

---

1 Flood, J (1996), "Megalawyering in the global order: the cultural, social and economic transformation of global legal practice", *International Journal of the Legal Profession*, volume 3, numbers 1 / 2, at p. 174.

3. Codes of Conduct

Corporate codes are adopted by corporations — usually retailers or producers of branded goods — to ensure that their suppliers and subsidiaries maintain minimum labor standards.

4. Incorporating Core Labor Standards

The key standards are the core ILO labor standards set out below. Guidance on these can be seen in the "Basic Code of Conduct covering Labor Practices", which was adopted by the executive board of the International Conference of Free Trade Unions (ICFTU) in Brussels in December 1997, and the International Trade Secretariat (ITS).

The text of the code was developed by the ICFTU/ITS Working Party on Multinational Companies in a process that involved extensive consultations with trade unions and other interested individuals and organizations. It aims to establish a minimum list of standards that ought to be included in all codes of conduct covering labor practices.

5. Development of a General Benchmark

A new "social accountability standard" — SA 8000 — is being developed by the Council on Economic Priorities accreditation agency. If it finds acceptance, it would provide a means for companies and consumers to ensure that the policy and practices of the companies whose goods they purchase meet minimum standards. This may be an attractive option for smaller firms.

6. European-Wide Codes of Conduct

In a number of industries, there has been an agreement on a code of conduct on a European-wide basis. The most notable is that reached in the textile industry between the European social partners in this sector.

There are also proposals before the European Parliament to research the feasibility of developing binding rules at the European level for all companies sourcing goods to apply the principles that would be contained in a code of conduct.

7. Core Standards Emphasized by International Labor Organization

Since 1995, the International Labor Organization (ILO) has been seeking to encourage as many countries as possible to sign "core" conventions of the ILO, including those relating to:

(1) The right of freedom of association and the protection of the right to organize;

(2) The right to organize and bargaining collectively;

(3) The abolition of forced labor;

(4) The respect of the minimum employment age regarding child labor;

(5) Equal pay for work of equal value; and

(6) Non-discrimination in employment.

8. Multilateral Agreement on Investment

The member countries of the OECD were until recently negotiating the terms of a proposed Multinational Agreement on Investment (MAI) to provide freer trade and capital flows by preventing discriminatory national arrangements against foreign direct investment.

During the negotiations, there was a strong lobby to have references to basic labor rights included in the text of agreements. There seems to be broad agreement on including references to key labor rights within the agreement.

D. MANAGING A MULTI-JURISDICTIONAL PROJECT

The key to managing a multi-jurisdictional project is to rise above the technical level and to have a clear method of working and a thorough understanding of how one's client or employer works. Much of what follows may seem familiar, but it still may serve as a reminder of good practice when instructing foreign lawyers.

There are many aspects to be considered in managing an international network. The most important is the contact or adviser choosen in each jurisdiction to assist you. As part of that choice, the following are important considerations.

1. One-Stop Shop or Manage It Yourself

If a client prefers to use a one-stop shop, there are no guarantees of quality from one jurisdiction to another. Author John Flood quotes a partner of an international law firm, who says:

> The problem with opening offices in each place is quality control. Look at "Baker & McDonalds". There are some of their offices which are no good and others you just would not touch at all . . . .

If one prefers to do it himself, he should develop a relationship with a network of existing or recommended contacts who specialize in labor law around the globe so that contracts will be readily available. Having a good working relationship with one's foreign adviser is a key to timely and expert advice delivered in a user-friendly way.

2. Know the Contact

It is easier for those who know each other already to respond and to deal with billing and cost issues more easily. All firms would like to be paid for their work in due course, and most firms have new client criteria or billing pre-requisites to ensure that their fee earners can be paid for the work. This may result in a time delay to the advice being sought.

In addition, a known contact is more likely to deliver the prompt and quality response that one requires. It is recommended that one get to know the other counsel personally and develop a relationship.

Instructing someone unfamiliar may lead to difficulties in the priority given to one's work over other work in which the foreign lawyer is involved. A personal relationship overcomes any such difficulties.

3. Language

Many foreign lawyers now speak English, which is the business language in many cases. It is always possible to find someone who speaks English. To ensure that he understands instructions, one should attempt to define any particular terms of art as simply as possible so that the foreign lawyer can understand the concept within the structure of his own system of law.

4. Timing

One should brief foreign contacts as soon as possible and build in realistic time lines for them to revert. Emergencies crop up, and they may not be available for part of a week when advice is really urgent.

In addition, bear in mind the cultural differences between countries and the ways of working and build these into reversion timetables. The countries in which advice is received quite slowly should be given a shorter time line to revert.

5. Availability

It is always a good idea to call before sending instructions to a foreign lawyer. This puts him on notice that the work is en route. This would also enable you to establish whether there is a public holiday in the country, usually because of a voicemail message at the other end of the telephone, and one can then factor this into your timing for the return of advice.

One will also be able to find out whether the individual is available and able to respond in the time required, as he may be on holiday or ill. One can then identify someone else to send the instructions to. On some occasions, a fax addressed to a particular individual will remain in his in-tray and may not be addressed in the time required for a response.

6. Cost Estimates and Budgets

Cost control is an important aspect of managing multi-jurisdictional projects. It is helpful to give the foreign lawyer a budget of either the number of hours' work required or the maximum cost which the project will bear for advice in that country. Usually, foreign lawyers will not exceed such a budget if they have accepted it in the past.

Alternatively, one may ask for a quote for the work up front and ensure that the foreign lawyer gives immediate notice if he is likely to overrun those cost estimates.

7. Uniform Briefs, Peculiar Issues In Particular Jurisdictions

It is useful to prepare a list of questions in relation to the advice that isrequired in as uniform a manner as possible, so that one can put the response into a report fairly easily. If possible, define terms as they may mean different things from country to country.

8. Follow-Up

It is quite useful to chase the foreign adviser to ensure that he is on time with the advice a few days in advance. If he has been distracted by other work, this usually prompts the foreign adviser into action and reinforces the need to receive the advice on time.

It is quite useful to give the foreign laywer a deadline which is at least two days before the work is really needed because one may have queries on the foreign adviser's advice which he will need to consider and respond to.[2]

---

[2] These notes are for general guidance only. Specific advice should be sought before taking action in any individual case.

CHAPTER 3
MANAGING EMPLOYEE LOYALTY IN THE 21ST CENTURY

Andrew J. Boling
Baker & McKenzie
Chicago, Illinois, United States

A. INTRODUCTION

A booming economy, a scarcity of skilled workers, and ever-deteriorating notions of employee loyalty have created an environment ripe for employee raiding and other forms of unfair competition. An increasing number of multi-national employers are experiencing this disturbing phenomenon outside the United States. This is perhaps because no country can match the United States for the ready availability of its sophisticated — and often severe — unfair competition laws.

In many respects, the erosion of employee loyalty can be tied to the significant collective redundancies and downsizings experienced by United States and European corporations in the 1980s and 1990s. Almost every state of the United States — except Montana — has long embraced the concept of at-will employment, which, in theory, means that an employer can arbitrarily terminate the employment relationship at any time and for any reason. Disregarding the at-will cloud which loomed over their employment, most employees in the United States shared an expectation of lifetime employment so long as they performed their work in a competent manner.

Indeed, until the 1980s, such expectations were usually borne out by reality. However, a troubled economy and pressures to increase profits resulted in the significant collective redundancies which served to dash the traditional model of the "organization man". These dramatic changes in the employment landscape have left in their wake a workforce in which self-interest now pre-dominates over institutional loyalty to the employer.

B. "HOSTILE TAKEOVERS" IN THE EMPLOYMENT CONTEXT

Attorneys often use the phrase "hostile takeover" to describe an unwanted solicitation to purchase or "takeover" a corporation. However, to an employment lawyer, "hostile takeover" more likely means the unsolicited appropriation of an organization's most precious asset — its human capital. Businesses increasingly use such "hostile takeovers" to inflict harm on the competition. Employee poaching is a very real — if not legitimate — means of competition in today's global business economy. Indeed, many businesses carefully survey potential battlefields in terms of the strength of a given country's unfair competition laws before declaring "corporate war" against a competitor.

This phenomenon is readily explainable when one compares the relative benefits of employee raiding versus other traditional forms of competition. Consider, for example, the advantages of enticing away a competitor's key employees versus the risk of criminal sanctions for predatory pricing as a means of inflicting competitive harm. Even in the United States, the potential damages for employee raiding are significantly less than the formidable civil and criminal penalties for predatory pricing.

If the competitive goal is to acquire the human talent of a competitor, selective employee raiding is certainly less expensive than an outright acquisition. Not only can a competitor avoid the payment of investment banking fees and other administrative costs associated with a transaction, but the competitor can also avoid payments for the goodwill of a business. Further, there is no need to pay a "control premium" and the raider will enjoy the opportunity to exercise significant discretion in identifying which assets are desirable and which are not. Employers opting to purchase a corporation for the purpose of obtaining discrete assets, in contrast, are invariably burdened with the problem of unwanted employees. Finally, a legitimate acquisition may not even be an option where a corporation is not publicly traded and there are no readily available means to obtain a majority interest of the corporation's shares.

1. Where Does this Occur?

Without question, employee raiding occurs everyday in virtually every jurisdiction. However, many employers find that unfair competition is most prevalent and problematic in emerging markets. Many emerging market countries have — at least when compared with laws of the United States and many European countries — either unsettled or unsophisticated unfair competition laws. Moreover, in many emerging markets, there is a premium to be placed on available managerial talent. The shortage of trained managers in the local country often provides an irresistible temptation to a company wishing to expand its operations.

Employers often find that Latin America in particular presents the most challenging environment for employee raiding. Many of the factors identified above are present in Latin America. In addition, many Latin American countries simply refuse to enforce covenants not to compete under the doctrine of "right to work". The concept of a person's "right to work" free of any restrictions is in fact embodied in the constitutions of many Latin American countries. This powerful "right to work" principle, when coupled with the relative dearth of unfair competition laws in Latin America, has made that region in particular a hotbed of employee raiding. As a practical matter, unless an aggrieved United States employer can protect its rights under United States law in a United States forum, it may be defenseless against extraterritorial employee raiding. A vivid depiction of the volatile dynamic created by the mixture of diminished employee loyalty, the use of employee raiding as a means of corporate expansion, and lax unfair competition laws can be found in the case of *Value Partners v. Bain.*[1]

2. Factual Background

Value Partners, an international consulting firm with headquarters in Italy, opened its Brazilian subsidiary in Sao Paolo, Brazil in 1994. Between 1994 and the end of 1997, the Sao Paolo office grew in size to over 20 employees producing gross sales of approximately US $5 million per year.

According to the complaint filed by Value Partners, Bain, a direct competitor, had no offices in South America until it opened an office in Mexico City in July 1997. In October 1997, Bain created a Brazilian affiliate, which established an office in Sao Paolo. Between October 30 and the first week of November 1997, almost all of the professionals and staff members of Value Partners' Sao Paolo office resigned to become Bain employees.

On November 27, 1997, Value Partners filed criminal charges in Brazil against many of the defecting employees. Then, on March 4, 1998, it also initiated litigation in federal court in New York. The allegations made by Value Partners, which Bain denied, included breach of trust and loyalty and the theft of confidential information. The lawsuit sought US $20 million in compensatory damages plus punitive damages in an unspecified amount. Bain promptly moved to dismiss under the doctrine of *forum non conveniens*. Under United States law, this concept allows the court to dismiss a case because it would be more conveniently and efficiently litigated in another location, either within or outside the United States.

3. The Court's Ruling

In ruling that the matter would be more properly adjudicated in Brazil, the court held that Brazilian civil law made adequate remedies available to Value Partners. The court also noted that almost all of the witnesses were located in Brazil and the vast majority of the conduct at issue took place in Brazil as well. Moreover, Bain agreed to consent to jurisdiction in the Brazilian courts.

As a practical matter, resolution of such a dispute in Brazil could work to the advantage of the "raider" in cases involving allegations similar to the allegations in *Value Partners v. Bain*. This is because Brazilian law, as is the case with many countries outside of the United States, does not offer the comprehensive injunctive

---

1 Value Partners v. Bain, 1998 WL 336648 (SDNY June 22, 1998). Value Partners filed another lawsuit against Bain, this time in a Massachusetts federal court. According to the 7 July 1999 *Wall Street Journal*, the court denied Bain's motion to dismiss under the *forum non conveniens* doctrine in an order entered on 6 July 1999.

relief and significant compensatory and punitive damages afforded under United States law for claims involving employee disloyalty.

4. Lessons From Value Partners

Employers everywhere should be concerned about strengthening — if not re-creating — stronger bonds between employees located in local countries and the corporate parent. In essence, there are two options available to employers. The first option is to create a proper corporate culture that fosters employee loyalty. The second is to establish appropriate legal procedures, including appropriate employment agreements. The prudent employer should of course try to pursue both options.

C. IMPORTANCE OF THE WRITTEN CONTRACT — CHOICE OF LAW CONCERNS

Choice of law is an issue of critical importance in any employment agreement. Although conventional wisdom suggests that local country law should always apply regardless of the citizenship of the employee working in the local country, the author would respectively suggest that multi-national employers would be well served to designate the law of their "home" country to the extent that the employer wishes to have any possible basis for adjudicating disputes in the home country or in some location other than in the local country.

Employers should do this knowing that in any labor dispute adjudicated in the local country, the "home country" choice of law designation will usually be disregarded and local law will prevail. However, for reasons explained at greater length below, use of the home country choice of law can have critical significance in terms of influencing the location of the litigation.

D. CHOICE OF FORUM

An appropriate choice of forum provision can sometimes be more important than the choice of law clause. If a business wants to adjudicate disputes in a location other than the local country, it is imperative that this is spelled out with specificity in the employment agreement. In the case of a United States employer, attempts should be made to spell out whether jurisdiction will be appropriate in both the federal and state courts of a given state or whether the exclusive remedy shall be in one or the other.

Although the competition may choose to fire the first shot in a distant locale, identifying a choice of forum in the employment agreement will allow the "target" company to have a say in where the final battle will be fought. In the case of *Value Partners*, there is no evidence in the record that it had a forum selection clause in its employment agreements. The absence of such a designation made it virtually impossible for this Italian-based company to adjudicate its dispute in the United States, where the disloyal employees were, in large measure, Brazilian and Italian nationals.

Using home country law in a home country forum can also help lay the predicate for a successful claim of tortuous interference with contract. In some cases, it may be too late or practically impossible to obtain any form of injunctive relief in the local country against disloyal employees. However, to the extent a multi-national employer has an over-arching dispute with another multi-national that does business in the home country, toughening the employment agreement with home country forum and law provisions will make it easier for a court in the home country to assume jurisdiction over a major commercial dispute between the two corporate competitors. Most corporations find that to the extent they have any sympathy at all before a judge or jury, it will be in their home location where they are often perceived to be a significant and positive economic force.

E. RACE TO THE COURT HOUSE

On discovering employee loyalty anywhere in the world, an employer should immediately consider initiating litigation in a home country forum. Having home country choice of law and choice of forum designations in the underlying employment agreement will make it easier to accomplish this objective. The "race to the courthouse" as it is often called is important if the employer wants to salvage any chance of adjudicating the dispute in the home country. If, as is often the case, the employer waits for the disloyal employee to file a trumped up labor claim in the local country, it could find the door to home country litigation slammed shut under the abstention doctrine.

United States courts will often "abstain" from exercising their jurisdiction in deference to an earlier filed action even if that action has been filed in a different country under different substantive and procedural rules. In evaluating where to initiate litigation, the employer should consider the relative advantages and disadvantages of the home country versus the local country. While an outcome may often be faster under local country laws, there will usually be significantly reduced sympathy for the foreign employer in the local country. Even though litigation in the home country may ultimately prove futile, employers may nevertheless derive several benefits even in defeat. Foremost among these potential benefits is the opportunity to distract the former employee from helping his new employer. If the former employee becomes embroiled in litigation outside the local country, he will be hard pressed to carry out his duties.

The extraordinary inconvenience of retaining an attorney in a different country and then dealing with the logistical difficulties inherent in transnational litigation will — during the pendency of the litigation — effectively preclude the employee from providing any meaningful assistance to his new employer. Indeed, the demands of comprehensive unfair competition litigation can often serve as a "*de facto*" injunction to prevent the disloyal employee — and his new employer — from obtaining a "head start" on their wrongful activities.

F. CLEARING THE FORUM NON CONVENIENS HURDLE

Having won the race to the courthouse, it is incumbent on an employer to insure that the home country tribunal will not refer the dispute to another location under the doctrine of *forum non conveniens*. Under the doctrine of *forum non conveniens*, a court, although it has the jurisdiction to entertain a dispute, will refuse to do so in deference to a more convenient forum which also would have jurisdiction over the parties.

To clear the *forum non conveniens* hurdle, the employer must persuade the home country court to hear the case. A contract with choice of law and choice of forum dedicated to the home country will often go a long way in clearing this step.

There are other strategies employers can pursue in an effort to keep the dispute in the home country. One such strategy is to pay a portion of the employee's compensation in the home country.

Tax considerations and local country currency rules allowing — and these are often very serious issues worthy of careful analysis — employers should consider a means of compensating the employee in the home country. Sometimes this will result in a direct payment from the parent corporation to the employee in the home country. The funds can be paid into a custodial account based in the home country. Access to the funds should be withheld pursuant to a written agreement until such time as the employee has successfully completed the foreign assignment. Forfeiture mechanisms should be built into the agreement. Such mechanisms would include forfeiture of the funds on any material breach of the agreement and forfeiture if the employee should make any claims against the company under local labor law.

Sometimes this system can be modified to accommodate the special facts arising with the employment of a local national. The local country employee should designate the custodian or trustee over the account. That employee should also appoint that custodian as his agent for service of process. Service in the home country on a home country entity may help to avoid potential service of process concerns that would otherwise arise under the Hague Convention.

Establishing a compensation system as described above may also provide the employer with a more legitimate basis for proceeding in the home country in the first instance. Even if the disloyal employee is thousands of miles away in a different hemisphere, there are funds within the home country's court over which the court could exercise *in rem* jurisdiction. Courts will often take a special interest and concern over property located within its jurisdiction.

Of course, even the most carefully planned and implemented scheme does not provide complete insurance against a local national or even an ex-patriot from pursuing relief and of securing relief under local law in the local country. However, creating formidable barriers as described above may often give an employee second thoughts before he or she embarks on a pattern of disloyal activity.

G. CONCLUSION

In a global economy where employee knowledge can be an employer's most valuable asset, the scenario alleged in the *Value Partners* case illustrates the sudden and devastating consequences of losing precious intellectual capital to a competitor. Although corrective action taken in response to employee disloyalty is often futile, it is never too late to take all appropriate pro-active and preventive steps to preserve employee loyalty, guard against unfair competition, and plan the best available route to the safe harbor of the home country judicial system.

CHAPTER 4

REPRESENTING THE EMPLOYEE WORKING ABROAD

Jack A. Raisner
Outten & Golden LLP
New York, New York, United States

A. INTRODUCTION

The objective of this chapter is to present a basic framework for the legal counselor who is advising and representing an expatriate employee. It focuses on practical issues faced when the client is a native of the primary legal counselor's home country, but is employed outside that country by a domestic, related, or foreign entity.

In the face of the rapidly changing landscape of global expansion, the legal counselor needs to adopt a pragmatic approach to assist the client in optimizing the overseas employment opportunity and minimizing the risks.

This overview reflects the author's United States-based perspective. It is intended as a tool to help transition any practitioner's knowledge of domestic employment law practice into practical advice for expatriate clients.

B. CLIENT'S SITUATION

1. Pre-Hire Stage

The practice of employment law on behalf of individual employees in the United States focuses mainly on problems that arise when the employment relationship is about to end, not begin. This is because the employment-at-will rule governs most employment relationships in the United States. It creates the presumption, held both by employers and employees, that employment is terminable at will, obviating the need to reach agreement on the contentious issue of the duration of the employment, for which employment contracts are usually sought. Accordingly, the employees who regularly sought legal advice at the point of hire tended to be CEO's, entertainment talent, star salespeople and only a few other key people. Lawyers began to serve the rest of the workforce only when terminations became challengeable under the emerging concept of wrongful discharge, which includes claims based on discrimination statutes, implied contracts and tort claims.

Recently, however, a strong economy and several other developments, including globalization, have caused contractual agreements to trickle down to lower levels of employees in the 1990's. Full employment, for example, has fed a wave of corporate raiding. This, in turn, has led to contractual offers to hire, since restrictive covenants cannot be enforced unless they are ancillary to contracts. As the workforce has become more insecure and fluid, so employers have offered contracts to a wider group of employees, to staunch the loss of intellectual property caused by the exodus of employees, as well as avoid the competition created by entrepreneurial ex-employees. Finally, employers have recognized the necessity of offering contracts to employees taking internal overseas assignments. The use of a contract may spring from the foreign employer's universal policies or because it is the norm in the practices of the destination. Or, the parties may recognize the need for greater predictability and security from one another, and thus sit down to negotiate an agreement.

Foreign assignments involve a host of risks and considerations that cannot be left to an at-will understanding. Expatriates who are sent overseas by a transnational employer will likely encounter a standard bundle of logistical concerns that will help them move and adjust. These employers will often have a whole office dedicated to standard issues. This department will set policy and handle the arrangements that entail special issues such as moving, housing, schooling, tax and benefits treatment and the like. Employers without such policies will have to work out these arrangements with the employee, but these non-contentious discussions do not necessarily require legal representation. This is because, at the outset of the relationship, the employer and the employees' interests are aligned in many ways. If the employer fails to observe laws concerning taxation, for example, it usually will bear the liability.

The issues that standard policies do not address are those that are most sensitive and particular to the individual:

(1) Security (i.e., the duration of the job and the grounds/penalties for early termination); and

(2) Compensation.

Of the two, the latter is more a business issue, which the employee often can negotiate. The job security issue, however, may entail the knowledge and interpretation of wide-ranging laws. In such cases, it may be prudent for the employee to seek an attorney's advice sooner rather than later.

2. Contracts and Employment-at-Will

Contracts in the United States usually take the form of offer (or service) letters, or full-fledged employment agreements. The purpose of the letter is to set down the basic terms of employment, including title and responsibilities of the job, the compensation arrangements, a term, and provisions for its early termination. Of prime importance to anyone hired to go overseas should be the provision specifying the duration of the employment. If that duration is not fixed, but rather left open, United States courts are likely to find the employment to be at-will. It will not matter that employee will have lifted stakes in moving abroad and be left "stranded" without a job, home and other essentials in the foreign country. The move abroad itself will not transform an at-will contract to one with an expectancy of duration.

For example, in a dispute that never made it to court, a United States company hired a female United States citizen to oversee its seasonal cruise business on a foreign resort island. The entire industry did its annual hiring before the start of the season. When her employer fired her midseason, purportedly because sales were weak, and she could find no other work, she claimed her contract had been violated. Only then did she give her offer letter to an attorney to look at and interpret. The contract did not specify any particular term of employment. Under the at-will rule, United States courts generally find that a contract that does not specifically fix the length of employment is terminable at will. The employee's only hope was that the courts of her foreign worksite would take a more hospitable view, otherwise, under United States law, she was left on a distant island, jobless and without funds to return home.

In the event that the employee's counsel is given the opportunity to negotiate the expatriate's contract, he or she will normally couch its language in familiar terms that reduce ambiguity, and place jurisdiction and the governing law in the home country. Of course, the attorney would be well advised to understand the laws of the foreign worksite, which on occasion may be more favorable than those of the home country. An attorney who knows, for example, that courts in the foreign jurisdiction will grant the client statutorily guaranteed severance pay or other allowances, for example, can direct his or her negotiation efforts to other benefits.

3. Job Security Issues Outside of the Contract

Legal counselors can do more than negotiate contracts for their clients at the outset of employment. They can turn the client's attention towards the non-legal, but often more critical considerations of career preservation and advancement. Whether they realize it or not, expatriates go out on a limb when they accept a position overseas. Experience has shown that jobs in foreign offices are simply more vulnerable than those in the home country. A fledgling foreign office can be opened with great fanfare one day, but become a forgotten outpost the next. Profitability can be very uncertain. The office's existence may ride on economic conditions in which slight downturns may spell doom. Foreign offices are more subject to whim than domestic operations; the business strategies that created the office can more easily change, regardless of the efforts or merits of those who run them.

Given the vicissitudes of expatriate employment, counsel should begin to lay the groundwork, in any initial discussions, for the client's future "return trip home" — to a position that preserves seniority, compensation, and prestige. As seasoned managers know, job security ultimately rests on "people" issues rather than legal ones. The client should expect that the absence will weaken and strain the all-important ties with the home headquarters.

"Out of sight, out of mind" is the expression commonly used to describe this costly phenomenon to the employee. The employee should not allow his or her relationship with those in the home office to be attenuated. The employee should have some plan of action for keeping in contact with the employer's decision-makers throughout the period, by frequent correspondence or other means. To keep the base of support alive, the employee should be prepared to send a steady flow of e-mail, letters, even birthday cards, and to make return visits whenever feasible. This may be as valuable as the employer's commitment to return him or her to some specific post at the end of the tour, and is essential when such a guarantee cannot be secured.

If a return position cannot be promised, the employee should seek "exit" payments and commitments, which ease reentry to the job market if termination rather than a transfer home takes place.

a. *Preparing for the New Culture*

Respect and sensitivity to the foreign culture is a must for expatriates and those who counsel them. Much has been written about cross-cultural differences between workplaces in foreign cultures and the need to expose and sensitize employees to them. Ideally, the international employment lawyer would serve to forewarn the client at the outset about these incompatibility issues. Doing so might avoid situations such as the following. An oil engineer of Arab nationality went to work in an American company's oilfields, which were leased from another Arab country, "the kingdom". Because many of his supervisors, who were natives of the kingdom, were, of course, Arabs, the engineer did not anticipate that he would be discriminated against, even though he did not share their nationality. The native Arabs and Americans filled the corporation's highest ranks. The engineer found he could not penetrate those ranks even after a career of superior performance. Had the client been apprised of this "glass ceiling" at the outset, he might have chosen to build his career in another locale.

In addition to career planning, the employee would do well to acquire the foreign language. Many expatriates, however, do not. With English fast becoming the international language of business, the United States employee may not take language acquisition seriously in the belief that one can get by with translation help without learning the foreign language. After all, the employee thinks, if foreign language skills were necessary, he or she would not have been posted to overseas assignment in the first place. The fallacy is that while this logic may apply when times are good, it leaves the employee vulnerable should the day come when the job picture sours. When an employer looks for flaws on which to base a termination, it will have little difficulty convincing a court that the employee was less able to handle the work as compared to bilingual employees who may have been retained or even hired to replace the expatriate. Instead of giving the employer this card to play, the client should embark on intensive language acquisition, as a matter of career development and the preemptive defense of his or her job.

b. Pregnancy and Other Leaves

Under United States law, employers are not to consider the fact that a female employee or a male employee's spouse is, or may become, pregnant. Although they are not supposed to, many nevertheless do. It may even become a topic of discussion. Although incautious discussions leave employers highly vulnerable to a discrimination suit, the stakes of not considering pregnancy at the outset of overseas employment are also high.

Pregnancy leave is different from other extended leaves of absence in terms of the considerations that go into taking an overseas job. Most leaves of absence in the foreign country will place both the employer and employee in a fairly undesirable position. Most health-related leaves of absence, however, are unexpected or unavoidable. In the rare case that an employee knows he or she is going to need a major medical procedure, it would probably be advisable, for purposes of receiving proper care, to discuss the impact of being in a foreign country before undertaking the assignment. Unlike other medical conditions, pregnancy is susceptible to planning, thus, there is an expectation that it will be considered, and perhaps even discussed at least by the employee with his or her mate in conjunction with accepting the foreign post. Staffing and logistical complications abroad may be so unwieldy that the discussion may even rise to the surface, as it did in the celebrated case of attorney Amy Cherry. She worked for the prestigious international law firm, Coudert Bros., until she was terminated 11 days after returning from a three-month maternity leave. In *Cherry v. Coudert*,[1] the attorney was given friendly advice by a firm lawyer before she left New York for a post in the firm's Tokyo office: it was not to become pregnant. The female head of the firm's associates committee issued this cautionary warning and defended it based on her prior experience with expatriate female associates. The Tokyo office was managed by a particular male partner who apparently had demonstrated his displeasure with females subordinates who took maternity leave. After becoming pregnant and giving birth in Japan, Ms. Cherry was discharged, or rather "transferred" to no where. She tried her case before a jury but reached a settlement just before the jury returned its verdict. In short, the female or couple going abroad should gauge the impact, inconvenience, and other issues that would seem to arise in connection with taking a leave and dealing with child-bearing during the foreign tour of duty.

C. TERMINATION OF EMPLOYMENT

The plaintiff's lawyer generally first hears from the client when a problem is at the boiling point and a discharge has either just occurred or is about to. Assuming

---

[1] "Coudert Lawyer's Bias Claim Goes to Trial", *New York Law Journal*, (July 22, 1996).

the employee has been able find the lawyer, the two need to address the pragmatic issue of opening private lines of communication with each other, so that they can deal with the rapid communications that ordinarily ensue when an employment termination is contested. Ideally, the client should have 24-hour access to portable, global cell phone service, especially where differences in time zones make calling at conventional times difficult. Many attorneys find the use of e-mail for highly sensitive attorney-client communications undesirable due to privacy and perhaps privilege concerns. Fax service will also be essential, especially where contracts or separation agreements are being discussed. Very often, the attorney will bring the client's case to conclusion without ever having met him or her.

1. Evaluating the Case

Typically, an employee arrives at the lawyer's doorstep bringing news of a termination that may be about to happen or has already occurred. The plaintiff's employment lawyer has the critical task of assessing the employee's legal rights as quickly as possible, ideally in the initial consultation. With this assessment, the employment lawyer can then discuss with the employee how this legal component may fit into the overall picture that confronts the employee. Many employees cannot frame their own objectives, no less arrive at a course of action, until their legal advisor presents their realistic legal options.

Under normal circumstances, an experienced employment practitioner should be able to give a rough sketch of the client's potential legal strategies in the initial consultation. This is because the employment practitioner is familiar with the governing substantive law and procedures in the relevant jurisdiction. At home, the identity of the employer generally is not a difficult issue. In the case of expatriates, however, sets of confounding variables often come into play. These questions often begin with basics, such as the identity and nature of the employer. While a domestic employee usually works for one employer, under one agreement, in one jurisdiction, to which one body of law applies, each of these factors can become uncertain and multi-layered in the expatriate employment relationship. This presents a whole new set of challenges for counsel who must expeditiously attempt to determine:

(1) Who is the employer?

(2) What is the operative employment agreement?

(3) What substantive law applies to the facts?

(4) What jurisdiction can hear the case? and

(5) What negotiation and/or dispute resolution routes exist?

Addressing these questions will not necessarily result in a single answer for each. International employment is often made complex by the presence of two, three or even more "employers", multiple letters of agreement, references to various applicable laws, and contacts with various geographic sites which can satisfy jurisdictional requirements in several locales. It is counsel's job to sift through, and sometimes mix and match combinations of these elements, to come up with the strongest assertable claims.

D. FROM PRINCIPLES TO PRACTICE

Below is an illustration of the role of the counselor in expatriate employment situations, who must typically identify, weigh, and combine these factors. Counsel's analysis seeks to yield the maximum number of realistic, assertable claims to arm the employee with legal leverage. He or she can then proceed to litigate unless a favorable termination package can be negotiated.

1. Facts

Josef K., an American citizen of Russian origin, began working for a European Bank (EB) in early 1998. A managing director of EB, Vladimir S., had twice interviewed him: first in Brussels, then in New York's Kennedy Airport. At the New York interview, he was shown his first contract, a "Consultancy Agreement" under which he would work for one year as a bank executive in Moscow, for the Russian subsidiary (RSub) of EB. He agreed to its terms with a handshake. It was then sent to his address in Connecticut, where he executed it.

This first Consultancy Agreement, dated January 1998 (1998 Agreement), was between Josef K. and Geneva Global Management Services (GGMS), a Swiss professional employment organization[2] used by the European Bank. A provision in the 1998 Agreement stipulated that the law of the United Kingdom governed the agreement. It also specified an annual incentive compensation bonus. At the end of 1998, Josef K. began to renegotiate a second one-year contract. His chief demand was a sharply increased bonus. He was not sent a new Consultancy Agreement at the end of the year and threatened to stop working and leave. While a new Consultancy Agreement was being negotiated, Vladimir S. sent Josef K. an interim agreement in the form of an executed letter of agreement on the stationery of R. Sub, dated December 12, 1998, which purported to renew employment until a new Consultancy Agreement could be generated. It did not include a choice of law clause, but did promise the increased bonus that Josef K. demanded. He signed the December 12 letter and returned it to Vladimir S. Finally, Josef K. was sent an unsigned, 1999

---

[2] A professional employment organization (PEO) contractually assumes employer rights, responsibilities, and risks of its clients, for whom the employee works, and establishes and maintains the employer relationship with the workers assigned to its clients. The PEO commonly assigns workers to client locations, and thereby assumes responsibility as an employer of the workers assigned to the location. The PEO typically reserves the right to direct and control, as well as hire and fire, the employees, and may share that responsibility with the client. It pays wages and employment taxes of the employee out of its own accounts, and reports, collects, and deposits employment taxes with the applicable government authorities. The employment relationship it establishes and maintains with the employee is usually intended to be long term, not temporary.

version of the "Consultancy Agreement", with somewhat different terms. It, too, came from SGMS, but this time specified that the law of Belgium governed the relationship. It contained the same bonus provision as the 1998 Agreement, and thus did not mention the increased bonus set forth in the December 12 letter. By this time, the employment relationship between 58-year-old Josef K. and his immediate supervisor in Moscow, 26-year-old, Igor, had deteriorated, as had the business of the Moscow office due to the downturn in Russia's economy. Before either party signed the 1999 Agreement, Igor terminated Josef. K.'s employment effective June 1, 1999. Josef K. was paid through that day, but received nothing toward his 1999 bonus.

Josef K. contacted an employment lawyer in the United States and sought advice. His choice of an American lawyer was practical, since he planned to return to the United States. He therefore preferred to prosecute any case he might bring in the United States. His prime objective, however, was first to negotiate as much of a severance as possible. He therefore wanted to know how much bargaining leverage he possessed at this point.

2. Issues

The task of the legal advisor is similar to that of a student taking a final examination in law school, i.e., to rapidly spot all the viable claims Josef may have, to bring them to bear in any ensuing negotiation. Once these claims are identified, the counselor examines each to see if they will be supported with the requisite facts and substantive law, and whether the most desired courts will be amenable to these claims under their jurisdictional, venue, and procedural rules. Finally, the counselor must contemplate the logistical complications that would be encountered in the pursuit of these claims. Once the attorney has a handle on this picture, the client and attorney can design a plan of action to approach the employer.

The first issue that the attorney must consider in framing the particular claims is the identity of the employer. In Josef K.'s case, which is typical, at least three entities arguably could be called his employer:

(1) The parent company, EB;

(2) The PEO, GGMS; or

(3) EB's Russian subsidiary.

Here, it is possible that all three bear employer liability.

The potential claims will be strongest where the employee has the greatest likelihood of bringing a sustainable action. In this case, Josef will want to know what are the best claims he can prosecute from the United States. Practical parameters such as these often frame the counselor's inquiry. Josef K.'s attorney in the United States will pose the following issues for initial research in connection with these claims:

(1) Which courts might have jurisdiction over claims against which entities; and

(2) Whether those entities have violated a provision of American law that can be heard in that United States.

In other words, Josef's K.'s United States attorney would begin to ask whether any of the three entities did anything that would give the United States courts a basis for extending jurisdiction to them. The problem with framing the strategy in this way is that it focuses overly on United States law, to the exclusion of other claims. As will be seen momentarily, the jurisdictional issues alone, in a case where the United States lawyer is seeking a foothold for the claims of one in Josef K.'s position can be fairly complex and time consuming to fathom.

That the same lawyer will have the ability to determine the client's best claims in the foreign jurisdiction will depend, of course, on the lawyer's range of expertise. The likelihood is, however that with international plaintiffs' employment law in its infancy, the home country lawyer will have to rely on foreign counsel's advice in the foreign jurisdiction to determine the viability of any claims there. The plaintiff may find it difficult to find suitable lawyers in a timely manner. At the present, no international plaintiffs' employment bar association exists to which requests for referrals can be lodged. The client must find a local lawyer to assay the claims in the foreign locale, as well as gauge the procedural and logistical issues that must temper the practical advice.

3. Analysis

The home country attorney will likely view the potential claims first through the lens of jurisdiction, which means determining whether the home country's courts and laws can extend to any of the "employers". For example, an individual or entity must usually either be a domicile of the jurisdiction or be doing business there. In the case of an expatriate, such as Josef K., the immediate employer (here the Russian subsidiary) is unlikely to be residing or doing any business in the United States, no less a state within it.[3] For the purposes of the "doing business" test, however, a foreign corporation that controls an entity, such as a branch or subsidiary in a state, such as New York, is considered to be doing business in New York. This jurisdictional rule directs the inquiry, therefore, toward EB, the Russian subsidiary's

[3] The plaintiff in the United States can seek the jurisdiction of the federal courts for only certain cases, or the state court, for most every case.

parent. If the parent or another subsidiary of the parent is doing business in New York, the parent arguably could be hauled into New York court to answer the claims brought by Josef K.

The jurisdictional tests do not end there. If EB was not considered to be domiciled in New York because it did not control a subsidiary doing business there, Josef K. could still attempt to show that EB transacted business in New York, which would subject it to New York's jurisdiction. This inquiry would focus on Josef K.'s second interview (with Vladimir in Kennedy Airport) when he was initially hired. New York CPLR, Section 302 (a)(1), sets forth the relevant jurisdictional requirements when suing a nonresident that is not engaged in ongoing business in New York, but which does transact some business here. Section 302 provides in pertinent part:

> (a) A court may exercise personal jurisdiction over any nondomiciliary who in person or through an agent:
>
> 1. transacts any business within the state or contracts anywhere to supply goods or services in the state . . . .

Unlike the CPLR, section 301 test, section 302 requires the showing of a connection between the injury and the New York transaction. The Court of Appeals has held that the New York transaction must "bear a substantial relationship to the transaction out of which the instant cause of action arose".[4] Under the Second Circuit's gloss, there must be a "direct relationship between the cause of action and the in-state conduct".[5] Misconduct "separated by time and geography" from New York does not arise out of a "transaction of business" under CPLR, section 302.[6] Courts have refused to find that a New York link in the chain of events leading to the claim is enough.[7]

In services contracts, an initial New York contact is ordinarily insufficient. Purchasing bus tickets in New York, for example, will not support a New York claim for an Arizona bus accident.[8]

Assuming there is substantial connection between the wrongful act (i.e., the discharge) and the New York transaction (i.e., had the New York contract been the only one, and the operative one at the time of Josef K.'s discharge), then a single, purposeful meeting in New York may be sufficient to be a "transaction" for section 302 purposes. The negotiation should be substantial in terms of quantity and quality.[9]

---

4 McGowan v. Smith, 437 N.Y.S.2d 643 (1981).

5 Beacon Enterprises, Inc. v. Menzies, 715 F.2d 757 (2d Cir. 1983).

6 Weinstein Korn Miller, section 302.05.

7 Weinstein Korn Miller, section 302.05. at p. 3–91.

8 Weinstein Korn Miller, section 302.05. at p. 3–91.

9 Lehigh Valley Indus. Inc. v. Birnbaum, 527 F.2d 87, 91 (2d Cir. 1975).

For example, a 45-minute exploratory meeting was held insufficient to constitute a transaction for business under Section 302.[10]

In the leading case, however, the Court of Appeals held that a one-day meeting in New York was sufficient to confer jurisdiction. In *George Reiner & Co. v. Schwartz,*[11] the New York employer corporation in New York interviewed the Massachusetts-based employee. He took back with him a written employment agreement creating a continuing relationship that ended when the employer terminated and sued him four years later. The court noted that the entering into the contract on that day was not "merely the 'last act marking the formal execution of the contract' . . . which might not, without more, be sufficient" to subject the salesman to New York's jurisdiction.[12] Also, the Court emphasized that he came to New York "purposefully seeking employment . . . with a New York employer that contemplated and resulted in a continuing relationship between them". The best argument in favor of obtaining New York jurisdiction over EB is that Josef K.'s meeting in New York with Vladimir was the purposeful commencement of the relationship out of which the breach of contract arose. The problems, however, are that:

(1) The New York meeting was not the only meeting that gave rise to the relationship;

(2) Josef K. did not come to New York to contract with a New York employer, thus the site of New York was arbitrary; and

(3) The agreement that Josef. K. Would insist is the operative one (with the higher pay and bonus guarantee) is not the 1998 agreement, but the 1998 agreement — represented in the December 12, 1998 letter from Vladimir — that was not transacted in New York.

Given this triangulated structure, Josef K. should attempt to establish as direct an employment link between himself and the parent as possible. Of course, in the present case, Josef K. might be able to show that the EB ultimately was his employer, despite the intervening PEO and the fact that he actually performed work for the subsidiary. Nevertheless, Josef K.'s most lucrative claims might not be against the parent. Under the contract with the PEO/parent he was not guaranteed a generous bonus. The official from the Russian subsidiary promised the bonus that he most wishes to enforce. The trick for Josef K.'s counsel would then be to try to have EB, the parent, answer in New York as the responsible party for the acts of the Russian subsidiary, by virtue of any branch of United States subsidiary that it operates in New York. In other words, Josef K. obtains the jurisdiction he wants because the European controls an American entity, and yet is answerable in liability only because it also controls another foreign (here, Russian) entity.

---

10 C-Life Group Ltd. v. The Generra Co., 652 N.Y.S.2d 41 (1st Dep't 1997).

11 George Reiner & Co. v. Schwartz, 394 N.Y.S.2d 844 (1970).

12 George Reiner & Co. v. Schwartz, 394 N.Y.S.2d 844 (1970), at p. 848.

These cases reveal why one of the greatest challenges of the plaintiff's attorney is to throw rope bridges between related entities to establish jurisdictional and liability footings on which to scale, based on the relationships between these entities. The court would examine the relationships between the parent entity to see whether it tightly controls both its New York and Russian affiliates, if there is such an entity with such relationships, under a multi-factor test that looks at whether the subsidiaries were co-owned, supported by, and controlled (in their staffing and other decision-making) by the parent. This inquiry is particularly common in discrimination cases and the tests, which are rather nebulous, are set forth in their clearest form in those statutes.

a. Bounds of United States Discrimination Laws and Corporate Control

In additional to his contract-based claims, Josef K. will want to explore his discrimination claims. The person who fired him was half his age. He will need to know whether the age discrimination protections found in United States law apply to his employment in Russia. The likelihood is that Josef K. will not be able to find that protection unless his employer was part of an United States-based entity. The question then becomes to what extent does a transnational company that has operations in the United States become liable to United States expatriates working in their operations outside the United States.

To answer this question, one must refer to the rules regarding extraterritoriality and corporate control found in those statutes. Indeed, the same rules that tie a foreign parent to the acts of its United States domiciled subsidiary for jurisdiction purposes can also make it liable for discrimination when claims are brought by United States citizens who work in the company's overseas operations

b. Age Discrimination in Employment Act

The Age Discrimination in Employment Act (ADEA) of 1967 was amended in 1984 to extend coverage to Americans working for United States employers in foreign locales. Three key provisions were added, as set forth below. Before 1984, the ADEA's coverage was considered coterminous with that of the Fair Labor Standards Act (FLSA), which specifically does not apply with respect to an employee whose services are "performed in a workplace within a foreign country".[13] This FLSA's coverage is still only domestic.

I. Definition of "Employee". For the purposes of the ADEA and FLSA, an employee includes "any individual who is a citizen of the United States employed by an employer in a workplace in a foreign country".[14]

---

[13] 29 United States Code, section 213(f).

[14] 29 United States Code, section 630(f).

II. Issue of "Control". The question of whether the United States employer is liable under the ADEA and FLSA for conduct abroad turns on the concept of control. the ADEA[15] provides that:

> (1) If an employer controls a corporation whose place of incorporation is in a foreign country, any practice by such corporation prohibited under this section shall be presumed to be such practice by such employer.
>
> (2) The prohibitions of this section shall not apply where the employer is a foreign person not controlled by an American employer.
>
> (3) For purpose of this subsection the determination of whether an employer controls a corporation shall be based on:
>
> (a) interrelationship of operations,
>
> (b) common management,
>
> (c) centralized control of labor relations; and
>
> (d) common ownership or financial controls.

Applying these rules, the court in *Denty v. SmithKline Beecham Corp.*[16] was faced with an American who worked domestically for a United States corporation that was controlled by a British one. He was denied overseas jobs by the British parent, he alleged, because of his age. He argued that the ADEA's coverage extended to the British parent because it was highly integrated with the American subsidiary. Focusing, instead, on the issue of "control",[17] the court found that the defendant British parent was not controlled by its American subsidiary; it was the other way around. Accordingly, the ADEA did not to apply to decisions of the British parent.

EEOC Policy Guidance is also instructive on the ADEA's extraterritoriality. In 1989, the EEOC issued a "Policy Guide on Application of ADEA and Equal Pay Act Overseas".[18]

c. *"Foreign Law Conflict" Defense*

To determine whether ADEA coverage will extend outside the United States, the legal counselor must also keep in mind a statutory limitation known as the "foreign law conflict defense".

---

15 29 United States Code, section 623(h)(3).

16 Denty v. SmithKline Beecham Corp., 907 F. Supp. 879, *aff'd*, 109 F.3d 147 (3d Cir. 1997), *cert. denied*, 118 S. Ct. 94 (1997).

17 29 United States Code, section 623(h)(3).

18 EEOC Policy Guidance, N-915.039 (March 3, 1989).

According to the ADEA:[19]

It shall not be unlawful for an employer . . .

(1) to take any action otherwise prohibited under . . . this section . . . where such practices involve an employee in a workplace in a foreign country, and compliance with such subsections would cause such employer, or a corporation controlled by such employer, to violate the laws of the country in which such workplace is located.

Illustrating this rule is *Mahoney v. RFE/RL, Inc.*[20] There, Radio Free Europe (RFE), a United States corporation, dismissed three United States citizen employees working in Germany pursuant to a German collective bargaining agreement that set a mandatory retirement age of 65. The three Americans filed ADEA claims and persuaded the District Court that, while the RFE might be contractually bound to retire Germans at age 65, no German law prohibited the employment of the 65-year old Americans. RFE argued that its "work council", which enforces its collective bargaining agreement, had rejected its prior attempts to carve out separate, nonconforming employment arrangements for American employees. The Third Circuit reversed, finding that the German law of contracts, which stood behind the collective bargaining agreement, was a conflicting "law" that RFE would be violating if it retained the Americans past 65. Due to that conflict, the Court held the ADEA inapplicable to the claims.[21]

4. Title VII

a. *Civil Rights Act of 1991*

In 1991, Congress overruled the Supreme Court's domestic-only interpretation of Title VII in the case of *EEOC v. Arabian American Oil Co.*[22] Congress adopted the ADEA's extraterritorial language, which it had used the year before in the Americans with Disabilities Act of 1990 (ADA). Title VII's now applies "with respect to employment in a foreign country . . . an individual who is a citizen of the United States".[23] Title VII covers discrimination against United States citizens abroad if engaged in by an American employer or by a foreign corporation controlled by an American employer.[24]

---

19 29 United States Code, section 623(f)(1).

20 Mahoney v. RFE/RL, Inc. 818 F. Supp. 1 (D.D.C. 1992), *rev'd*, 47 F.3d 447 (D.C. Cir. 1994), *cert. denied*, 116 S. Ct. 181 (1995).

21 Further analysis of the "foreign law conflict" defense can be found in the EEOC Compliance Manual, Notice 915.046, EEOC Compl. Man (December 5, 1989).

22 EEOC v. Arabian American Oil Co., 499 U.S. 244 (1991).

23 42 United States Code, section 2000-e(f) (Title VII); 42 United States Code, section 12111(4)(ADA).

24 42 United States Code, section 2000e-(c)(1) (Title VII); 42 United States Code, section 12112(c)(ADA).

As for the important issue of control, Title VII uses the four-part ADEA test.[25] Title VII also borrows ADEA's "conflict with [local] law".[26]

b. *Employment Opportunity Commission Guidance*

The United States Equal Employment Opportunity Commission (EEOC) issued its "Enforcement Guidance on Application of Title VII and ADA to Conduct Overseas and to Foreign Employers in the United States" on October 20, 1993.[27] According to the EEOC, an American corporation is one that "has numerous contacts here", even if it is incorporated elsewhere. Such contacts include its principal place of business, dominant shareholders, officers and directors.

According to the EEOC, a foreign corporation would be controlled by an American corporation, and thus be covered under Title VII, if it satisfies the same four-part standard used under the ADEA. Thus, the following hypothetical foreign corporation would be controlled by a United States corporation, according to the EEOC:

(1) The United States corporation owns 25 per cent of the foreign corporation's stock;

(2) The board memberships of the two corporations overlap;

(3) The United States corporation sets human resources policies for the foreign corporation;

(4) The United States corporation's representatives visit and inspect the foreign corporation's operations; and

(5) The United States corporation dictates changes in marketing and sales strategy.

The EEOC also acknowledges a "Foreign Law Conflict" Defense. According to the EEOC, a foreign law for the purposes of this defense is one that is codified. Thus, the EEOC shares the view of the reversed district court in *Mahoney*.[28] Given that many foreign cultures observe strict employment requirements that are part of their customs or religion, but that are not codified as law, the EEOC's position could

---

[25] 42 United States Code, section 2000e-(c)(1) (Title VII); 42 United States Code, section 12112(c) (ADA).

[26] 42 United States Code, section 2000e-l(b) (Title VII); 42 United States Code, section 12112(c)(1)(ADA).

[27] Title VII/ADA Policy.

[28] Mahoney v. RFE/RL, Inc., 818 F. Supp. 1 (D.D.C. 1992), *rev'd*, 47 F.3d 447 (D.C. Cir. 1994), *cert. denied*, 116 S. Ct. 181 (1995).

leave employers with no exemption when an American expatriate employee's rights collide with the mores and practices of a foreign country.

E. CONFLICT OF LAWS

What happens when conflicting laws from multiple jurisdictions are implicated in a termination? As any international practitioner knows, the inquiry into applicable claims often leads to conflict of law questions. Although this chapter will not even begin to review this area, it should be noted that many countries have labor laws, particularly wage and hour statutes that decisively will preempt any conflicting, less-protective foreign law, even when the employee is a non-citizen expatriate. In Josef K.'s case, even if he were to bring EB to court in New York, for example, he probably would have difficulty arguing that New York law applies to his contract claims as opposed to Russian law or the law stipulated in the agreements. The first signed contract makes United Kingdom law operative. The second, unsigned formal contracts invoke the law of Belgium. In between, there is the signed, Igor letter, which is silent as to the governing law. That letter comes from Russia and contemplates employment there. It is reasonable to assume that the law of one of those three locales applies, but which one is a more complex question.

F. CONCLUSION

As graphically illustrated by Josef K.'s case, today's transnational employment trends place an increasing number of challenges before the legal counselor when the client works for foreign entities. As more United States companies and expatriates venture abroad, these multifaceted employment questions will become more common.

Some say the globe has become so small that hardly an inch remains unexplored. At the busy crossroads of global commerce, however, the expatriate employee stands in one such pocket, where the world's employment laws intersect and so many questions abound. It might be hoped that as employers send expatriates abroad and compete globally for the best employees, they will carry with them their best practices. As these expatriates per force influence their foreign surroundings they will raise the standards of employee protections to higher, more harmonious, levels. Although the expatriate's migration may resemble a leap into the unknown today, he ultimately may be paving the way towards a new, enlightened era in global labor standards.

CHAPTER 5

CONFLICTS OF LAW AND CHOICE OF LAW ISSUES IN CROSSBORDER EMPLOYMENT DISPUTES

David Greene
Edwin Coe Solicitors
London, England

A. INTRODUCTION

Sixty years ago, "working" abroad was suddenly enforced on millions of people worldwide. Between 1939 and 1945, worldwide hostilities led to the mass movement of "workers" around the world. The resulting interface between nationalities was alternatively friendly or aggressive.

After the World War I, nations withdrew behind their borders and put up the shutters as the rebuilding process commenced, national stereotypes having been fuelled by six years of hostilities. A global war economy attempted to revert to its pre-War state. Nothing was quite the same, however.

The world started to examine how such an event could be avoided in the future. The seeds of the modern global economy had been planted. The United Nations, the European Union and the European Convention for Human Rights are all the products of attempts to avoid such hostilities in the future, to provide methods of settling differences between nations and to protect human rights.

B. WHAT IS CROSSBORDER EMPLOYMENT?

The phrase "crossborder employment" is rather like the eponymous elephant; you know it when you see it but it is rather difficult to describe. Some questions might be raised as to whether there is such a thing. It is not the purpose of this chapter to explore that issue.

One might say that any employment with a foreign element falls within the band of crossborder employment. This is true to a large extent but can be taken too far. For instance, an American national working in the United Kingdom for an English subsidiary of a Danish company might be a very domestic matter subject straightforwardly to English law.

On the other hand, a French national working in the United Kingdom will in the same circumstances be subject simply to English law but that English law might be subject to an examination purely on the grounds that the employee is a French national and therefore entitled to the protection and benefits of the Treaty of Rome under the articles providing freedom of movement and establishment.

Although difficult to define, for our purposes, the presence of a foreign element will be all-important. For example, the nationalities of the employer and employee may differ or the contract may be performed outside the domicile of either the employee or employer or the parties may have chosen an applicable jurisdiction or law other than that applying where the contract is performed.

C. WHAT IS A CROSSBORDER EMPLOYMENT DISPUTE?

Again, it would be simple to answer that such a dispute must relate to contractual relationship between employer and employee with that foreign element. It is not, however, only driven by contract. Important liabilities, for our purposes, may arise in tort. Indeed, it is often these that give rise to the most difficult jurisdiction and choice of law problems.

Whether it be contractual or tortious, however, such a dispute, notwithstanding that it has a foreign element, may be a very domestic matter. Taking again our American employee working in England for a Danish employer, the employee in question would be entitled to rely on his rights under English domestic legislation, even if the parties had agreed to apply American law to the contract. The fact that the employee is an American national may make absolutely no difference to those rights and entitlements.

It is a strange irony that from a European point of view while borders within the European Union are being taken down the borders around the European Union are being strengthened and we can now talk realistically of fortress Europe. As far as the law relating to employment is concerned the European can see a world divided into two — European Union and non-European Union.

D. CROSSBORDER EMPLOYMENT WITHIN THE EUROPEAN UNION

The Treaty of Rome guarantees certain freedoms. Article 48, for instance, provides for the free movement of workers. Article 52 provides for the right of establishment. These basic freedoms have themselves produced legislation within the European Union supporting and imposing them. For instance, the freedom of movement of workers is supported by the Rome Convention on the Law Applicable to Contractual Obligations (the Rome Treaty).

The Brussels and Lugano Conventions on the Recognition and Enforcement of Judgments arise not from a basic freedom guaranteed by the Treaty of Rome but by article 220 of the Treaty. Article 220 invoked the signatory States to insofar as necessary enter into negotiations with each other with a view to securing for the benefit of their nationals the simplification of formalities governing the reciprocal recognition and enforcement of judgments of courts or tribunals and of arbitration awards.

Any lawyer now working on an employment contract or dispute related to it, whether truly domestic or with a foreign element, has increasing reference to European legislation. This European legislation has equal importance to domestic legislation. The result is that often the simplest of employment disputes can lead to very complex considerations of both domestic and European legislation.

This area of law has seen an exponential growth over the past 20 years but remains in an early stage of development. Domestic law remains constantly in question on the basis of its compliance with European law. From an English point of view, a small bomb is being placed into this circle by the codification of the European Convention for Human Rights under the Human Rights Act 1998. Few, have yet to fully understand the significance of that piece of legislation on all walks of life including employment.

Traditionally, when looking at a contract with a foreign element, lawyers would consider three elements of the contract in determining the way forward in a dispute:

(1) Jurisdiction;

(2) Choice of law; and

(3) Recognition and enforcement of any judgments or awards.

1. Jurisdiction Questions in the European Economic Area

With respect to jurisdiction in the European Economic Area (EEA), that is in the European Free Trade Area (EFTA) and the European Union (EU), the first question to be asked by the lawyer is where will the dispute in relation to the employment contract will be resolved — in which forum. The author's broad comments about the position within the European Union originate from an English point of view and his experience gained from an English perspective.

Within the European Union the correct forum for the resolution of a dispute is determined either by the Brussels Convention or (in relation to EFTA and European Union states) the Lugano Convention.

From an English point of view these Conventions and their incorporation into English legislation (Civil Jurisdiction and Judgments Act 1982) in some respects confirmed practice in the courts of England and Wales as to jurisdiction and in other respects altered it substantially. As with any Common Law jurisdiction the process of precedent gave the court much scope to adapt to the particular circumstances what was felt to be 'just'. The codification under the Brussels or Lugano Conventions removed much of that discretion. Both the Brussels and Lugano Conventions apply to contracts of employment.

Under both Conventions, the basis of jurisdiction is that of "domicile". Surprisingly domicile is not then defined within the Convention and it is left to each individual contracting state to determine exactly what domicile means. Thus, despite the attempt to produce a common system among the contracting states the lawyer advising may or must seek advice in another jurisdiction as to the local regulation of 'domicile'.

The Conventions codify the principle that the question of jurisdiction revolves around the right of the defendant to be sued in their own jurisdiction. Thus, it is the domicile of the defendant that is the defining criteria. If the defendant is not domiciled in the contracting state then generally the Conventions do not apply.

Although domicile is the general determining factor as to where a defendant is entitled to be sued, in relation to contract that person may also be sued in another contracting state if within that other state the contract is to be performed. In individual contracts of employment the place of performance for that purpose is where the employee habitually carries out his work.[1] In *Shenavai v. Kreischer,*[2] the European Court of Justice seeks to define what an employment contract is.

One can immediately see that there may well be remaining difficulties, particularly in establishing where someone "habitually" carries out his work. For this purpose article 5(1) of the Brussels Convention also provides that where an employee does not habitually carry out work in any one country, the employer may also be sued in the courts of a place where the business which engaged the employee was or is now situated. The Lugano Convention provides slightly differently since it speaks of the place of business through which the employee was engaged.

There is an important difference between the two Conventions. The Lugano Convention does not limit the jurisdiction to actions by the employee against the employer but the 1968 Convention does.

It should be noted how the provisions of the two Conventions sit with the Rome Convention on the Law Applicable to Contractual Obligations. Under the Rome Convention on the Law Applicable to Contractual Obligations, without an express or implied choice of law, a contract of employment is governed by the law of the country:

(1) In which the employee habitually performs the contract; or

(2) If the employee habitually performs the contract in two or more places, the law of the country in which the place of business through which he was engaged is situated.

---

1 Ivenel v. Schwab, Case 133/81 [1982] ECR 1891. The ratio for this decision has since been codified in article 5(1) of the Brussels and Lugano Conventions.

2 Shenavai v. Kreischer, Case 266/85 [1987] ECR 239.

Thus, there will be a marrying of the three Conventions.

2. Ousting Jurisdiction

The parties one or more of whom is domiciled in a contracting State can oust the jurisdiction of the court that would normally have jurisdiction in accordance with the Convention and the court chosen by the parties may have exclusive jurisdiction.[3] Such a jurisdiction clause is governed by the law applicable to the contract.[4] The ousting agreement must be in writing and must be unambiguous.

This European jurisdictional rule[5] and its effect has interesting consequences in relation to employment. Throughout the European Union, it is quite common for domestic legislation to contain provisions which prevent parties from contracting out of the jurisdiction of the domestic courts. The European Court has decided, however,[6] that an agreement as to jurisdiction falling within this rule must be given effect notwithstanding provisions such as this within domestic legislation.

In *Sanicentral GmbH v. Collins*,[7] a contract between a French worker and a German employer conferred jurisdiction on the German court, thus depriving the French courts of jurisdiction despite the fact that the jurisdiction clause was void by French law. The court on that occasion said that it was not attempting to affect rules of substantive law but said that:

> In matters of civil jurisdiction, the national procedural laws applicable to the cases concerned are set aside in the matters governed by the Convention in favor of the provisions thereof.

One matter that should always be considered when dealing with international conventions is their interpretation. Generally, the court will only look at the enacting statute and the text of the convention within it. If, however, the convention is not included within it or the statute the court may look at the convention to interpret it. Further, the court may look at decisions in other jurisdictions and the convention in other languages. In England, this is a whole new ball game with the House of Lords decreeing that the English courts should adopt continental methods of interpretation.[8]

---

3 Brussels and Lugano Conventions, article 17.

4 The Rome Convention has no application to such a clause.

5 Brussels and Lugano Conventions, article 17.

6 Sanicentral GmbH v. Collins, Case 25/79 [1979] ECR 3423.

7 Sanicentral GmbH v. Collins, Case 25/79 [1979] ECR 3423.

8 James Buchanan & Co. Ltd. v. Babco Forwarding and Shipping (UK) Ltd. (1978) AC 141.

E. CHOICE OF LAW ISSUES IN THE EUROPEAN UNION

Having determined the correct forum for determining a dispute, the next question is what law will be applicable to the relationship between employer and employee.

Within the European Union, the Rome Convention on the Law Applicable to Contractual Obligations applies. Article 6 of the Convention contains special provisions in relation to individual employment contracts. As a whole, however, under the Rome Convention the parties are free to make a choice of the applicable law. If there is no choice of law, then in accordance with article 6(2) the law governing the contract of employment will be:

(1) The law of the country in which the employee habitually carries out his work in performance of the contract, even if he is temporarily employed in another country; or

(2) If the employee does not habitually carry out his work in any one country, by the law of the country in which the place of business through which he was engaged is situated.

However, if it appears from the circumstances as a whole that the contract is more closely connected with another country then the contract will be governed by the law of that country.

Difficulties of interpretation arise from article 6(2). For instance, what amounts to "habitually" or "temporarily"?[9] Further, where for the purposes of article 6(2)(b) is "the place of business through which he was engaged". Indeed, what is "engagement"?

These are not necessarily new problems. The English court has dealt with some aspects of them even before the inception of the Rome Convention. In *Sayers v. International Drilling Company*,[10] an employee was hired through an English agent on behalf of a Dutch company to carry out work in Nigeria, although the employer retained the right to change the place of employment. In that case the Court of Appeal said that Dutch law should apply because the contract of employment had the closest and most real connection with Dutch law.

It is not clear whether the Court of Appeal would make the same decision under the Convention. It might be said that one of the factors that may determine the law governing the contract would be the protection offered to the employee under that law where everything else is in balance. In *Sayers*, however, the court chose a law (Dutch law) which provided less protection to the employee than English law.

---

9 Rome Convention, Article 6(2)(a).

10 Sayers v. International Drilling Company [1971] 1WLR 1176.

There was an exclusion clause which limited liability. The clause was void under English law but valid under Dutch.

Under the Rome Convention, as with the Brussels Convention, the parties are free to select a law to govern the contract.[11] This freedom to choose the law, however, is limited in that it cannot have the effect of depriving the employee of protection given to him by mandatory rules of law that would have been applicable in the absence of the selection of an alternative law to that which would normally govern under the rules of article 6(2).

Thus, the chosen law "shall not have the result of depriving the employee of the protection afforded to him by the mandatory rules of law which would" apply in the absence of a choice.

Thus, in examining such a contract, the advisor will have to consider what protections are lost as a result of the choice of law. This is not an easy question. An immediate difficulty arises if competing laws provide different types of protection. Can the employee enjoy the protection of both laws? Further, what are the relevant rules relating to employment protection that are safeguarded? It appears that these rules "consist not only of the provisions relating to the contract of employment itself, but also to provisions such as those concerning industrial safety and hygiene which are regarded in certain member states as being provisions of public law".[12]

This gives some general picture of the mandatory rules envisaged but in the end it is for the national law to determine whether the rule is mandatory. Rules that may appear mandatory on the face of it might not be mandatory on further examination. Thus, the unfair dismissal laws of England are mandatory rules unless the employee is ordinarily working outside Great Britain.

There are no special rules under the Rome Convention as to the formal validity of a contract. Thus, article 9 of the Rome Convention will apply. Accordingly, whether or not a contract is valid will be determined either by the law which governs the contract or the law of the country in which the contract was concluded. This may of course lead to questions of validity under a number of laws, particularly where the contracting parties are themselves in different jurisdictions and the law of choice is different. As long as the contract is valid under one of the appropriate laws, it will be valid for the purposes of the Rome Convention.

Of course, a claim by an employee may not be in contract alone; it might be a collateral claim in tort, as there was in *Sayers v. International Drilling Company*. Article 5 (3) provides that jurisdiction is conferred on the courts where "the harmful

---

11 Rome Convention, Article 6(1).

12 *The Giuliano-Lagarde Report.*

event occurred". What amounts to a tort may cause some difficulty — a tort in one jurisdiction may be a contractual claim in another.

In *Kalfelis v. Schroder*,[13] the European Court of Justice tried to answer this question. It decreed that what is a tort or delict is not to be determined according to national law but as an autonomous concept covering:

> . . . all actions which seek to establish the liability of a defendant and which are not related to a 'contract' within the meaning of article 5(1).

As with so much, this remains a question for the domestic court.

F. JURISDICTION IN NON EUROPEAN ECONOMIC AREA STATES

If the Brussels or Lugano Conventions have no application in determining a particular jurisdiction for the contract, one must fall back on the domestic law as to the assertion of jurisdiction. In most jurisdictions the parties to a contract can submit to the jurisdiction but it is an important distinction as to the timing of the submissions i.e., the difference between *prorogatio fori proprii ante litem natam* and *prorogatio fori proprii post litem natam*. In the absence of a choice of jurisdiction expressed in the contract, jurisdiction will be determined in accordance with particular domestic provisions including when there is tacit submission; such as in England, taking a step in the proceedings.

In England, jurisdiction is very much based on service of the originating process, either within or outside the jurisdiction, i.e., England and Wales. In other states jurisdiction might depend on whether assets of a party are held within the jurisdiction. It is an infamous example that if a non-resident leaves his umbrella in Sweden the Swedish court assumes jurisdiction over him for a debt in any amount.

This example should remind United States lawyers that even if jurisdiction is asserted, the result may be unenforceable in another jurisdiction. It may be said that the exercise of the jurisdiction by that court and the granting of a judgment lead to an exorbitant judgment because there are few, if any, assets held within the jurisdiction of judgment.

Similarly, there may be public policy reasons why a judgment is unenforceable in another jurisdiction. By way of example, a judgment that is penal (such as penal damages in the United States) may be unenforceable in other jurisdictions such as England. The jurisdiction in which enforcement is sought may similarly determine that there was insufficient connection between the defendant and the court giving judgment.

From an English point of view, it is felt that the United States is one of those jurisdictions which is more willing to assume jurisdiction over a dispute.

---

13 Kalfelis v. Schroder, Case 189/97 (1988) ECR 5565.

Domestically within the United States, many have what are known as "long arm" statutes that provide for wide ranging jurisdiction foreign to European standards — for example, section 302 of the New York Civil Practice Law and Rules.

Even in less adventurous and assertive jurisdictions, courts may seek to extend their jurisdiction even if it be by requiring parties to discontinue proceedings in a foreign court.

There may be many factors to be taken into account by a court as to the exercise of its jurisdiction. One of the areas of growth within practice has been the development of the concept "*forum non conveniens*" within Common Law jurisdictions. The author's own purely anecdotal experience is that the United States courts have been more ready recently to dismiss attempts to found United States jurisdiction with the attraction of higher damages on the basis of *forum non conveniens*.

The disaster in Bhopal was an infamous example of a refusal by the United States courts to try a claim. Indeed, the general doctrine of *forum non conveniens* to compel or enable the court to refrain from adjudicating on the merits only because adjudicating abroad would be more convenient is a concept much more associated with Scottish law (which has strong ties with continental law) than English law.

Although there may be good arguments against taking jurisdiction for *conveniens* reasons, with the growth in social legislation affecting employment, the court may well take into account the form of relief available within a particular jurisdiction and the protection given to employees by that jurisdiction before exercising its discretion in favor of another jurisdiction. Despite the limitations of its application generally in Common Law jurisdictions, the application of *forum non conveniens* requires the identification of the forum in which the case could be suitably tried for the interests of all the parties and for the ends of justice.[14]

The other matter that will be of primary importance in consideration of questions of jurisdiction will be whether proceedings have been commenced already in another jurisdiction.

As well as the question of remedies available within the other jurisdiction, the court might look at methods of funding the proceedings. In England, recently, the court has taken into account the availability of Legal Aid as one of those factors.

As now applies under the Brussels and Lugano Conventions, the parties are generally free to determine a jurisdiction by agreement. The courts will generally not allow a party to go back on its word. However, in deciding whether to allow this (the claimant will be more strictly bound), the court must apply its own rules as to whether its jurisdiction can be excluded and assess the consequences of such

---

14 Spiliada Maritime Corp v. Cansulex Ltd [1987] AC 460.

exclusion; is it compelled or merely enabled to refuse a decision on the merits and on what factors should it base its decision?

It is a question of interpretation of the law applicable to the jurisdiction clause whether the clause is exclusive or non-exclusive. In the United States and Scotland, the principle of *forum non conveniens* may be one consideration. Certainly since the decision in the Supreme Court in *Motor Ship Bremen v. Zapata Off-Shore Co.*,[15] the United States courts appear more willing to give cognizance to a choice of jurisdiction clause.

As with the two Conventions, jurisdiction will depend on the nature of the claim. The claim, although connected to the contract of employment, may be truly a claim in tort. Whether it is or not must be determined by the domestic court based on domestic law. If it is a tort there may be a competition between *lex loci* and *lex loci delicti*. This may arise, for instance, where there is a clause within the contract excluding liability for the tort.

G. CHOICE OF LAW IN NON EUROPEAN UNION STATES

Some of the considerations that have already been covered apply equally to the consideration of the applicable governing law. Each jurisdiction has its own general rules for the identification. Those rules might be, for instance, the law that has the closest and most real connection with the contract. In relation to an employment contract, the proper law would govern such questions as:

(1) The terms to be implied into a contract;

(2) The circumstances in which the employee was entitled to remain on the employer's premises and to receive wages or other forms of compensation;

(3) Whether notice of termination is effective; and

(4) Whether an exemption clause in the contract is valid.

The development of social legislation, however, has affected these general rules quite substantially. That social legislation has been regarded as of primary importance. In England the Employment Rights Act 1996 provides specifically at section 203 (1) that any provision in an agreement will be void insofar as it purports either to exclude or limit the operation of the 1996 Act or to preclude any person from bringing any proceedings before an industrial tribunal.

Thus, a contract which purported to restrict an employee's rights in connection with pregnancy and confinement would be overridden by section 203(1) even if the

---

15 Motor Ship Bremen v. Zapata Off-Shore Co., 407 US 1.

contract were governed by a foreign law under which the term in question was valid. However, section 203(1) does not apply to employment outside Great Britain.

The legislation may imply into the contract certain obligatory clauses.

It is important, however, to differentiate between procedural requirements and substantive requirements of law.[16] Procedure such as whether to grant injunctive relief is for the *lex fori*.

Outside statutory provisions, however, the court should apply the law of choice even if the effect might be regarded as contrary to principles under the law of the forum.[17] In an employment contract the court may have regard to the relative bargaining positions of the parties and whether the choice of law derives from some economic duress.

Once again, the question of the application of a choice of law will depend on the nature of the claim and the remedy being sought, as different rules will apply between a claim in contract and a claim in tort. Interesting problems may then arise if there is a contractual clause excluding or limiting liability for the tort, as there was in *Sayers*. Then, the court must consider whether liability can be excluded either under the *lex fori* or the *lex delictii*. Having decided that issue, the court will consider the validity of the clause itself under the law of choice.

Even more problems may arise if the claim in tort is settled and the tortfeasor released; what law applies to that release? It may be the law appropriate for the tort or the law of the contract of release. More difficulty then arises as to the law relating to the release of a joint tortfeasor.

H. CONCLUSION

Jurisdiction and applicable law questions relating to the relationship between employer and employee raise very complex legal issues. They are unique because of the increasing amount of social legislation that regulates that relationship and the sensitivity of legislators and courts that arises from a perceived disparity in bargaining power and the potential for exploitation. As the global economy gathers pace, this complex area of the law will become ever more important to the employment lawyers' practice.

---

[16] Monterosso Shipping Co. Ltd v. ITWF (1982) IRLR 468.

[17] Sayers v. International Drilling Company [1971] 1WLR 1176.

Part II

Global Talent Management — Harmonizing Employment and Benefit Practices in an Employer's Global Operations

CHAPTER 6

DEVELOPING GLOBAL EMPLOYMENT POLICIES AND PROCEDURES

Robert J. Mignin and Steven A. Miller
Seyfarth, Shaw, Fairweather & Geraldson
Chicago, Illinois, United States

A. A GLOBAL PERSPECTIVE

Rapid advancements in technology, the expansion, integration, and interdependence of global businesses through mergers, acquisitions, and investments, the lessening of territorial and political barriers, the opening of markets through regional and global trade agreements, and the emergence of new markets and economic powers have all contributed to the growth of multinational companies.

The most significant change to affect global business in recent years is the rapid change in communication technologies. With the punch of a few keys, individuals are now able to conduct sensitive and complicated business transactions and communicate to customers, suppliers, business partners and fellow employees across thousands of miles without regard to geographic, political and cultural boundaries. This global growth and expansion of business has, in turn, placed pressure on multinational companies to adjust and change operations to increase business efficiencies. This, in turn, has resulted in many companies considering, developing, and implementing uniform global employment policies and practices to allow them to better manage their global workforce.

One impediment to uniform global employment policies has been not only the difference in culture and custom but also the perceived difference between labor and employment standards and laws applicable to employees in various countries. Despite these perceived legal disparities, many multinational companies have already adopted more general global "codes of conduct" in an attempt to harmonize and globalize their business and corporate culture, ever mindful of local laws, traditions and customs. These global businesses realize that despite real and/or perceived "legal" differences, their business goals and objectives remain essentially the same regardless of the country in which they operate:

(1) Maintaining an efficient operation;

(2) Ensuring a consistent, uniform and high quality product or service;

(3) Marketing products and services to appeal to local customers and cultures;

(4) Managing a global workforce in a manner which engenders loyalty, creativity and high performance; and

(5) Effectively competing in a global, compared to a local or regional, marketplace.

Global codes of conduct typically set forth general standards for a company's ethical business operations. These codes often encompass prohibitions on child labor, forced labor, and discrimination in employment. Some global codes also address employee health and safety issues, ethical behavior, environmental practices, freedom of association, the right to organize and bargain collectively, and workplace privacy. These codes are viewed by many companies as not only good for public relations but as a means of improving workplace conditions and the quality and loyalty of the global workforce.

Critics have opined that while the concept of global codes of conduct may be a sound business idea, there are simply too many legal and cultural obstacles to implementing and enforcing a viable and consistent set of uniform global employment policies and practices. Indeed, such critics argue that employment laws differ so significantly from country to country and the difference in customs, cultures, and language is so great that a uniform employment code is impossible.

When addressing the issue of uniform global employment policies and procedures, the question confronted by many multinational companies, however, is not what the host country's law provides or requires, but what is the company's core culture and value system and how important is it to the company to instill this culture to its employees on a worldwide basis, despite the impediments of local law, custom, and culture.

There are many issues surrounding the creation and adoption of global employment policies and procedures. The purpose of this chapter is not to explore every aspect of that debate. This paper simply examines a number of "substantive" employment issues common to all global employers and discusses some of the issues multinational companies may encounter in implementing global employment policies. A checklist of "practical" issues that should be considered when preparing and implementing global workforce policies is also attached.

B. ESTABLISHING GLOBAL EMPLOYMENT POLICIES AND PROCEDURES

1. Policies Prohibiting Employment Discrimination

Laws that prohibit discrimination in the workplace and provide some form of equal employment opportunities are common to many countries. These concepts have also been recognized in a number of international treaties and covenants.

Nevertheless, discrimination laws vary considerably because they are typically based on the host country's culture, political and economic systems. These disparities can present difficult business issues for multinational companies assessing whether to apply their employment policies that prohibit workforce discrimination and harassment to operations in countries where such conduct is not necessarily illegal.

Despite the potential legal conflict and differences in culture, many companies believe that the prohibition of discrimination in employment, even in countries where discrimination might be tolerated, is not only the morally correct practice, but a sound business practice, because employees who are free from discrimination:

(1) Are more efficient and productive;

(2) Achieve their greatest potential; and

(3) Are best able to assist the company in earning higher profits through increased efficiency and lower turnover.

Nevertheless, the following discussion highlights some of the cultural and political issues that multinational companies confront when drafting non-discrimination employment policies.

a. Sex Discrimination and Sexual Harassment

Sex discrimination and sexual harassment present unique challenges to companies adopting and fashioning global employment policies for the simple reason that differences in cultural norms often make it difficult to globally define what is "acceptable" or "unacceptable" conduct. What is tolerable or acceptable in one culture may be construed as offensive or discriminating in another. Even translating the United States concept of "sexual harassment" in some cultures can be a daunting linguistic challenge. While many countries have some type of law prohibiting sexual discrimination, the scope of the laws' coverage may differ considerably. Within Latin America, for example, Peru defines sexual harassment as a "dishonest act" that affects the dignity and moral values of the workers. Costa Rica, on the other hand, has a broad sexual harassment law that extends beyond the workplace.

Other conflicts arise because sexual harassment covers a broad range of activity, ranging from displaying pornographic materials to rape. Moreover, while many countries have some type of law addressing gender equality, such laws may be routinely ignored due to paternalism or other conceptions about the role of women in the workplace. Some countries, such as Japan, have laws allowing women to be discriminated against in certain employment terms — such as salary.

Regardless of these potential legal and cultural conflicts, the emotional and psychological impact of sex discrimination and sexual harassment, on both women and men, and the resulting loss of productivity and potential legal liability, has caused many multinational companies to implement (or consider implementing) global anti-discrimination and anti-harassment policies. Such policies not only prohibit discrimination and workplace sexual harassment but they establish procedures for enforcement and conducting investigations. Some multinational companies now maintain a toll-free number or e-mail address for employees who wish to bring complaints of this nature to the attention of management.

Global policies which prohibit sex discrimination in the workplace are supported by a number of international treaties, conventions and pronouncements which specifically recognize the rights of women to be free of discrimination and sexual harassment in the workplace. These conventions and treaties have formed the basis for court decisions protecting women from sexual harassment in the workplace. For example, India's Supreme Court recently expanded the country's legal definition of sexual harassment to include an employee's unsuccessful attempts to touch a female employee. Because India does not have any sexual harassment legislation, the court based its decision on two international treaties:

(1) The 1979 Convention on the Elimination of All Forms of Discrimination Against Women; and

(2) The Beijing Declaration from the Fourth, United Nations Conference on Women.

Moreover, the legal systems of many countries are increasingly influenced, if not directly based on, the laws and court decisions in the United States, England, and other western nations. Indeed, many of the constitutions of developing nations are directly modeled after the principles contained in the United States Constitution. Courts from other countries often look to the United States for guidance in such areas as sex discrimination and harassment. For example, in Malaysia, a conservative and predominately Muslin country which has no laws specifically prohibiting sexual harassment, a plaintiff recently prevailed in the country's first sexual harassment suit. The Industrial Court based its ruling on the decisional law of United States courts. Sexual harassment legislation in Canada and Australia is also based on United States case law and precedent.

For all these reasons, the barriers to adopting global employment policies addressing sexual harassment and sex discrimination may not be as problematic as critics assume.

b. Disability Discrimination

Many companies have also adopted employment policies that protect disabled employees from discrimination in the workplace. Laws governing workplace disability protections and the provision of accommodations for individuals with disabilities vary from country to country.

In the United States, the Americans with Disabilities Act of 1990 (ADA) provides comprehensive protection to disabled employees. The ADA exposes employers to financial liability for failing to make "reasonable accommodations" for persons who are disabled or who are perceived to be disabled. Some European countries, however, such as Germany, utilize a statutory quota system, which requires employers to include a certain percentage of disabled workers in their workforces.

A company doing business in Germany must implement a quota system or be subject to a monthly fine. In Germany, disabled employees have the right to refuse to perform any work in excess of normal working hours and receive special protection from dismissal. The French Labor Code also contains extensive regulations concerning disability discrimination and an affirmative action requirement. Several other European countries have also enacted legislation prohibiting employers from refusing to offer employment on the grounds of an applicant's health or state of disability.

While the specific nuances of the laws of the host country will have to be taken into consideration, there does not appear to be any business or legal reason why global employment policies cannot be created to address these concerns. Indeed, the concept of disability discrimination may be easier to transfer to other cultures than such concepts as sexual harassment.

c. *Age Discrimination*

Some countries specifically prohibit age discrimination in the workplace, while other nations do not have any such laws. For example, in Japan, employment decisions can, and often do, take into consideration an employee's age. An applicant is required to place his or her age on his or her resume. Promotions and salary raises are based on loyalty and seniority, of which age is an implicit part. In addition, companies can use age requirements in classified job advertisements and they often have mandatory retirement ages. These practices are common in those countries where there are no prohibitions on using age as a basis for employment-related decisions.

These differences, however, should not impede a multinational company's desire to adopt a global policy that prohibits discrimination on the basis of age. While a host country may have specific laws regulating retirement, there is nothing precluding a multinational company from adopting a policy which precludes using age as a basis for hiring and promotional decisions. Even though the local culture may have preconceptions about age, policies can still be created which rely on objective factors and direct the appropriate decision-makers to ignore the employee's age.

2. Policies Regulating Employee Discipline and Termination

Job security and employee termination are often cited as some of the most dramatic differences between the United States and other countries' employment laws. The "at-will" employment doctrine still dominates most employment relationships in the United States. Under this doctrine, employment is terminable "at-will" without notice, for any reason, or no reason at all, by either party. Indeed, although union collective bargaining agreements provide some job security, an estimated 75 to 80 per cent of all individuals employed in the United States are considered "at-will" employees.

Conversely, countries which have adopted the International Labor Convention (ILC) provide employees with protection from arbitrary dismissal. Under the ILC, employees must be given a valid reason for their dismissal. The German Termination Protection Act, for example, prohibits a German company with more than five employees from terminating employees without "acceptable" reasons. Terminations based on economic reasons, behavioral reasons, and personal characteristics of the employee all constitute "acceptable" reasons. Despite these provisions, German employers have often found it difficult to terminate employees and easier to pay employees a "redundancy payment" to avoid litigation or as an incentive to sign a waiver. As a result, German employers are now using time-based employment contracts to limit their exposure.

Similarly, in France an employee can only be terminated for a "real and serious" reason. A reason is "real" when it is true and objective and "serious" when the reason for the dismissal makes it impossible to continue the employment relationship. Employee dismissals can also be based on personal or economic reasons. In addition, employees may be terminated for failing to satisfy reasonable production standards or for engaging in conduct that results in a loss of confidence or ignores health and safety rules.

Japan also protects employees from arbitrary dismissal. Japanese courts use an "abuse of right" standard to determine if a termination decision is invalid. Under this theory a dismissal which is not reasonable "in light of the circumstances of the case and prevailing social norms" will be held invalid. This often makes it difficult to discharge a marginal worker because the prevailing norm is that it is wrong to discharge an employee because he or she is incompetent or unproductive.

While the "at-will" standard may appear harsh and arbitrary, it is not the practice of United States employers to arbitrarily terminate employees for no reason. Employees are protected from being terminated on a number of statutory and public policy grounds. Indeed, as a practical matter, almost all large United States companies have some form of rules of conduct and performance standards which set forth standards for termination (i.e., theft, dishonesty, workplace violence, acts of moral turpitude). When disciplining employees for any other reason, however, such companies typically follow progressive discipline. Terminating employees for no reason at all, although lawful, is not the standard practice in the United States.

A standardized termination policy and procedure, such as that presented by the ILC, would alleviate some of the confusion surrounding global termination proceedings. However, because some nations, especially the United States, have been reluctant to relinquish the "at-will" status of their employees, the disparity between "at-will" termination proceedings and those of countries who have adopted the ILC, or similar standards may create some difficulties for multinational companies developing global termination and discipline policies and procedures.

3. Policies Setting Wages, Benefits, and Working Hours

Because of worldwide economic and political disparities, there is little consensus or uniformity on wages, hours, and employee benefits. Indeed, the differences between developed, underdeveloped, and developing countries are significant and complex. Notwithstanding these disparities, many multinational companies have adopted certain minimum standards and compensation policies that apply on a global basis.

These policies are supported by several international conventions and treaties, such as the International Covenant on Civil and Political Rights and the International Covenant on Economic, Social and Cultural Rights, which declare fair wages, a decent living, safe and healthy working conditions, rest periods, and reasonable limitations on working hours to be fundamental human rights.

4. Policies Protecting Employee Privacy and Confidential Business Information

The advent of technology in the workplace has brought concomitant issues regarding employee privacy and business security. In addition to traditional telephone communications and omnipresent computers, employees now use voice-mail, send instantaneous e-mail, "surf" the globe-spanning Internet, and access and utilize global electronic bulletin boards. With global bulletin boards, employees and social organizations are now able to post both positive and negative comments about the business practices of multinational companies.

Many companies have now taken advantage of technological advances to monitor the workplace and their employees in an effort to guard against potential abuse, misconduct, theft, and other concerns. Moreover, recent advances in medical testing allow for the examination of human genes to predict future illnesses and psychological testing to screen out applicants with current or potential mental impairments. Employee monitoring raises privacy concerns in countries where an employee's right to privacy is statutorily recognized or where there is an applicable international or bilateral treaty. Many European and non-European countries include a right to privacy in their Constitutions, while others recognize privacy protections in their statutes and Common Law.

When adopting global employment policies protecting privacy and confidential business information, multinational companies must be cognizant of national and local laws regulating medical, drug, and psychological testing, the interception of data, and workplace searches and surveillance, to name only a few of the regulated areas. While countries have different definitions and parameters for the right to privacy, many multinational companies are adopting basic policies protecting privacy in the workplace.

5. Policies Regulating Health and Safety in the Workplace

Many companies have adopted or are considering adopting global employment policies that address employee health and safety issues, such as:

(1) Health and safety rules and procedures;

(2) Illegal drug and alcohol policies and testing;

(3) No-smoking policies;

(4) Environmental awareness issues; and

(5) Workplace violence and inspection policies.

Some of these policies lend themselves fairly easily to standard global employment policies, such as policies for reporting on the job injuries and workplace inspections. For example, the Maquiladora Standards of Conduct outline a number of health and safety practices that can be transformed into global codes and employment policies.[1] Some of the principles included in the Maquiladora Standards include:

(1) Disclosing to employees and the public the chemical identity of all chemicals used and the amount of waste materials stored on the premises;

(2) Providing health and safety training;

(3) Providing adequate ventilation systems; and

(4) Arranging for health and safety inspections by outside consultants.

6. Employment Dispute Resolution Mechanisms

With the increase in the volume and expense of employment-related litigation, companies doing business globally face constant challenges to monitor and control employee claims and litigation costs. One effective way to control employment claims is through internal dispute resolution procedures and mandatory arbitration of employment disputes.

Generally, an internal dispute resolution procedure is a non-adjudicatory, voluntary, "investigative" type of process that gives employees the opportunity to

---

1 The Maquiladora Standards were proposed by an alliance of United States and Mexican church, environmental, labor, and human rights activists and are directed at United States multinational companies that operate in Mexico along the United States–Mexican border. To date, one United States multinational company has adopted the Standards.

raise their job "grievances". As long as this type of procedure does not result in binding decisions or take away any employee rights, it is an appropriate topic for a global employment policy.

Mandatory arbitration may be cheaper, quicker, less time-consuming, less formal and less public than litigation. It is an excellent tool for controlling the risk of a large employment case and adverse public relations. Nevertheless, laws between countries vary significantly as to the legality of mandatory arbitration agreements. Some European countries forbid them entirely, subject to narrow exceptions with certain classes of executives. In other countries, such as Germany, local labor courts have exclusive jurisdiction over individual employment contract disputes — thereby taking away the ability to implement a mandatory procedure.

The law in other countries, such as the United States, is in a state of flux. In the United States the legality of any particular arbitration agreement is dependent on the jurisdiction, how the agreement is drafted, whether the agreement is contained in a collective bargaining agreement or individual employment contract, and whether the agreement deprives the claimant of any significant legal rights. These considerations do not necessarily lead to a uniform approach. Establishing global policies that incorporate alternative dispute resolution procedures is not an impossible task but will have to take into account the legal and cultural particularities of the host country.

C. FUTURE OF GLOBAL EMPLOYMENT POLICIES

Despite legal, cultural, and political barriers, more and more global businesses are considering implementing not only global codes of conduct but uniform global employment policies and procedures to create a common corporate culture and increase business efficiency. Some of the employment policies that may be subject to "globalization" include:

(1) Policies which require employees to act with honesty, integrity, and an ethical sense;

(2) Policies which prohibit employees from engaging in any act or behavior that is illegal under the laws of the United States, the host country or international law;

(3) Policies which establish uniform standards and criteria for hiring, performance evaluations, discipline, and termination;

(4) Policies which establish uniform standards with regard to job eliminations, layoffs, plant shutdowns, and mergers and acquisitions;

(5) Policies which recognize basic human rights and prohibit discrimination and harassment in the workplace;

(6) Policies which establish employee training programs;

(7) Policies which establish fair wages, benefits and compensation, and reasonable work hours;

(8) Policies which recognize employees' freedom of association and the right to join or not join labor unions;

(9) Policies which recognize employees' right to privacy in the workplace, while at the same time outlining the parameters of that right, such as retaining the ability to monitor employees or conduct workplace inspections or drug testing for legitimate business reasons;

(10) Policies which recognize the right of multinational companies to maintain strict confidentiality of intellectual property and trade secrets; and

(11) Policies that establish global dispute resolution procedures.

Despite the real or perceived differences in law, custom and culture, multinational companies are no longer finding it efficient or acceptable to manage their global workforce on a country by country basis using individual employment contracts, varying workplace standards or local policies, rules, and regulations. Such piecemeal approaches fail to address a company's global corporate culture, employee loyalty and retention, and other business considerations.

Moreover, with the rapid advancements in communication and technology, governments, international organizations, employers, consumers and investors are becoming increasingly aware of the personnel and employment practices of multinational companies. With this awareness comes heightened demands and expectations that multinational companies act more socially and ethically responsible.

This chapter has highlighted some of the issues multinational companies must address when formulating global employment policies and procedures. The key to implementing global employment policies will be overcoming cultural stereotypes and providing proper training to employees, supervisors, and all levels of management not on the differences, but on the similarities of global workplace conduct and behavior.

Based on the increased integration of the global marketplace and political community, and the emergence of new communications technologies, we believe that more and more multinational companies will be exploring ways to implement uniform global employment policies and procedures which transcend cultural and political boundaries and further enhance a company's ability to successfully operate its business in the new world marketplace.

APPENDIX

CHECKLIST FOR PREPARATION OF GLOBAL EMPLOYMENT POLICIES AND PROCEDURES

1. Practical Issues

(1) Preparation of new policies versus the revision of existing policies

(2) Employer style, culture, values, and history

(3) Employee morale and loyalty

(4) Political, cultural and religious issues in a particular country

(5) Dissemination, translation, and interpretation

2. Type of Employer

(1) Private sector, government contractor, public employer

(2) Service sector or manufacturing

(3) Multi-facility, international

(4) Union or non-union

3. Applicable Laws

(1) International and bilateral treaties (FCNs, GATT, NAFTA, MFN, environmental treaties, European Union policies)

(2) Guidelines of the International Labor Organization (ILO), the Organization for Economic Cooperation and Development (OECD), and the United Nations Charter

(3) National, state, local laws

(4) Choice of law

(5) Citizens, non-citizens, expatriate employees

4. "Plain Language" Rule

(1) Written to be understood — "plain language" — avoid legalese

(2) Self-contained document

(3) Translate, implement, and train in accordance with local laws, customs, traditions, and a company's corporate culture

5. Form of Document

(1) Table of contents

(2) Removable and insertable pages

(3) Dated pages

6. Coverage of Global Employment Policies and Procedures

(1) Must be explicit

(2) Hourly, salaried, executives, management, and labor

(3) Part-time, full-time

(4) Temporary, irregular, regular (not "permanent")

(5) Current employees versus new employees

(6) Unionized or non-unionized

7. Legal Effect of Global Employment Policies and Procedures

(1) Not a legal document—provides policies that employees and managers are expected to follow

(2) Employer has right to change or revise

(3) Consideration

8. Consistency with Other Company Documents, Policies, and Procedures

(1) Supervisor manuals

(2) Procedure manuals

(3) Employment forms (e.g., applications and offer letters)

(4) Benefit plans, booklets

(5) Codes of conduct, mission statements

CHAPTER 7

SATISFYING MULTINATIONAL REDUNDANCY OBLIGATIONS DURING CROSSBORDER FORCE REDUCTIONS

Edmund M. Kneisel and Charles M. Rice
Kilpatrick Stockton LLP
Atlanta, Georgia, United States

A. INTRODUCTION

Economic downturns, technological changes, and the restructuring of a business can all have profound effects on the workforce needs of an employer. When these or other factors convince an employer that its existing workforce is too large or too expensive to maintain, the employer must face the often difficult and distasteful task of reducing the size of its workforce, consistent with the operational needs of the company. How the employer achieves this "downsizing", or "right sizing" to accomplish a force reduction, known in many countries as a "collective dismissal", can vary dramatically depending on the local laws and on local customs and culture.

Until recently, most business operations tended to be based entirely in one country, and employers contemplating a reduction in force had no need to consult the laws of any nation other than their home country. The past two decades, however, have witnessed the elimination or reduction of many impediments to crossborder operations. The strengthening of the European Union and the reduction of trade barriers through such treaties as NAFTA have spawned a proliferation of multinational operations designed to take advantage of a global marketplace. As a result of the increased incidence of multinational operations, the volatility of the local economy in many countries, and the growing acceptance of downsizing as an appropriate response to a business's fiscal problems, crossborder and even worldwide force reductions are becoming increasingly common.

Because laws dealing with the termination of employment and collective dismissals often differ substantially from country to country, crossborder force reductions typically take substantially more advance planning than terminations implemented in a single country. When the laws of multiple countries are involved, employers often find it difficult, if not impossible, to adopt a uniform plan for implementing a force reduction at all locations. Before suggesting solutions to this problem, it is essential to become generally familiar with the laws that may apply.

B. OVERVIEW OF LEGAL IMPEDIMENTS TO EMPLOYEE TERMINATIONS

1. Employment Laws from the Global Perspective

In the United States, there are relatively few legal restrictions on the termination of employment, and collective dismissals and layoffs are culturally accepted as a routine part of doing business. As a result, employers in the United States are relatively free to implement force reductions quickly and with few legal impediments. The primary legal restraints on this discretion are federal and state anti-discrimination statutes prohibiting United States employers from basing termination decisions (as well as other employment actions) on an employee's race, color, religion, sex, national origin, age, or disability. In addition, some laws protect "whistleblowers" against retaliatory discharge.

Apart from the prospect of claims for unlawful discrimination and retaliation, United States employers have few legal concerns when terminating employees. In general, persons hired for an indefinite term are classified as employed "at-will" and may be terminated for any reason, good or bad, that is not otherwise prohibited by law.

Individual employment agreements modifying the "at-will" rule are rare in the United States, and labor unions represent less than 14 percent of the total United States workforce, with their greatest strength in heavy industry. Even at unionized facilities collective bargaining agreements typically do not prohibit employers from implementing a force reduction. These agreements often do, however, contain very specific provisions for selecting the employees for layoff during a force reduction, typically using seniority as the primary selection criterion. The least senior employees in a department or job classification are the first to be discharged, and more senior employees often have the right to displace or "bump" less senior employees who were not selected for layoff.

The National Labor Relations Act governs labor-management relations generally. It imposes a duty on United States employers to bargain with unions over the terms and conditions of employment, but generally there is no duty to bargain over a force reduction decision unless it involves subcontracting or relocating work historically performed by the unionized employees being adversely affected. However, even if an employer has no duty to bargain over the business decision to restructure, it still must bargain over the effects of the decision on its unionized employees. "Effects bargaining" may cover such subjects as severance pay, enhanced early retirement benefits, pay for accrued but unused vacation, preferential rehiring rights, and outplacement services.

In contrast to the United States, most European countries provide substantial "job security" protections for employees, and the concept of termination without just cause meets with considerable cultural resistance. European employment laws usually prohibit unjust dismissals and often impose significant procedural requirements (advance notice and consultation requirements) and financial disincentives (mandatory severance pay and social benefits) on the termination of employment. Consequently, European employers have traditionally approached the restructuring of a business with a strong emphasis on minimizing the effects on the workforce. The favored means of downsizing has been through attrition, voluntary retirement, and reductions in working hours rather than through sudden, large-scale job eliminations and terminations.

Large-scale force reductions are uncommon and quite difficult to achieve in other parts of the world because of strong cultural attitudes opposing terminations unrelated to employee wrongdoing and because of extensive social, severance, and indemnity benefits and penalties that must be paid on termination. In several countries, such as Pakistan and Zimbabwe, employers must obtain the approval of a government agency before terminating employees without just cause; in Egypt, employers must obtain government approval of plans to reduce operations. Many countries in Asia and the Middle East impose onerous procedural requirements on collective redundancies and some countries, such as Pakistan and Kenya, impose strict standards for selecting employees for redundancy.

2. Legal Restrictions on Employee Terminations

a. *Termination for Cause and Other Limitations on Dismissals*

The concept of termination at will for any reason or no reason is virtually unknown in industrialized countries other than the United States. In most countries, statutes prescribe the circumstances in which the unilateral termination of the employment relationship by the employer may occur; and an employee who is terminated in the absence of those circumstances ordinarily may sue the employer for damages and, possibly, reinstatement. Aside from limitations imposed by an individual or collective employment contract, the particular grounds for terminating an employment relationship vary significantly. Most countries do, however, permit an employer to dismiss an employee for "just cause", "good cause", or some related concept requiring an objective and reasonable basis for deeming the employee unsuitable for continued employment.

Some countries, particularly those in Latin America, codify an exclusive list of factors constituting just cause for dismissal.[1] For example, the Labor Code of Colombia identifies 15 circumstances constituting just cause, ranging from falsification of documents and acts of violence, insult, or ill-treatment, to any habitual vice of the employee that impairs discipline in the workplace. In Europe, detailed listings of the grounds for just-cause termination are rare. Instead, the question of

---

1 In the United States, only individual contracts or union agreements provide the primary protection against unfair (as opposed to discriminatory) dismissal, usually adopting a "good cause" standard for discharge. However, United States collective bargaining agreements typically do not prohibit employers from terminating or laying off employees in connection with a force reduction.

whether a particular factual situation constitutes just cause for termination is left up to a court or other tribunal. For example, French courts have recognized that appropriate reasons for dismissal include the incompetence of the employee, the failure of the employee to achieve necessary results such as a sales quota, the violation of safety rules, acts of dishonesty, and the disclosure of confidential company information to third parties.

Just cause for termination typically requires misconduct or poor job performance by an individual employee. In addition, employers are often entitled to dismiss employees when the continuation of the employment relationship is made impossible by *force majeure*, such as a fire or flood. In a few countries, however, even *force majeure* may not justify a termination. For example, an Egyptian tribunal required an employer to continue employing and paying its employees even though a fire had destroyed their workplace. Economic necessity is not "cause" for termination in some countries, but many countries do recognize redundancy of employees as an appropriate and lawful ground for termination.

The statutory restrictions on termination often are not universally applicable. In Germany, for example, employers with 10 or fewer employees are not subject to the employment termination laws; and in Portugal, a simplified dismissal procedure applies to employers with 20 or fewer employees. Frequently, statutory protections against dismissal do not apply to probationary employees during the first three to six months of their employment. In the United Kingdom, employees with less than two years of continuous service cannot claim unfair dismissal. High-ranking managers and directors in policymaking positions are also frequently excluded from the statutory protections against dismissal.

b. Discrimination Laws

Most industrialized countries prohibit employment discrimination based on certain protected factors, such as sex, race, marital status, religion, political affiliation, pregnancy, disability, national origin, age, and union activities. In most countries, other statutory and contractual protections against termination tend to diminish the importance of the anti-discrimination laws; however, in the United States, the discrimination laws are the principal protection invoked by terminated employees.

Damages awards for successful claimants can be substantial, and may include backpay, and, in some cases, compensatory and punitive damages. Accordingly United States employers pay close attention to the statistical impact of their termination criteria on women, racial and ethnic minorities, and older workers.

c. Employees Entitled to Special Protections

Laws in many countries often go beyond nondiscrimination requirements and actually impose special limitations on termination or special procedures for terminating employees in certain, protected categories. The most commonly recognized categories of specially protected employees are set forth below:

(1) Union officials — In many European and Latin American countries, employees serving as union officials cannot be dismissed except for certain reasons specified by statute.

(2) Members of works councils and other employee representatives — Several European Union countries provide special protections and procedures relating to the dismissal of "employee representatives" in general, thereby broadening the protected category beyond union officials.

(3) Pregnant women and new mothers — Many European and Latin American countries restrict an employer's right to terminate a female employee during her pregnancy or during a fixed period following the birth of her child.

(4) Disabled employees — Some countries give special protection to disabled employees or employees who are on a disability leave.

(5) Employees nearing retirement — Some countries, particularly those in Latin America and Eastern Europe, provide special protections against termination to employees who are nearing retirement age.

(6) Employees serving in the military or returning from military obligations — Many countries throughout the world provide special protections against termination to employees who are absent from work because of military service or who have recently returned to work from military service.

3. Procedural Requirements for Employee Terminations

a. Notice Requirements

Many countries require employers to provide advance notice of an employment termination, including, in some countries, notice of termination to a union or works council or to a government agency. Ordinarily, the notice must state with specificity the date on which employment will end and the reasons for the termination. The required notice period may range anywhere from one day to two years or more. In relatively few countries, a single, uniform period of notice applies to all terminations for which notice is required.[2] In Chile, for example, the labor code provides a standard 30-day notice period applicable to all situations requiring a termination

---

[2] There is no United States law imposing a general requirement of advance notice of individual terminations, but federal law and the laws of some states require employers to give employees advance notice of certain plant closings and mass layoffs.

notice. In some countries, the notice period depends on whether the terminated employee is a blue-collar worker or a white-collar worker. In Austria, blue-collars workers are entitled to 14 days' notice, whereas white-collar workers are entitled to anywhere from six weeks to five months of notice, depending on their seniority.

Most countries requiring advance notice of termination give employers the option of paying the employee in lieu of notice. Thus, if an employee is entitled to three months of notice before termination, the employer can dismiss the employee without notice by paying the employee the full amount (often, both wages and benefits) he or she would have earned during the three-month notice period.

In a few countries such as the Philippines, however, the notice period is not waiveable, and an employer cannot avoid the obligation of providing advance notice by paying the employee in lieu of notice. It may be possible in some of these countries to place the affected employee on a fully paid "leave of absence" for the duration of the notice period, thereby effectively ending the employee's active service at the beginning of the notice period.

b. Severance Indemnities and Social Benefits

Most countries require the payment of specified severance or "social" benefits on the termination of employment. The nature and amount of these benefits and the circumstances in which they are due vary widely.[3] The most common type of mandatory severance benefit is a lump-sum severance payment or "severance indemnity", as it is often called. A severance indemnity typically is payable whenever an employer unilaterally dismisses an employee for reasons other than serious misconduct. In a few countries, statutory programs require payments to employees in a much broader range of circumstances, including separations by mutual agreement or retirement.

Moreover, several Latin American countries, such as Colombia and Brazil, require employers to establish accounts, either in a bank or simply on the employer's books, in the name of each employee and to pay into each account, either monthly or annually, a fixed percentage of the employee's earnings. These "social benefit" accounts accumulate interest and periodically are adjusted for inflation. When an employee's employment is terminated, the employee is entitled to receive all of the money in his or her account. If the account is not maintained, the terminating employee may sue the employer to recover the equivalent amount.

The severance indemnity typically is payable directly from the employer to the employee on separation and is calculated pursuant to a statutory formula, usually based on earnings and seniority. Even in countries that apply relatively simple formulas, such as one week's salary for each year of employment, the "salary" used

---

[3] In the United States, severance pay is required by statute in only a few states and then only in limited circumstances.

in computing the severance indemnity may include more than base weekly wages. In many countries, the amount used to compute the severance indemnity is an "integrated salary" composed of numerous payments and the value of fringe benefits provided to the employee. The period of service used in calculating the severance indemnity also varies widely. In some countries, only the employee's service in the country where the termination occurs is counted. In others, all of an employee's company service is counted, regardless of where that service occurred.

4. Special Laws Regulating "Collective Dismissals"

a. Termination Based on Redundancy

Nearly all European countries and, indeed, most countries throughout the world recognize redundancy, or the elimination or restructuring of a job due to economic, business, or technical reasons unrelated to the performance or conduct of the employee, as a valid reason for terminating the employment relationship, regardless of whether the redundancy affects a single employee or a group of employees. However, many countries prohibit dismissals for redundancy when there is another available job to which the employee can be transferred.

The obligation to seek alternative jobs for an employee who is being made redundant sometimes includes an affirmative duty to train the employee for an available position. The redundancy laws of some countries are quite specific. In Portugal, for example, an employer considering a dismissal for redundancy must, in addition to seeking alternative work for the affected employee, consider other alternatives to dismissal, including the following:

(1) A temporary layoff of all or some employees;

(2) A temporary reduction in working hours for all or some employees;

(3) Retraining the affected employee for other jobs;

(4) Early retirement; and

(5) Termination of employment by mutual agreement with the payment of an agreed-on sum to the affected employee.

Japan similarly requires employers to exhaust all available alternatives to dismissal for redundancy, including the relocation of personnel and the solicitation of voluntary retirement.

b. Defining Collective Dismissals

In addition to statutes regulating terminations for redundancy, the laws of many countries impose special requirements when several employees are declared redundant as part of a "collective dismissal".[4] Statutes addressing collective dismissals usually apply only to employers with a designated minimum number of employees, which varies widely. In the United States, the Worked Adjustment and Retraining Notification Act (WARN) is a form of collective dismissal law requiring advance notice of plant closings affecting 50 or more employees and "massive" force reductions affecting 500 or more workers or 50 or more workers who constitute at least one-third of the workforce at a single site. WARN applies to employers with at least 100 full-time employees.

In several European nations, such as Austria, Belgium, and Finland, employers with as few as 20 employees are covered by collective dismissal statutes. In other countries, coverage depends on the number of employees dismissed within a fixed time period. For example, European Union Directive 75/129 suggests a flexible approach, triggering collective redundancy laws when as few as 10 employees are dismissed within a 30-day period from local establishments employing 20 to 100 workers, but using 30 dismissals as an automatic trigger, regardless of the size of the workforce. Collective dismissal requirements in the United Kingdom are triggered when 20 or more employees are made redundant at one establishment within a period of 90 days.

c. *Notice Requirements for Collective Dismissals*

Special forms of advance notice usually are required for collective dismissals. For instance, in the United States, WARN requires employers to provide 60 days' advance notice of a plant closing or mass layoff to the employees being terminated (or to the labor union representing such affected employees) and to the state and local governments in the locations where the plant closing or mass layoff will occur. Like WARN, notice requirements triggered by collective dismissals in other countries usually require the employer to serve advance notice on labor unions representing the affected employees, a government agency or court, or, in the European Union, a works council.

The mandatory notice or "cooling off" periods ensure a reasonable amount of time for the employer to consult and negotiate with employees' representatives and government agencies while hostile attitudes created by the announcement of a planned collective redundancy dissipate. Typically, employers must provide notice of a planned force reduction to employees' representatives or governmental agencies before serving individual dismissal notices on the employees themselves.[5] In

---

4 European Union Directive 75/129, article 1(1), defines a "collective dismissal" as a termination for one or more reasons not related to the individual workers concerned during a specified period.

5 An arguably premature "public" announcement of the closing of a Renault automobile plant in Belgium created substantial adverse publicity, labor unrest and strikes, numerous legal disputes including criminal proceedings, and even led to the adoption of a new "Renault" law clarifying the notice requirements. The Renault experience is described in a paper presented by Carl Bevernage, "The Closing of Renault Vilvoode Revisited", *Aba Int'l Lab. and Empl. Sec.* (April 20, 1998, as revised).

some countries, the governmental entities that receive notice play a direct role in reviewing compliance with the applicable laws. Employers may be required to obtain governmental approval of a redundancy plan before affected employees can be notified, and some governmental authorities may suspend for a period of time or even bar indefinitely an employer's implementation of a collective dismissal.

d. Negotiation and Consultation Requirements

The primary purpose of the required notice is to give the recipients an opportunity to consult or negotiate with the employer regarding the terms of the collective redundancy. The European Union's Council Directive 98/59/EC[6] provides that when an employer is contemplating collective redundancies, it must consult with the affected employees' representatives in good time for the purpose of reaching an agreement. These consultations must address ways to avoid collective redundancies or reduce the number of employees affected, as well as ways to mitigate the consequences of collective redundancies, such as by redeploying or retraining the redundant workers. The European Union Directive requires employers to supply the employees' representatives, including government authorities, with all relevant information, including:

(1) The reasons for the anticipated redundancies;

(2) The number of categories of workers to be made redundant;

(3) The number and categories of workers normally employed;

(4) The period over which the anticipated redundancies will be effected;

(5) The criteria proposed for selecting employees for redundancy; and

(6) The method for calculating any redundancy payments other than those required by applicable national legislation or practice.

e. Selection of Affected Employees

Employers generally are free to decide what segments or departments of their business will be affected by the collective redundancy and, subject to consultation and negotiation with a union or works council, the number of employees to be released. However, selection of the particular employees affected often is governed by carefully prescribed standards. For example, some collective dismissal laws require strict adherence to seniority, subject only to the proviso that the employees who are retained must be capable of performing the remaining work of the employer. In addition to seniority, collective dismissal laws often establish a variety of "social considerations" affecting terminations.

---

6 Council Directive 98/59/EC of July 20, 1998.

Such laws may give special preference to employees who have families with two or more dependents, employees with the longest uninterrupted service, students, veterans, and disabled employees. Other "social considerations" frequently found in collective dismissal laws include the age of the employee, the education level of the employee, and the likelihood that the employee will be able to obtain other employment.

5. Application of Laws to Non-Nationals

a. *Territorial Application of Laws*

The employment laws of a particular country typically apply to all individuals employed within that country's borders, regardless of nationality. However, some countries have special laws that apply solely to citizens of the country or to non-citizens. For example, in Saudi Arabia an employer that terminates the employment of a non-citizen may become liable for settling the individual's debts in Saudi Arabia. Other countries may grant special repatriation rights to foreign nationals, requiring the employer to pay the employee's transportation costs back to the home country or to the country in which the employment contract was made.

b. *Extraterritorial Application of Laws*

Employers with multinational operations must pay close attention to the extraterritorial application of a country's employment laws. In some cases, an expatriate employee may be protected by the laws of his or her home country as well as the laws of the country in which the employee works. For example, most federal anti-discrimination statutes in the United States apply to United States citizens employed overseas by a United States corporation or its overseas subsidiary.[7] Thus, when United States citizens working for a U.S.-owned company or affiliate anywhere in the world are affected by a force reduction, the employer must consider its obligations under United States laws prohibiting discrimination, as well as under local redundancy laws in the country of employment.

Some redundancy laws and laws requiring the payment of social and indemnity benefits to terminated employees may apply to a country's nationals who are employed and terminated outside that country. The extraterritorial reach of such laws can be felt when a multinational corporation with operations in an employee's home country transfers or seconds the employee to a foreign country, dismisses the

---

7 Affiliates of United States companies also may be covered. Thus, according to the Equal Employment Opportunity Commission, the federal agency charged with enforcing most United States antidiscrimination laws, a non-United States corporation in which a United States corporation holds only a minority interest may be subject to the United States laws if the United States corporation exercises certain control over the activities and policies of the non-United States corporation. Munger, "Employment Issues for Multi-National Employers and Employees: Extraterritorial Application of U.S. Employment Laws to U.S. Citizens Working Outside the United States", 1998 *ABA Section on Labor and Employment Law Report* (August 4, 1998).

employee in the foreign country, and then repatriates the dismissed employee to his or her home country. Once back in his or her own country, the former employee may sue the employer under that country's laws for wrongful dismissal or unpaid severance indemnities. To avoid this situation, the multinational corporation should plan to satisfy the redundancy (or anti-discrimination law) of the employee's home country, as well as the law of the country where the employee was dismissed.

C. MINIMIZING LEGAL RISKS IN CROSSBORDER FORCE REDUCTIONS

1. Advance Planning

The diverse legal standards and procedures relating to employment terminations and collective redundancies around the world frequently make the planning and implementation of a crossborder force reduction a costly and time-consuming process.

Employers can, however, reduce the legal problems and impediments associated with crossborder force reductions by anticipating the possibility of such an event at the outset of foreign operations and planning accordingly.

2. Familiarization with Local Laws and Practices

Before employing individuals in any foreign country, an employer should become familiar with the employment laws of that country, paying special attention to the laws and local customs relating to termination of employment.

Relevant information can often be obtained from the foreign country's embassy or consulate, employer associations in the foreign country, law firms in the foreign country, or law firms with an international practice.

3. Careful Drafting of Individual Employment Contracts

Outside the United States, employment contracts are common; and some countries require contracts for virtually the entire workforce. Even when contracts are not mandatory, employers should consider using them for at least the following reasons:

(1) Contracts may avoid disputes regarding local labor laws — Make sure that the contract covers the subjects required by the local labor code, including all procedural requirements for execution of the contract. Otherwise, labor courts may accept the employee's testimony about the terms of the employment relationship as conclusive.

(2) Choice of law clauses may be enforceable — When a multinational company reasonably anticipates transferring or seconding employees between countries, a choice-of-law provision stating that the employment contract will be interpreted under the laws of a particular country may be desirable. However, the employer should not assume that the provision will be enforceable in all countries.

(3) Compensation agreements can minimize severance-indemnity liability — Compensation packages for highly paid employees can sometimes minimize exposure to excessive severance indemnity by setting forth the statutorily defined "integrated salary" used to calculate the indemnity. In addition, contracts may specify that severance indemnities will be set off against benefit payments under the laws of the employee's home country, thereby reducing the employer's net financial outlay in the event of redundancy.

(4) Assume that local laws will apply to non-citizens — Regardless of choice of law clauses and nationality, a "host" country's employment laws ordinarily apply to all employees working in that country. As a result, multinational employers should not assume that the following common practices will avoid application of the host country's laws:

(a) Transferring employees to another country in anticipation of termination — Transferring the employees to a country with more favorable employment on the eve of termination does not minimize liability because the transferred employee may return to the country of his or her principal employment and file suit. Moreover, courts in the transferee country may characterize the transfer as a sham and award appropriate relief, including damages for unjust dismissal.

(b) "Seconding" employees — "Seconding" an employee by employing an individual on the payroll of a company in one country, but assigning the individual to work for a related company in another country, may qualify the employee for benefit plans not available in the host country; but seconding generally does not affect application employment laws of the host country.

(5) Voluntary separations by mutual consent — In most countries, employers and employees are free to negotiate the end of their employment relationship by mutual consent. Indeed, special severance agreements are becoming increasingly common in the United States; but if those agreements contain releases or waivers of certain rights, they may be strictly regulated by statute, such as the Older Workers Benefit Protection Act that governs releases of federal age discrimination claims.[8] Moreover, in some countries, terminations on "mutual consent" do not permit an employer to avoid paying mandatory social

---

[8] Age discrimination waiver programs must be carefully structured to avoid paying the departing employee money that can be used later to fund a wrongful termination lawsuit. *Oubre v. Entergy Operations, Inc.*, 118 S. Ct. 838 (1998) (employee need not tender back severance benefits received before suing to set aside an invalid waiver). Kneisel and Silver, "The OWBPA After Oubre: Employer Remedies When Workers Challenge ADEA Waivers", 24 *Employment Relations Law Journal* 73 (1998).

benefits and a severance indemnity. As a result, to achieve a voluntary separation on mutual consent, it is generally necessary to offer a severance package in excess of the amount the employees could reasonably expect to receive under the statutory standards otherwise applicable to collective dismissals.

(6) Use release agreements, where permissible — Because it is often impractical for an employer to develop a single severance package for all employees affected by a crossborder force reduction, severance offers normally must be tailored to satisfy the laws and customs of each country where employees are affected. To minimize the risk that a redundant employee may accept a generous severance incentive package, purport to resign, and then sue the employer for wrongful dismissal, the employer should, whenever possible, condition the offer of the severance package on the employee's execution of an enforceable release agreement.[9] In countries in which release agreements are not enforceable or are considered offensive or culturally inappropriate, there may be other documents that can be executed to minimize future liability. For example, forms acknowledging receipt of all payments owed to employees affected by the collective dismissal may help to eliminate further controversy over that often important issue.

D. CONCLUSION

In sum, pundits may speak of a global market place and the ever-shrinking "global village", but there is still considerable variation among the labor laws that apply to crossborder redundancies and collective dismissals. Accordingly, employers faced with a global restructuring must be aware of the concepts summarized herein and become familiar with the laws of each jurisdiction in which that employer's workers are employed.

Knowledge of local culture, attitudes and legal requirements, together with appropriate pre-planning with qualified legal counsel or other consultants, will significantly reduce the unexpected costs and other problems that can be encountered when restructuring a multinational workforce.

---

[9] In the United States, a release of discrimination or wrongful discharge claims must be "knowing and voluntary". At a minimum, this means that the employee must be aware that he or she is releasing claims against the employer and that the release was not obtained through fraud, coercion, or duress. The Older Workers Benefit Protection Act establishes specific requirements that must be satisfied before a release of age discrimination claims will be considered "knowing and voluntary". Kneisel and Piar, "The Impact of OWBPA's 'list' Requirements on the Enforceability of ADEA's Waivers", 22 *Employment Relations Law Journal* 73 (1998).

CHAPTER 8

EUROPEAN UNION HARMONIZATION OF EMPLOYEE BENEFITS, SOCIAL SECURITY, AND SECONDMENT

Patrick Thiebart
Caubet Chouchana Meyer
Paris, France

A. INTRODUCTION

Countries, economies, and people are coming closer as free markets spread, competition extends on a worldwide basis, finance moves faster and ever more freely, communications are easy and widespread, transforming the world into a "global village".

Such a situation of globalization has led since 1945 to a more thorough international cooperation at the economic level and, within this framework, to the creation of several free trade areas, such as:

(1) European Free Trade Association (EFTA);

(2) North American Free Trade Agreement (NAFTA);

(3) *Mercado Común del Sur* (MERCOSUR);

(4) Economic Union of Central Africa (EUCA);

(5) Economic Community of Western African States (ECOWAS);

(6) Central American States Organization (OCAS);

(7) Association of South East Asian Nations (ASEAN); and

(8) Pacific Bureau for Economic Cooperation (PBEC).

EFTA was created in 1960, in reaction to the creation of the European Economic Community in 1958 and the integration of the economies of its member states. Now, the remaining members of EFTA are Norway, Iceland, Switzerland and Liechtenstein. The other original member states have been integrated into the European Union.

NAFTA so far has only integrated the United States of America, Canada, and Mexico and MERCOSUR has as member states Argentina, Brazil, Uruguay, and Paraguay.

This chapter will focus on the European Union, which traces back in its origins, after the World War II, when France, Germany, Italy, Belgium, the Netherlands and Luxembourg, in short succession, created the Coal and Steel European Community, EURATOM, and the European Economic Community, to avoid any further repetition of conflicts which bled Europe in the first half of the 20th century, before being joined successively by the United Kingdom, Denmark, and Ireland (in 1973) and then by Greece (in 1981) Portugal and Spain (in 1986), and lastly by Austria, Sweden and Finland (in 1995).

On November 1, 1993, the European Economic Community changed its name to the "European Union". This change is not purely formal; it reflects the willingness of the 15 current European Union member states to no longer be a mere economic organization but to become a political institution more focused on, *inter alia*, the well-being of its citizens, better employment in the Union, and on the improvement of the working conditions of employees.

Indeed, one of the features of the European Union internal market is that the European Union citizens may enjoy the right to decide to work, to become established and to be seconded, at any time and in any member state.

To this end, European Union legislation is supposed to guarantee social security protection for the migrant European Union worker and his family, comparable to the level afforded to the nationals of the host country.

B. PREREQUISITES TO THE HARMONIZATION OF EMPLOYEE BENEFITS, SOCIAL SECURITY, AND SECONDMENT

There is no single answer to the question whether the European Union may serve as a model. This is due to the diversity of situations in which each free trade area is placed. For example, all the member states of EFTA are developed countries with efficient and reliable social security schemes. NAFTA combines two developed countries (the United Staes of America and Canada) and one developing country (Mexico). Most, if not all, the members of MERCOSUR are still developing countries.

We must ask whether these free trade areas intend to be more than economic organizations seeking to establish fair conditions of trade between member states. This is doubtful for an economic organization such as NAFTA due to the lack of economic homogeneity between its member states. This is also doubtful for a country such as Switzerland which has refused to join the European Union and even to sign the Porto Agreement of May 2, 1992.

The Porto Agreement entered into between the member states of the European Union and the member states of EFTA (with the exception of Switzerland) has given rise to the European Economic Area (EEA).[1]

The main point of the Porto Agreement is that as from January 1994, the four fundamental freedoms of movement (for goods, finance, services, and workers) provided for in the European Union Treaty are operative throughout the EEA. Thus, individuals are entitled to live, work, and offer services throughout the EEA.

In this respect, the Porto Agreement is, so far, the sole example of transposition of the European Union social security rules outside the European Union itself. Indeed, article 29 of the Porto Agreement provides that the principles governing social security laid down in article 51 of the Treaty of Rome, as well as all the European Union regulations on social security on migrant workers adopted before December 31, 1993 will be applicable to all the countries having ratified the Porto Agreement, including Norway and Iceland.[2]

Social progress within any free trade areas requires necessarily a certain co-ordination with other common policies. No common social policy can be successfully implemented if it is not closely connected with the other policies of the free trade organization. Indeed, it is important to make sure that measures of a social nature adopted or proposed in certain sectors do not conflict with other measures.

As far as the European Union is concerned, social policy is more particularly coordinated with the European Union economic, regional, agricultural and industrial policies.

1. Economic and Financial Policy

Needless to say, better employment rates at the Union and national levels is an essential condition for an effective social policy.

Furthermore, to maintain the social protection of persons with low incomes, the common economic policy must try to keep inflation at a relatively low level so that incomes grow more or less in the same proportion as the cost of living.

---

1 The European Economic Area includes the 15 European Union member states, plus Liechtenstein, Iceland, and Norway.

2 These two countries have made specific declarations restricting the scope of application of the Porto Agreement.

As far as the European Union is concerned, the European Union Commission has always considered that social benefits must progress at the same pace as the standards of living of the working population.

Moreover, it seems obvious that no harmonization of employee benefits and social security policies is conceivable without already (i) high or relatively high standards of living within the member states of the free trade organization and (ii) efficient national social security schemes.

2. Regional Policy

Certain regions within the free trade organization may suffer from structural underemployment, high unemployment, and substantial emigration, as it is the case in certain European Union member states (e.g. Ireland, Portugal, Greece or Corsica in France).

Such a situation may lead to the creation, as is the case in the European Union, of a social fund aimed at improving employment opportunities for workers, increasing their geographical and occupational mobility within the European Union and thereby raising the standards of living.

3. Agricultural Policy

The free trade organizations wishing to use the European Union as a model could rely on the European Commission's main goal in the common agricultural policy, i.e., equality for self-employed workers and employees in the agricultural sector with regard, *inter alia*, to social security.

4. Industrial Policy

As outlined in the European Commission's memorandum of May 3, 1973, the industrial development must form part of an overall plan to improve the quality of life, working conditions, and the environment so as to make possible the harmonization of the national social security schemes.

C. PROCESS OF HARMONIZATION OF EMPLOYEE BENEFITS SOCIAL SECURITY, AND SECONDMENT

Due to the reluctance of the member states to modify even slightly their social security policies, the harmonization of employee benefits and social security will not lead to their total uniformization.

It is a difficult task to reconcile disparate social systems, because member states are not prepared to modify their social security systems which are part of their sovereignty. It is particularly so because the scope of application of each national social security system is traditionally limited to its territory. In such a case, an employee regularly working in a given country will trigger coverage under the social security legislation of that country only, national social security schemes are generally based on the traditional model of the family, which implies direct and indirect discriminations against women and, more particularly, female workers.

In light of the foregoing, one of the main goals of the European Union regulation has been to put into effect in the member states the principle of equal treatment for men and women as regards access to employment, working conditions and social security.

In this respect, article 4(1) of Directive 79/7 of December 19, 1978, provides that the principle of equal treatment means that there should be no discrimination whatsoever on grounds of gender either directly or indirectly by reference in particular to marital or family status, as regards, *inter alia*, the scope of the schemes and the conditions of access thereto, and the obligation to contribute financially to the said schemes.

More particularly, the equal-pay principle for men and women has been deemed to be of significant importance to the development of the social policy of the European Union inasmuch as it has been interpreted widely and, for example, extended to statutory and occupational security benefits.

However, given the complexity and diversity of social security systems within the European Union, the principle of non-discrimination has been introduced gradually.

Furthermore, it should be borne in mind that discrimination is not limited to gender discrimination: free trade areas willing to use the European Union model will, more likely than not, need to fight against discriminations found in national social security legislations towards citizens of other member states. Indeed, the achievement of equal treatment requires measures to eliminate nationality as a condition of eligibility for benefits.

That is why article 6 of Directive 79/7 requires the member states to adopt the measures necessary to enable all persons, who consider themselves to have been wronged by discrimination prohibited under the Directive in the context of the awarding of social security benefits, to establish the unlawfulness of such discrimination and to obtain the benefits to which they would have been entitled in the absence of discrimination.

On the basis of Directive 79/7, the European Court of Justice has ruled that a member state is required to make reparation for the loss and damage caused to an individual for the delay in payment of a social security benefit, when that delay is the result of discrimination prohibited by the Directive.

A 1997 survey of the transposition of the European Union directives in the social field into national laws shows significant differences between European Union member states in the percentage of Directives properly transposed into national laws.

Apparently, only Finland would have a 100 per cent record. Sweden, Germany and Denmark have communicated that 96 per cent of their legislation would comply with the European Union regulation. The Netherlands have also communicated a 94 per cent rate.

However, the number of Directives properly transposed into national legislations is not as high in the other member states and in particular in Spain, Portugal and Greece. The harmonization of employee benefits and social security will not lead to total uniformization of the social security policies of the member states.

Due to the "natural" reluctance of the member states to amend their social security policies, the improvement of living and working conditions pursued by the European Union Authorities has never been envisaged as leading to a total uniformization of the domestic social systems based on a mere alignment of laws and regulations with those of the member states which appear to be the most advanced.

In this respect, article 51 of the European Union Treaty does not aim at harmonizing the social security schemes of the member states but its object is to co-ordinate them, since it provides in substance that the Council adopts in the social field the measures necessary for the establishment of the free movement of workers, by instituting, *inter alia,* a system enabling the migrant worker and his heirs to totalize all the periods taken into account by each national legislation under which the worker has been employed.

Accordingly, the goal pursued by the European Union authorities is a gradual adoption of a minimum standard of social protection, which can be improved on a regular basis, without depriving the member states from their sovereignty and national priorities in the social field.

There is, indeed, no compelling reason to transfer to supra-national authorities responsibilities that can be assumed more effectively at other levels and, in particular, at the national one.

For instance, notwithstanding the harmonization of the national social security policies, the European Union member states retain their competence in the sphere of social security and, in particular, remain free to regulate the terms of affiliation to their own social security scheme, provided, however, that there is no discrimination between the nationals and the other European Union citizens.

In the same vein, the European Court of Justice has ruled:[3]

> . . . social policy in the current state of community law is a matter for the Member States, which enjoy a margin of discretion as regards both the nature of the protective measures and the detailed arrangements for their implementation . . . .

1. Harmonization Process

No harmonization can result from the mere functioning of a free trade area. The articles of the Treaty of Rome in 1958 dealing with social issues in the newly born European Economic Community were initially quite limited.

Indeed, at the time of the signature of the Treaty, it was assumed that harmonization in the social field would mainly result from the functioning of the Common Market (i.e., the creation of the European customs union and the European economic integration) rather than from the provisions of the Treaty.

This view of the Founding Fathers of the Treaty of Rome is reflected in article 117 of the Treaty, which provides:

> Member States agree on the need to promote improved working conditions and an improved standard of living for workers, so as to render harmonization possible while the improvement is being maintained.

They believe that such a development will ensure not only from the functioning of the common market, which will favor the harmonization of social systems, but also from the procedures provided for in this Treaty and from the approximation of provisions laid down by law, regulation, or administrative action.

Accordingly, it appears from the second paragraph of article 117 that harmonization will flow as a natural consequence from the successful operation of the Common Market, which was a very optimistic point of view.

This explains why few specific measures were prescribed in the Treaty of Rome for the harmonization in the social field. Apart from articles 48 and 51 (which deal respectively with the free movement of workers and social security for migrant workers) and article 117, the only articles dealing with social issues were found in:

(1) Article 118; and

(2) Articles 123–125.

Article 118 requires the Commission to promote:

(1) Close collaboration between the member states in almost all fields of social policy; and

---

3 Commission of the European Communities v. Kingdom of Belgium, May 7, 1991.

(2) Harmonization of social policies in the European Union.

Articles 123–125 relate to the European Social Fund. The European Social Fund is used for financing member states' operations promoting the improvement of workers and increasing their geographical and mobility within the European Union.

2. Harmonization of Social Policy

Various factors have influenced harmonization of the social policies of the member states.

Several new steps have been taken by the European Union Authorities and the member states. As the Community developed and the economic situation in Europe worsened, it became apparent at the beginning of the 1970s that specific social measures had to be adopted.

a. *Regulation Number 1478/71*

As early as 1971, the European institutions and the member states realized that in the absence of a social security system favorable to the migrant workers, specific measures concerning social issues had to be taken simultaneously with those dealing with economic integration.

Indeed, the free movement of workers provided for in article 48 of the Treaty of Rome could not be implemented if the worker would in effect lose his social security benefits as a consequence of his decision to work outside his country of origin. In such a case, workers would be reluctant to move away from their home country.

To this end, the European Council adopted, on June 14, 1971, Regulation Number 1478/71 regarding the application of social security systems to employed people and their families moving from their home country to another European Union member state. Under this Regulation,[4] which is still in force, a person employed in the territory of a member state is subject to the legislation and eligible for the social benefits of that state (health benefits, old-age pension or invalidity pensions, unemployment benefits) even if he resides in the territory of another member state.

The rationale of these provisions is clear: to give priority to the legislation of the member state of employment in which the employed person contributes to the social security scheme.

However, as far as family benefits are concerned, other rules are applicable. Indeed, where a pensioner or a deceased worker has been subject to the laws of more

---

4 Regulation Number 1478/71, June 14, 1971, article 13–2.

than one member state, the family benefits for dependent children are to be paid in accordance with those of the state in which the pensioner, or the orphan of the deceased worker resides. However, this does not take away the right to get higher benefits awarded under the legislation of another member state to which the pensioner, or the orphan of the deceased worker, had previously been subjected to.

In such circumstances, a supplement equal to the difference between the two amounts is payable by the latter member state.

Needless to say, such a system cannot operate satisfactorily without a close cooperation between the member states. This condition is of the utmost importance for any free trade area wishing to take advantage of the European Union experience.

As far as social security for workers on secondment is concerned, the Community instrument for coordination is also Regulation Number 1408/71 and, in particular, its article 143, which provides that a worker posted to another member state "to perform work there" for the business to which he is normally attached continues to be subject to the social security of the country in which his employer is established during his posting provided that:

(1) The employee performs a given employment task on behalf of his employer;

(2) The anticipated duration of the work there does not exceed 12 months, which can be renewed once if the original mission is not achieved within the original 12-month period due to unforeseen reasons; and

(3) The employee must not be sent to replace another employee who finished his own temporary mission before the arrival of a new employee.

The same rules apply to self-employed persons. The Commission has recently proposed that Regulation Number 1408/71 be extended in its entirety to nationals of third countries, including the rules applying to postings of employed and self-employed persons. Currently, the social security conditions are governed by a complex system of bilateral agreements.

Since the adoption of Regulation number 1408/71, the European Union has taken considerable steps forward in the sphere of social policy: the Single European Act, the 1989 European Social Charter, and the Protocol on social policy incorporated in the European Union Treaty by the Amsterdam European Council.

b. *European Social Charter 1989*

Inspired by the will of the European Union institutions to enable those of the member states having the least developed social policies to gradually fill the gap with the others, the European Social Charter was adopted in Strasbourg on December 8 and 9, 1989, by all member states (with the sole exception of the United Kingdom).

In its first chapter, the European Social Charter enumerates the fundamental rights of European Union workers, which can be transposed in any other free trade area willing to use the European Union as a model:

(1) The improvement of the working conditions;

(2) Any European Union national, including any person being unemployed, is entitled to benefit from an appropriate social protection;

(3) The equality of treatment between men and women should be guaranteed; and

(4) Any worker must benefit from a satisfying health and social security protection at his workplace.

The European Social Charter reflects the concern of the member states not to be compelled to amend their own social security policies against their will since it has no binding effect on its signatories, which have only agreed the necessity to reach minimum social policy objectives.

However, this has led the same countries to enter into the Protocol and the Agreement on Social Policy simultaneously with the signature of the Maastricht Treaty on the European Union.

c. *Protocol on Social Policy*

The Protocol on Social Policy provides essentially that the European Union and the member states shall have, *inter alia*, as objectives, the promotion of employment, and improved living and working conditions. In pursuit of these aims, the Council may adopt directives setting minimum requirements for gradual implementation.

d. *Amsterdam Treaty*

Entered into on October 2, 1997, the Amsterdam Treaty is the first treaty signed by the European Union member states which gives priority to the social aspect of the European Union integration over the economic one, in particular by implementing a coordinated social strategy at the European Union level, aimed at ensuring a higher level of employment.

3. Role of the European Court of Justice

The European Court of Justice has set two important principles on which free trade areas may rely to implement the preeminence of the free trade area regulation over that of the member states, namely:

(1) There is direct applicability of certain articles of the European Union Treaty; and

(2) European Union law prevails over any inconsistent national legislation.

a. *Direct Applicability*

The European Court of Justice has ruled that certain articles[5] may have a direct effect which can be invoked directly by individuals before national courts to set aside the application of any inconsistent national provision.

Accordingly, the fact that certain provisions of the European Union Treaty are formally directed to the member states does not preclude individuals from taking advantage of the rights resulting from these provisions, provided that they prove to have a standing to do so.

In this respect, the European Court of Justice has considered, in its decision *Sabena v. Defrenne,*[6] that the principle laid down in article 119 of the Treaty may be invoked before the national courts even against a private employer, to ensure protection of the rights granted by this article to individuals, in particular as those types of discrimination arise from legislative provisions or collective bargaining agreements.

Consequently, legal provisions as well as contractual provisions (whether collective or individual) which are in breach of article 119 must be disregarded by national courts.

b. *Supremacy of European Union Law*

In respect of European Union law prevailing over any inconsistent national legislation, the European Court of Justice has ruled that the implementation of the European Union law is an obligation for all the member states and the national judges.

The preeminence of European Union Regulations over national law is also highlighted by the fact that the national judges must refer to the European Court of Justice when they have a doubt on the meaning or the extent of the European Union law.

On April 24, 1980, the European Court of Justice ruled:

> . . . when the member states lay down the conditions creating the right or the obligation to become affiliated to a social security scheme, they are under an obligation to comply with the provisions of the Community law in force . . . .

---

5 Article 119, which contains the principle that men and women should receive equal pay for equal work, is such a provision with direct effect.

6 Sabena v. Defrenne, European Court of Justice, Case 43/75.

4. Directives

Directives have proven to be a flexible instrument for harmonizing national social legislations. Considering the complexity and diversity of social security systems, which are an impediment to harmonization, any change toward the harmonization — as already seen — must be introduced gradually.

In this respect, European Union Directives are an important instrument for harmonizing the national legislation. This approach could inspire free trade areas.

Indeed, when an EU Directive is adopted, member states are obliged to take all the necessary steps to ensure that their national legislation complies with the objectives pursued by the directive within the required time-frame. Member states failing to transpose Directives into national laws are likely to be taken to the European Court of Justice by the European Commission.

The European Court of Justice has already imposed fines against member states for lack of implementation of European Union law.

It follows that, in applying a national law and in particular the provisions of a national law specifically introduced to implement a European Union Directive, national courts are required to interpret their national law in light of the wording and the purpose of the Directive. As of January 1997, 54 Directives had been adopted in the social field, of which 50 had come into force.

Another distinctive feature of a directive is that its provisions can be invoked directly in legal proceedings initiated by an individual against a member state, provided that the provisions of the directive are unconditional and sufficiently precise.

The European Court of Justice has also decided that a member state in default of the implementation requirement may be held liable for the tort to employees who suffered a damage resulting from the late or incomplete implementation.

Among the important Directives adopted so far is Directive 79/7 which provides the progressive implementation of the principles of equal treatment for men and women in social security matters. Directive 79/7 does not allow member states to keep in force, after the expiry of the period for implementation, the effects of their earlier national legislation which, under certain circumstances, excluded married women from old-age insurance cover.

D. CONCLUSION

The European Union member states have realized that economic expansion is not an end in itself but should result in the improvement of the quality of life as well as of the standards of living.

Because this point of view is now shared by an increasing number of countries, EFTA has now been reduced to a minor organization with only four members, whereas the European Union has gained five member states since 1986, without mentioning all the other countries wishing to become members of the European Union (Bulgaria, Cyprus, the Czech Republic, Estonia, Hungary, Latvia, Lithuania, Malta, Poland, Romania, Slovakia, and Slovenia).

Therefore, if the transposition of the European Union social model into free trade areas depends of course on objective and technical criteria (economic homogeneity between the member states and high standards of living), it is also, and above all, a question of political will.

CHAPTER 9

IMPORTING EMPLOYEE BENEFIT CONCEPTS FROM OTHER LEGAL SYSTEMS: THE LATIN AMERICAN EXPERIENCE

Miguel A. Zaldívar
Steel Hector & Davis LLP
Miami, Florida, United States

A. INTRODUCTION

An increasing policy of multinational corporations in recent years has been to extend to the local employees of their branches and subsidiaries located in Latin America certain employee benefit plans that were implemented in the corporations' home countries (typically the United States or the United Kingdom). Some of these plans include stock option plans, variable compensation plans, profit-sharing plans and safety incentive plans.

To efficiently implement these plans in Latin America and to avoid unintended windfalls derived from the highly protective labor statutes in effect in these countries, the plans should be:

(1) Implemented in compliance with local legal requirements;[1] and

(2) Analyzed in light of the benefits provided in the local labor statutes[2] to ensure that:

(a) Unintended increases of the amount of each of these benefits are not derived from the implementation of the plan;

(b) The plan benefits do not become vested rights of the employees, contrary to the intent of the employer; and/or

(c) The plan does not create an employment relationship or contract between the parent company of the local branch or subsidiary and the beneficiaries of the plan.

---

[1] For example, those set forth in the securities, exchange control, tax, social security and labor laws.

[2] These may include, mandatory profit sharing pay, vacation pay, holiday pay, christmas pay, severance, overtime payments and indemnity in lieu of termination notice.

In practice, prior to the implementation of the plan only a superficial analysis of the local Latin American labor statutes has been conducted by many multinational companies resulting in an increased number of labor disputes between management employees (normaly the beneficiary of these plans in the region) and the employer and/or the employer's non-local parent company.

The focus of this chapter is on the impact that Latin American labor statutes will have as a result of the implementation by a multinational company of a typical employee benefit plan.

B. LATIN AMERICAN LABOR LAW PRINCIPLES

The labor legislation of most Latin American countries contemplates the following principles:

(1) Vested rights theory;

(2) Broad definition of salary;

(3) No waiver of employee rights (public policy); and

(4) The principle of *in dubio pro operario*.

1. Vested Rights Theory

In many Latin American nations, if an employee receives a benefit two or more consecutive years, the employee would have the right to receive similar amounts in subsequent years, irrespective of the employer's unilateral determination to the contrary. Non-payment of the benefit in the following year(s) could be considered a constructive dismissal. In addition, unless specific provisions allowed by local law are expressly incorporated to the relevant plan, the "vested right theory" could prevent an employer from amending or terminating the plan in the future.

For instance, payment of a "one-time annual bonus" for two or more consecutive years, at approximately the same time during the course of the year and for the same motives, becomes a legally recognized right in most countries in Latin America. Whenever the same benefit is paid to an employee over the years, there is a greater risk that local labor authorities, unions and even employees would consider the benefit to have vested as an annual right to a payment entitlement.

2. Broad Definition of Salary

In general, salary is broadly defined to include any compensation an employee receives for rendering his or her services, regardless of the form of compensation agreed to. Salary thus includes, but is not limited to, commissions, premiums, stock awards, bonuses, expense allowances, statutory and contractual profit sharing and vacation bonuses. Also characterized as compensation are meals and housing, allowances therefor, and any other kind of benefit or perquisite which the employee receives in consideration for his or her services.

In the event that a benefit plan contemplates actual payments or benefits in kind to be provided to employees, if possible, it should be designed so as to prevent such benefit to constitute "salary" under the broad definition contemplated in Latin American labor legislation. Otherwise, benefits provided under the plan would be added to the basis for calculating the employee's statutory entitlement to other "social" benefits, including, among other things:

(1) Statutory profit-sharing payments;

(2) Christmas bonuses (*aguinaldo*);

(3) Vacation pay and vacation bonus;

(4) Overtime and night shift premiums;

(5) Severance;

(6) Indemnity in lieu of termination notice;

(7) Holiday and Sunday pay;

(8) Maternity allowance; and

(9) Bonuses and other benefits provided in the individual employment contract and in the collective labor agreement of each subsidiary or branch.

If it is not possible under local labor law to exclude benefit awards from the definition of salary, prior to the implementation of the plan the employer should assess whether such awards would affect the employee's entitlement to additional labor benefits[3] to better quantify the actual cost derived from the implementation of the plan and the actual benefits provided to the employees of the particular subsidiary where the plan would provide a windfall to local employees.

3. Non-Waiver of Employee Rights

The provisions of the local labor statutes and regulations are categorized as essential to public welfare, and their waiver in individual agreements or benefit plans is therefore prohibited. As a result, if, for instance, a benefit plan is treated by local law as one of the many "statutory labor benefits" provided in the local legislation, the plan may not be amended, modified or terminated by the parties.

---

3 An example would be an increased severance pay on termination of employment.

4. In Dubio Pro Operario

The labor statutes of many Latin American countries expressly establish the protective principle *in dubio pro operario*, according to which:

(1) In case of conflicting laws, the labor statutes will prevail whether they are substantive or procedural; and

(2) Where there is doubt as to the application of various rules in effect (e.g., the labor statutes and a benefit plan) or as to the interpretation of a given rule, the determination most favorable to the employee shall be applied.

C. PRACTICAL CASE

The following practical case is instructive in allowing an analysis of some overseas labor legal requirements. With the purpose of inducing employees to remain with a multinational company (the "Company"), the Company decided to give to certain key senior management employees a phantom stock award (the "Award") payable in cash based on a number of phantom stock units (PSUs) whose value is determined based on the value of the shares of common stock of the parent corporation. After careful consideration of other alternatives, including the implementation of a regular stock option plan, the Company opted for implementing a phantom stock award plan (the "Plan") in Latin America for essentially two main reasons:

(1) The human resources retention objective, in the judgment of the company, could have been equally accomplished with either plan; and

(2) On analysis of the relevant Latin American statutes, the phantom stock award option enables the company to manage the plan in a more similar fashion to its United States plan than the local statutes would have allowed if a pure stock option plan would have been implemented.

Following below is a summary of some of the key issues that had to be analyzed pursuant to the local labor statutes prior to the design, drafting and implementation of the plan:

1. Awards under the Plan: Not Part of the Employees' Salary

Awards were designed so as not to be considered part of the employees' salary to prevent that they become part of the basis used to calculate other employee benefits such as statutory severance pay.

2. Conditional Awards

The vesting of the Awards was made conditional on the beneficiaries remaining in the Company as employees for a certain number of years provided in the Plan and on their execution of certain Plan documents and releases prior to actual payment of the Award.

3. Registration with Local Authorities

Most countries do not require approval or registration of phantom stock option plans.

4. Amendment and Termination of Plan

In several countries, the Company would not be able to unilaterally amend or terminate the Plan, unless it is to provide greater benefits for the employees. In some countries, for instance, the unilateral amendment or termination of the Plan by the Company would constitute a constructive dismissal.

5. Additional Rights

The Plan had to be designed so that its implementation would not create additional rights in favor of the employees beyond the payment of the Award.[4]

6. Form of Implementation of the Plan

The company's preference was to implement the Plan as any other written policy of the corporation. In some countries that was possible, in others additional documentation was required (e.g., amendments to existing written employment contracts).

7. Union Fees

An analysis had to be made prior to implementation of the Plan to confirm whether union dues would have to be deducted from Award payments made to the employees. On review of relevant statutes and collective labor agreements it was determined that the deduction was not required.

8. Choice of Law

Generally, the local labor statutes do not allow for the Plan to be subject to the legislation other than that of the countries where the employee renders his or her personal services.

Other examples of practical cases include the implementation of a:

(1) "Variable Compensation Program" by a multinational company in a Latin American country.

(2) The implementation of an Annual Profit Sharing Plan for a year.

---

[4] For example, the Plan should not create vested rights to the entitlements.

In the case of a Variable Compensation Program, the international draft plan had to be amended prior to implementation and payment had to be categorized as a statutory benefit ("mandatory profit sharing") to prevent employee entitlement to both benefits.

In the case of an Annual Profit Sharing Plan for a year, to minimize the risk that the annual profit sharing payment (as contemplated by the multinational company) be considered a legally recognized "vested right", it was recommended that it be labeled as a gratuity (*gratificación*) to the employee. The gratuity consisted of a one time bonus, equal to a percentage of each employee's base pay. Gratuities are defined in most Latin American labor statutes as a special kind of voluntary payment made by an employer to the employees as a reward or incentive and are subject only to the terms and conditions provided by the employer. Gratuities that are paid one time as a lump sum payment for special reasons (such as the benefit contemplated by the multinational company in this case) are not considered the equivalent of a bonus and do not grant any legal rights to employees for further payments of this nature.

In summary, prior to implementing a global employee benefit plan in Latin America, the unintended implications that might result from the plan and the legal requirements for the implementation of the plan should be carefully analyzed in coordination with counsel that specializes in the area in order to fully assess the cost and local consequences resulting from its implementation.

Part III

Employment Issues in Crossborder Business Transactions, Mergers, Acquisitions, and Free Trade

CHAPTER 10

EMPLOYMENT ISSUES IN CROSSBORDER AND INWARD INVESTMENT MATTERS

Fiona McLaren
Clyde & Co.
London, England

A. POST-ACQUISITION EMPLOYMENT ISSUES

The purpose of this chapter is to give a brief overview of some of the employment issues that can arise when acquiring a business within the United Kingdom for those who are not familiar with the United Kingdom legal framework.

Those seeking to acquire a business in the United Kingdom do so either by purchasing the shares of the company or by acquiring the assets of the business. The method chosen determines the employment issues that arise. If the first method is chosen, a share purchase, then there is a change only in the identity of the shareholders and not in the identity of the employer. The new shareholders take over the position of the previous shareholders. For those employees there is no change. They remain employed by the same employer on unchanged terms and conditions.

The alternative method, an asset purchase, is less straightforward. As a result of European wide legislation, acquiring assets may also mean acquiring employment liabilities.

All Member States of the European Union are subject to a number of European wide Directives that seek to regulate, among other things, employment practices. These include the Acquired Rights Directive, which seeks to safeguard the interests of employees where an "undertaking" is acquired. In the United Kingdom the Acquired Rights Directive has been implemented as the Transfer of Undertakings (Protection of Employment) Regulations 1981 (TUPE). All rights, liabilities, duties, and obligations arising out of the employment contracts are transferred to the acquirer so that TUPE provides that where there has been a "relevant transfer" then the employment contracts are, in effect, novated. The acquirer of the undertaking steps into the shoes of the employer.

The issue of whether or not there has been a "relevant transfer" is therefore a key issue and what amounts to such a "relevant transfer" has been the subject of much case law. It is a question of fact on each case, but the European Court of Justice in *Spijkes Gebroeders Benedik Abattoir CV*[1] stated that the following factors should be taken into account:

(1) The type of undertaking;

(2) Whether any tangible assets have been transferred;

(3) The value of intangible assets transferred;

(4) Whether the majority of employees have been transferred;

(5) Whether customers and work-in-progress have been transferred; and

(6) Whether there is any similarity between the activities of the undertaking before and after the transfer.

No one factor carries more weight than any other. The type of undertaking is important since in a labor-intensive undertaking, few tangible assets may be transferred. There can, nonetheless, be a transfer if the acquirer takes on the majority of the staff previously employed.

Assuming that the acquisition is a "relevant transfer" for the purposes of TUPE, what exactly is transferred? TUPE operates to create a statutory novation of the contracts. This means that all contract terms transfer with the exception, currently, of pension rights. Not only do the contracts transfer as a whole, but also any claims arising out of those contracts transfer. For example, if the old employer has not paid wages or has not paid accrued holiday, this liability passes to the acquirer. Any claims that arise from facts that pre-date the transfer will, nonetheless, be the acquirer's liability, e.g., a sex discrimination claim relating to a pre-transfer act is the liability of the acquirer.

This, in effect, puts the acquirer of an undertaking in the same position as an acquirer of shares. There are, however, some significant extra obligations on the acquirer when purchasing an undertaking rather than shares.

Where there is a "relevant transfer", there is an obligation to consult either with a recognized Trade Union or, if there is no recognized Trade Union, with an elected representative on behalf of the workforce. This means that sufficient time must be built into the purchase program to allow an election to be held as well as sufficient time prior to completion to consult. This consultation must take place as soon as practicable prior to the transfer and it must take place with a view to reaching agreement on prescribed topics.

---

1 *Spijkes Gebroeders Benedik Abattoir CV* ECJ (1998) 2 CLMR 486.

The seller must explain the reason for the transfer, when it will take place, and the "legal, economic and social implications" which it will entail for the affected employees, i.e., any effect on pay and benefits, whether redundancies are likely, and whether relocation will arise. Regulation 10 (3) of TUPE requires the acquirer to give the seller sufficient information to enable the seller to undertake meaningful consultation.

The primary purpose of the consultation is to inform the employees of the "measures" that the transferor or the transferee foresee taking in connection with the transfer. During the consultations the transferor must consider the views of the Trade Union elected representative and reply to their proposals or representations explaining, if necessary, why the proposals or representations are being rejected. Failure to consult or inform the Trade Union or other employees' representatives can lead to financial awards against the seller.

Not only does an acquisition that is governed by TUPE involve more employment issues than a share acquisition prior to transfer, there are also significant differences in post transfer obligations. Generally, where assets are acquired the new owner of the business will want to make a reduction in the number of staff. A TUPE transfer is an additional hurdle in an employer's way.

Under United Kingdom law, and most European systems of law, there are procedures that must be followed to avoid financial penalty for a dismissal. This applies equally to situations where there is insufficient work for the workforce as in any other type of dismissal. However, where TUPE applies, any dismissals resulting from the acquisition of the business not only must meet the normal statutory tests of fairness contained in the Employment Rights Act 1996, but also must be for an economic, technical, or organizational reason entailing changes in the workforce.

Essentially, this means that the decision to dismiss the employees must have been a sensible business decision founded on the ongoing conduct of the business.[2] The most common example of an economic, technical, or organizational reason will be the need for the transferee to make employees redundant post transfer. Dismissals are unfair, though, if the primary reason for the dismissal is to facilitate a particular transfer or to improve the prospect of any transfer taking place.[3]

If the new owner of the business does not want to "downsize", they may well wish to change the terms and conditions on which staff are employed. If the acquirer of the business owns other businesses within the United Kingdom and wishes to amalgamate these then it is likely that the acquirer will want to employ all staff on the same terms and conditions. Here, TUPE creates another problem. As TUPE

---

2 Wheeler v. Patel, (1987) IRLR 211.

3 Harrison Bowden Ltd v. Bowden, (1994) ICR 186.

provides that all staff must be employed on the same terms and conditions before and after the transfer and this is a mandatory rule of law, any change in terms is ineffective and the terms cannot be changed even if the staff consent.[4]

It is not simply a question of letting time pass before changing terms after a transfer. If there is any causal link between the change in terms and the transfer, the change will be ineffective. The effect of this was graphically illustrated under United Kingdom law in *Credit Suisse v. Padiachy*.[5] There, a TUPE transfer occurred and employees agreed new terms and conditions where, although the employees were arguably better off following the renegotiation, the new terms were not effective as the employees were not entitled to waive the mandatory protection afforded to them under TUPE.

It is thought that the only effective way to change employee terms and conditions following a TUPE transfer is to dismiss them unfairly and then re-engage them on the new terms which will be effective despite the provisions of TUPE.[6] As a TUPE transfer will have occurred, the acquirer of the business will have inherited claims for unfair dismissal for all those staff who were dismissed because of the transfer and then re-engaged.

One must evaluate how likely staff are to bring such claims and to weigh up the financial cost of potential unfair dismissal claims against financial and organizational benefits in harmonizing terms and conditions. With the maximum level of compensation for unfair dismissal increasing to £50,000 in late 1999, the costs of imposing the changes in terms and conditions in this manner need to be carefully considered.

B. ISSUES IN PRACTICE

1. Case Study

a. *Facts*

Alphabet Inc., a United States-incorporated company, operates its manufacturing business globally. In the last three years, it has been growing by acquiring companies throughout Europe, particularly concentrating on the United Kingdom.

Twelve months ago, Alphabet Inc. acquired Alpha Limited by buying the shares of that company. Last month, it completed the acquisition of the assets of Beta Limited taking over the lease of the factory, all the stock, ongoing customer orders, and the majority of staff. Alphabet Inc. now wish to rationalize the operation

---

4 Foreningen af Arbejdsledere I Danmark v. Daddy's Dance Hall A/S, (1998) 315 ECJ.

5 Credit Suisse v. Padiachy, (1998) IRLR 504.

6 Wilson v. St Helens, (1998) 3 WLR 1070.

in the United Kingdom by running Alpha Limited and the business of Beta Limited as one. The intention is that the business carried out at Beta Limited would be moved to Alpha's premises. This would include the staff but in fact only the sales and accounts teams are required. They would be expected to relocate some 50 miles.

One-third of the total staff of Alpha Limited and Beta Limited are excess to requirements and will have to be made redundant.

Alphabet Inc. want to employ all remaining staff on the same terms and conditions, which will mean making significant changes to the current contract terms of both Alpha Limited and Beta Limited's employees.

b. Issues

Do the TUPE Regulations apply to the acquisition of Alpha Limited?

TUPE does not apply to acquisitions by way of share purchase.

Do the TUPE Regulations apply to the acquisition of the assets of Beta Limited?

The acquisition is by asset purchase and, therefore, TUPE may apply to the transaction.

Consider the factors in accordance with the *Spijkers* test: tangible and intangible assets are transferring as are the majority of employees and customers and work in progress. It seems the activities before and after transfer will be the same. On this basis, TUPE will apply to the acquisition of Beta Limited.

TUPE applying to the acquisition of assets of Beta Limited has various consequences. Individuals employed by Beta Limited immediately before the transfer automatically become the employees of Alphabet Inc. on the terms and conditions they previously held.

Alphabet Inc. will inherit Beta Limited's rights and liabilities in relation to those individuals.

Collective agreements made by or on behalf of Beta Limited with a Trade Union recognized by Beta Limited continue with Alphabet Inc.

Alphabet Inc. should have provided Beta Limited with relevant information about the relocation and redundancy to allow Beta Limited to consult with recognized Trade Unions or elected employee representatives concerning the transfer.

Issues relating to redundant staff will also arise: Are the redundancies connected to the transfer? If so, the dismissals are automatically unfair unless the reason for the dismissals is an economic, technical, or organizational reason entailing changes in the workforce (ETO). Even if the reason for the dismissal is an ETO reason, the dismissals are only fair if reasonable in the circumstances. The relocating staff may also be redundant.

Changing the terms and conditions of staff who move also raises questions. The TUPE regulations protect employees of Beta Limited. One must ask whether the changes are connected to the relevant transfer. If so, consent to these changes is invalid as TUPE is a mandatory rule of law.

A possible solution for the employer might be to dismiss employees and re-engage them on new terms.

TUPE does not apply to Alpha Limited's transferred employees. Their terms can therefore be changed by consent.

C. CONCLUSION

Anyone thinking of acquiring a business in the United Kingdom should take proper counsel as to the employment issues that might arise. Whatever the method of acquisition, whether it be through buying the assets or buying the shares, the acquirer will effectively stand in the position of the old employer and will be bound by existing rights and obligations. It is always worth investigating what these are so that the true financial cost of employees' contracts, for example, can be measured at the outset.

If acquiring through assets, then there will be an extra dimension that needs to be taken into account; the acquirer needs to understand the additional hurdles that may have to be met and the possible additional costs involved because of these hurdles.

CHAPTER 11
EMPLOYMENT ISSUES IN INTERNATIONAL DEALS — THE BRAZILIAN PERSPECTIVE

Isabel C. Franco and Esther Kauffmann
Demarest & Almeida
New York, New York, United States

A. INTRODUCTION

1. Background

Labor law in Brazil was influenced by the transformations in Europe and by the concern of various countries' in creating legislation to protect workers, and particularly a commitment made by Brazil with the International Labor Organization (ILO).

The ILO was created in 1919, at the end of World War I, at the time of the Peace Conference, which convened first in Paris, then at Versailles. The initial motivation was humanitarian. The condition of workers, more and more numerous and exploited with no consideration for their health, their family lives, and their advancement, was less and less acceptable. The second motivation was political. Without an improvement in their condition, the workers, whose numbers were ever increasing as a result of industrialization, would create social unrest, even revolution. The third motivation was economic.

Because of its inevitable effect on the cost of production, any industry or country adopting social reform would find itself at a disadvantage *vis-à-vis* its competitors. Another reason for the creation of the ILO was added by the participants of the Peace Conference, linked to the end of the war to which workers had contributed significantly both on the battlefield and in industry.

In Brazil, during the 1920s and 1930s, all these elements, combined with important domestic factors, such as the pro-labor policy of the government and the industrial growth in the country, triggered the creation of a series of protective labor laws. However, only in 1943 were the laws compiled in the Consolidation of the Brazilian Labor Laws (*Consolidação das Leis do Trabalho* — CLT).

The CLT was created by Getúlio Vargas, a Brazilian populist president and leader of the labor party. The legal structure created by the CLT reflects not only the premises of Italian fascism from the early 1930s (of which Getúlio was an admirer), but also the positivism of Augusto Conte and the post-bellum principles of the ILO.

The CLT was complemented at that time by principles of labor law developed by legal scholars. The CLT is the primary legal system that rules labor relationships, currently containing more than 900 articles. Among the chapters forming the CLT, there are important norms relating to:

(1) General Labor Safety Norms;

(2) Daily and Weekly Working Hours, Minimal Wage and Vacation Norms;

(3) Medicine and Occupational Safety Norms;

(4) Special Norms for Labor Tutorship;

(5) Norms for Labor Nationalization;

(6) Norms for Women's Labor Protection;

(7) Norms for Labor Protection of Underage Persons;

(8) Norms for Individual Employment Contracts;

(9) Workers' Union and Trade Association Norms and Classification; and

(10) Workers' Union and Trade Association Contribution Norms.

Additionally, the CLT contains rules on the whole legal system supporting the labor courts, such as related agencies and their operation, also asserting the norms that rule labor judicial proceedings.

Although the CLT was enacted in 1943, through the years the Brazilian legal system has been modified with the creation of a number of laws and regulations ruling certain issues such as the right to strike. With the enactment of the new Federal Constitution in 1988, new labor rights were added to the body of the CLT. There are other sources of regulations, which are respected by the Brazilian legal system:

(1) Collective Bargaining and Collective Labor Agreements;

(2) Precedents of Superior Labor Court; and

(3) Norms issued by the Ministry of Labor.

One of the most significant characteristics of the Brazilian labor system is that, to a great extent, it preemptively regulates labor management relations. However, negotiations between employers and employees, resulting in collective bargaining and collective labor agreements, are already a strong alternative, deriving from more flexible rules and regulations.

2. Labor Benefits

The right to strike is guaranteed by the Constitution. Basic labor rights granted to the employee are the following:

(1) Normal working week of 44 hours, limited to a maximum of eight hours per day or six hours a day for any work performed in continuing rotation working shifts;

(2) After one year of work, paid vacation of 30 days per year, plus an extra one-third of that amount as bonus;

(3) Mandatory minimum wages, the value of which is set by law and periodically adjusted. Currently, the minimum wage is R$ 136 (US $1 equals approximately R$ 1.7);

(4) A yearly bonus, called 13th salary (*13º salário*), which corresponds to one-twelfth of the December salary for each month worked during the year;

(5) Participation in the profits of the company, under terms and conditions to be negotiated in each case between the employer and the employees' union;

(6) Overtime pay of at least 50 per cent;

(7) Paid maternity leave of 120 days (reimbursed to the employer through Social Security);

(8) Paternity leave of five days;

(9) Prior notice of dismissal of at least 30 days;

(10) Unemployment insurance;

(11) Retirement (following recent changes, after age 70 for men or age 65 for women or after 35 years of social security contributions for men or 30 years for women;

(12) Approval of collective norms;

(13) Employment-related accident insurance;

(14) Workers' Compensation Fund; and

(15) Provisional tenure for members of the Internal Commission for Accident Prevention, employees victims of employment-related accidents, and pregnant employees.

3. Social Contributions — "Labor Charges"

Brazilian companies are subject to significant social security contributions or charges, due to employment contracts, as follows:

(1) Social Security Contribution (*Instituto Nacional de Seguridade Social* — INSS) equal to 24 per cent to 25.90 per cent of the payroll must be paid by the company to the National Institute of Social Security. Additionally, employees pay eight per cent to 10 per cent, deducted from their salaries and paid by the company.

(2) Workers' Compensation Fund (*Fundo de Garantia por Tempo de Serviço* — FGTS) equal to eight per cent of the amounts paid by the company to its employees must be deposited by the employer in the Workers' Compensation Fund of the employee with the Federal Savings Bank (*Caixa Econômica Federal*). If an employee is dismissed without cause, the employee receives the Fund and the employer must pay the employee a penalty corresponding to 40 per cent of the total amount deposited in the Fund. The Fund is also received by the employee on his retirement.

(3) Social Integration Plan (*Programa de Integração Social* — PIS) is a 0.65 per cent tax on gross revenues from the sale of goods, provision of services, or results of transactions on third parties' account. Gross revenues do not include canceled sales or services, unconditional discounts, and taxes withheld on accounts of third parties. PIS is not levied on the exportation of goods or services, as long as the proceeds from such exportation are brought into Brazil.

(4) Contribution for Financing of Social Security (*Contribuição para Financiamento da Seguridade Social* — COFINS) was recently increased from two per cent to three per cent of the gross revenues, one-third of which may be offset against the Social Contribution on Profits — CSL. COFINS is not levied on the exportation of goods or services.

(5) Social Contribution on Profits (*Contribuição Social sobre o Lucro* — CSL) consists of a 12 per cent tax on adjusted net profits (as of May 1, 1999), calculated monthly or annually (pursuant to the option for income tax made by the taxpayer) and is not deductible from income tax.

4. Effects of Labor Charges in the Employment Relationship

The mandatory and fixed benefits may represent practically over 100 per cent of an employee's salary depending on the collective bargaining agreement, i.e., an employee with a salary of R$ 100 may cost over R$ 200 for the employer, creating a significant obstacle for the expansion of jobs.

As a result of these charges, Brazil is a country with a very high payroll cost. Some benefits, such as the 13th salary, are practically non-existent in other countries. In such other countries, the institution of bonuses and profit-sharing plans are more used with the intention to stimulate productivity. In Brazil, profit-sharing plans have started to be used by companies quite recently.

Although these costs are very high in Brazil, the quality of the benefits is low. In an effort to provide the social security system with a more consistent cash flow, on December 15, 1998, both the House of Representatives and the Senate enacted an amendment to the Brazilian Constitution (no. 20) altering the Brazilian system of social security and establishing the rules for the transition period. According to these new rules, fewer people will qualify to receive retirement pension and more types of benefits and income will be subject to taxation. These changes will likely impact the employment relationship, causing employers to cut benefits granted to employees.

The labor system in Brazil is highly protective of employees resulting in a long tradition of litigation where employees almost always claim their rights in labor courts. It is estimated that six to seven out of ten employees usually claim labor rights in court. Sometimes the employee goes to court long after quitting the job, due to financial conditions or to difficulties finding a new job.

In this scenario, Brazil appears to be the leader of conflicts between employers and employees. The stance of the labor courts in Brazil ends up stimulating conflicts. For example, in 1997, labor courts examined 1.5 million labor suits whereas in Japan that number was only 1000.

On the other hand, as a consequence of the high costs borne by companies related to the so-called "labor charges", the flexibilization of labor rights resulting in collective agreements has grown substantially, as has the number of companies adopting outsourcing.

Notwithstanding, due to the recent crises affecting Brazil and the high unemployment rates especially in the urban centers, there is a clear tendency in recent decisions rendered by the Superior Labor Court towards accepting flexibility as an important element in the current phase of development of employment relationships. In fact, as demonstrated below, new laws are also being enacted in that direction.

5. New Measures

In 1998, the unemployment rate in Brazil averaged 7.59 per cent, one of the highest rates since the early 1980s, with the exception of 1992 when the failure of the Collor stabilization plan plunged the economy into recession.

In light of these recent economic difficulties, the government has issued new measures that clearly demonstrate the tendency to flexibilize labor relations. This flexibility is expected to have a positive effect on the employment rate.

a. Temporary Employment Contracts

Law Number 9,601 of January 21, 1998,[1] introduced temporary employment contracts. Temporary employment has reduced some "labor charges" of the companies — from 55.4 per cent over the salary to 37 per cent — and the monthly deposits of the Workers' Compensation Fund — from eight per cent to two per cent.

When terminating a temporary contract, the company is also released from the payment of prior notice and from the penalty of 40 per cent of the balance of the Workers' Compensation Fund. The Law allows a significant reduction in social benefits paid by employers when contracting workers for a maximum period of two years.

b. Part-Time Employment Contracts

Provisional Rule Number 1,779 of January 13, 1999 regulates the part-time employment contracts, i.e., those which do not exceed 25 hours per week. Part-time employees are not allowed to work overtime. The aim is the creation of new jobs since 99 per cent of labor suits usually contain a claim for overtime payment.

c. "Bank of Hours"

Provisional Rule Number 1,779 has created the "bank of hours". Pursuant to such concept, the overtime of one day can be compensated by less work time on another day, within the period of one year, with a daily limitation of 10 hours.

This system can only be utilized if approved by a collective agreement, signed between the employer and the respective employee union. The bank of hours is intended to be used by companies in low periods of activity, through the reduction of daily working hours without the reduction of salaries and the creation of a "bank of hours" that can be used in periods of high activity. If the system is implemented in periods of high production activity, the daily working hours can be extended to a maximum of two hours. These overtime hours will be compensated through the granting of vacation periods or through the reduction of the working hours in the near future.

The compensation of the "bank of hours" must be made during the validity of the employment contract. In other words, if the employee is dismissed without the proper compensation, the employee will have the right to receive any credited hours

---

1 Law Number 9,601 of January 21, 1998 regulated by Decree Number 2,490 of February 4, 1998.

plus a compensation established by the collective agreement. This compensation cannot have a value of less than 50 per cent of the value of the regular working hour.

d. Suspension of Employment Contracts

The same Provisional Rule also created the possibility of suspension of the employment contract. According to this provision, the employment contract can be suspended from two to five months for the participation of the employee in a course or professional qualification program offered by the employer.

The employer has the obligation to pay 80 per cent of the salary of the employee during this period and to reintegrate the employee after the program is completed.

B. MERGERS AND ACQUISITIONS

There are many different labor issues involved in an acquisition or in a merger of a Brazilian company, depending on the employer's decision to:

(1) Keep the employees of the Brazilian company under the same employment conditions;

(2) Terminate their employment contracts, paying to employees all labor rights required by law; or

(3) Terminate their employment contracts paying all legal labor rights and granting a severance package with benefits such as extension of the health insurance for a certain period, additional indemnification, and payment of expenses with professional placement.

1. Successor Liabilities

Since the labor liability may remain not only with the target company but may reach the other participating companies as successors, during the process of decision making, the status of labor rights of the employees of the target company should be seriously taken into consideration.

Due to potential claims for pending labor benefits, an evaluation of the status of each employee on a case-by-case basis is recommended to verify possible liabilities in case of termination. For example, if an employee in the target company has not consumed his/her vacation leave over the period of time established in the law, the employer is subject to a payment of vacation days in double plus fines.

In certain cases, previous employers may have created compensation mechanisms which, although accepted by employees at a given moment, may not be in full compliance with the law, even when sometimes such mechanisms may benefit the employees. Therefore, a full due diligence work in the target company is highly recommended, encompassing not only existing liabilities but also possible claims. In examining the target company, the methods used by it *vis-à-vis* its employees as well as the existence of labor disputes are a significant indicator of what liabilities may arise in the future, after the merger or the acquisition.

2. Statute of Limitations of Labor Rights

In Brazil, as a general rule, the statute of limitations for labor rights is five years for any violation with a time limit of two years after the termination of the employment contract for the claims to be brought in court. There are certain labor rights for which the statute of limitations is longer as, for instance, for payments into the Workers' Compensation Fund, where it is 20 years.

In any case, a labor settlement is only enforceable if done in court. That means that a private agreement with an employee is never a guarantee that the employee will not subsequently bring a claim in court. This system works against the motivation of the parties to settle out of court, and the employees know that the courts will likely protect them if they initiate a suit even if they had a severance settlement.

C. DOING BUSINESS IN BRAZIL

When looking at Brazil for business opportunities, one should have in mind the two basic ways to do business:

(1) In the country; or

(2) With the country.

Each one of these situations originates distinct labor consequences. Doing business in Brazil encompasses direct investments in the Brazilian territory, which may, for example, require the incorporation of a company or, alternatively, involve applications in portfolio investments.

By doing business in the country, a foreign investor is expected to set up a wholly owned subsidiary, acquire a Brazilian company, or associate with a Brazilian company in a joint venture.

It is important to point out that Brazilian labor law requires that at least two-thirds of the personnel of a company with three or more employees must be Brazilians. This proportion must be maintained at all levels in the company. In addition, at least two-thirds of the payroll must be paid to Brazilians. For purposes of these rules, an alien residing in Brazil for more than 10 years and/or having a Brazilian spouse or child is considered Brazilian.

1. Hiring a General Manager

Any company established in Brazil must have a manager who must be a Brazilian resident, who may be a foreigner holding a proper permanent visa. Whether the general manager is to be an officer or director of the company, pursuant to Brazilian labor law there are two ways to hire a general manager: as an employee general manager or as a statutory general manager. The employee general manager can be either:

(1) A person who is hired by an employer to render the services as general manager or officer under an employment agreement; or

(2) In the case of a company already in existence, a person who is already an employee under an employment agreement and is promoted as general manager or officer under such employment agreement.

The employee general manager will be entitled to all labor rights. The statutory general manager is nominated as a general manager or an officer through a resolution adopted by the partners or shareholders, deliberating on his/her elected position. Since the general manager or officer is considered as a business person who personifies the figure of the employer, the compensation is not referred to as "salary" but as *pro-labore*, the value of which is determined by the partners or shareholders.

It is important to emphasize that a statutory general manager is not considered an employee and, therefore, he/she is not entitled to any of the labor rights granted to an employee general manager. The statutory general manager merely has a statutory and not a labor relationship with the company.

2. Visa for Foreign Workers

Currently, the Brazilian authorities maintain a strict immigration policy in defense of Brazilian workers. There are two types of visa a foreigner may apply for to work in Brazil, namely:

(1) Permanent visas; and

(2) Temporary visas.

a. *Permanent Visas*

Permanent visas are granted only to:

(1) Personnel who are transferred to Brazil from foreign companies to work in their subsidiaries; or

(2) Managers or officers (occupying positions established in the local company's charter or by-laws as explained above).

No permanent visas are granted to foreigners intending to work as department heads, foremen, technical managers, or similar positions. The Brazilian company in which the foreigner will occupy a position as a manager or an officer must prove that the foreign affiliated company has invested at least US $200,000 paid into the capital stock of the Brazilian company.

Foreigners who are married to Brazilian citizens or have Brazilian children may apply for permanent visas, provided that they have a job offer in Brazil.

b. Temporary Visas

Temporary visas may be granted for a maximum of two years for foreigners who will perform scientific or technical functions in Brazil pursuant to a labor contract.

Such visas are renewable once for an additional two-year period, without the need to leave the country, by authorization of the Ministry of Justice; thereafter, the bearer of the temporary visa may apply for transformation of his/her visa into a permanent visa, provided that all legal conditions are met.

D. DOING BUSINESS WITH BRAZIL

Doing business with Brazil may be another form of presence in the country, without actually creating a local establishment. It usually comprises sales by the foreign company to a Brazilian party, through sales arrangements, distributions, licenses, technology transfers, and franchises.

There are several different ways to sell products in and to Brazil by using an intermediary person or entity, some of which are ruled by specific regulations and others by general laws. The investor should carefully evaluate which method of business is more appropriate for each purpose and heed its labor consequences. Among the main types of intermediaries, special reference should be made to agents and distributors, each one of which is subject to a different legal treatment. As a general rule, the Brazilian approach to these transactions is that, in an agency, an agent just collects orders from clients of the manufacturer (the principal) and places these purchase orders with the principal.

A distributor, on the other hand, buys the products from a manufacturer and resells them to its own customers. Although not specifically considered employees, if the relationship is not clearly defined otherwise from the outset, there may be risks of labor-related claims.

1. Agents

In an agency relationship, a self-employed individual or legal entity (agent) acts on behalf of one or more legal entities or persons (principal), on a regular basis, as intermediary in commercial transactions by negotiating proposals and orders and transmitting them to the principal, regardless of whether the agent's actions are related to the completion of these transactions. No employment relationship exists between agent and principal and this condition should be clearly stated in the agency agreement. The agent should always act on behalf of the principal and only within the powers granted by the latter.

Under no circumstance should an agent be treated as the principal's subordinate. Subordination is one of the elements characterizing an employment relationship. Brazilian courts have upheld that subordination exists whenever the agency's activities are closely inspected on a regular basis and controlled by the principal. If the agency is characterized as an employment relationship, the principal will be subject to labor laws, and social and welfare contributions. Most importantly, if the principal is domiciled or incorporated outside Brazil, he may be characterized as doing business in Brazil, a situation which will trigger taxes not levied on an agency relationship.

The agent acquires the right to a commission whenever a client makes total or partial payment to the principal for the products under the agency. Commissions are usually either a floating percentage or a fixed commission based on the sales price.

In case of termination of the agreement, the indemnification payable to the agent will depend on whether:

(1) The agreement is terminated with or without cause; and

(2) The duration is for a determinate or indeterminate period of time.

a. *With-Cause Termination*

If the agreement is terminated with cause, at any time, no indemnification is owed to the agent by the principal. The courts will decide, however, whether or not termination was for fair cause on evidence supplied by the parties in an eventual lawsuit (if the agent resists termination). In certain cases, the parties may be entitled to losses and damages pursuant to the Brazilian Civil Code, and the principal has the right to retain commissions owed to the agent as a means of off-setting the losses incurred as result of the agent's behavior.

The law lists the events considered just causes for the principal and/or agent to terminate the agreement; however, the parties may establish in the agreement other events considered causes for termination of the agreement.

In agreements for an indeterminate period of time, the law does not provide for a specific prior notice. The contractual provisions should be observed; in any event a prior notice is always advisable.

b. Without-Cause Termination

In the case of without-cause termination, if the agreement is for a determinate period of time, the agent will be entitled to:

(1) The average of the monthly commissions received up to the date of termination multiplied by half of the months remaining to the expiration of the agreement; and

(2) Any losses and damages effectively incurred and duly proven.

If the agreement is for an indeterminate term, either party may terminate the agreement if it has been in force for more than six months on:

(1) Thirty days' notice; or

(2) Payment of one-third of the commissions received by the agent in the preceding three months, unless otherwise defined in the agreement.

2. Distributors

Distributorship is a relationship in which a manufacturer agrees to sell its products to a distributor, an individual, or a legal entity, with special advantages and on a continuing basis, for further resale of these products by the distributor to third parties in a defined geographic area, at the distributor's own account and risk.

The distributor does not receive any commission and usually makes its profits out of the difference between the price sold to consumers and the one paid to the manufacturer. The distributor is a reseller who acquires the products from a manufacturer and promotes their sale.

There is no specific legislation regulating the general distribution relationship in Brazil, except for laws specifically dealing with sales of automobiles and software products. For this reason, the distribution agreement must be drafted very carefully, and in detail, allowing the parties to bargain their own terms and avoiding any elements which may be considered tantamount to the employment relationship. The termination of the agreement will depend on whether it is with or without cause, and if the duration is for a determinate or indeterminate period of time.

Agreements with a definite term are considered automatically terminated at the end of the term and no compensation is due to the distributor. On the expiration of the term, the parties should cease their contractual activities and consider their relationship ended. Even though the agreement may contain an expiration date, it is advisable for the parties to give each other a prior written notice indicating their intention of renewing or canceling the agreement. Such notice will substantiate the continuance of their relationship in writing — thus defining other terms and conditions — or confirm the discontinuance of their obligations.

Agreements with an indefinite term may be terminated by either party, without just cause, at any time, preceded by a reasonable notice.

3. Independent Contractors

Foreign investors usually establish themselves in Brazil by incorporating a Brazilian company. That is to say that a foreign company, as such, cannot be registered in Brazil. Unlike other countries, the use of branches in Brazil must be approved by the Brazilian President, which is a rather complex, time-consuming and unusual procedure. Without any registration, the foreign company is unable to pay any social security benefit to eventual local assistance. If the foreign company establishes a relationship with a Brazilian employee, social security charges would result from it. Since the foreign company is not able to collect them, it cannot have any type of employment relationship in Brazil.

However, the foreign company can hire a person as an independent contractor. In this case, the independent contractor will have the burden to pay all legal benefit charges and all applicable taxes. Preferably, the independent contractor should take the form of a duly incorporated company.

It is important, however, to carefully draft the agreement with an independent contractor. Words that indicate a subordination relationship, such as "salary", "13th salary", "vacation" and, especially, "employer" and "employee", should not be used.

CHAPTER 12

EMPLOYMENT ASPECTS OF FREE TRADE AGREEMENTS IN BUSINESS TRANSACTIONS AND PERSONNEL TRANSFERS

Sergio Karas
Karas & Associates
Toronto, Ontario, Canada

A. INTRODUCTION

The mobility of the labor force is a key element for the success of an international enterprise. To facilitate the transfer of senior personnel and international business people from one country to another, several instruments have been devised to assist in carrying out those objectives.

The most notable are the North American Free Trade Agreement (NAFTA) and the General Agreement of Trade in Services (GATS).

B. TEMPORARY ENTRY UNDER THE GENERAL AGREEMENT ON TRADE IN SERVICES

The General Agreement on Trade in Services (GATS), one of three components to the Agreement Establishing the World Trade Organization (AEWTO) promulgated on January 1, 1995, provides expedited and simplified entry procedures for admission to signatory countries for business purposes and employment for individuals from 122 countries. The temporary entry provisions of the GATS consist of Annex 1B (to the World Trade Agreement), which sets out the signatories' commitments, the economic sectors and/or services to which the agreement applies, and the member nations.

The most valuable feature of the GATS is simply that qualification of a foreign worker under its provisions permits entry without a job validation or foreign worker record. To qualify under the GATS, the applicant must be a citizen of and resident in a member nation listed in Appendix A to Annex 1B of the AEWTO.

The member nation need not be the same for both aspects of this qualification to be satisfied (i.e., the applicant may qualify as a citizen of one nation and as a resident of another nation, so long as both nations are member nations for purposes of the GATS).

To qualify under the GATS, prospective applicants must be entering a member nation to engage in a business activity in one of the following sectors:

(1) Business services;

(2) Communications services;

(3) Construction services;

(4) Distribution services;

(5) Environmental services;

(6) Financial services;

(7) Tourism and travel-related services; and

(8) Transport services.

It is important to ensure that the specific occupational services relating to the applicant are enumerated. For example, legal, accounting, and engineering personnel are found under the Business Services section, while Communication Services has the largest listing of computer-related services.

Three types of businesspersons qualify for admission under the GATS:

(1) Business visitors;

(2) Intra-company transferees; and

(3) Professionals.

1. Business Visitors

Under the GATS, they are citizens of a member nation who will stay in a member nation for qualifying purposes without:

(1) Obtaining remuneration from within the member nation; or

(2) Engaging in making direct sales to the general public or supplying services.

Qualifying purposes are participating in business meetings, establishing business contacts, including negotiations for the sale of services and/or other similar activities including those to prepare for establishing a commercial presence in the member nation. The service provider must be located in a member nation.

The applicant may not be remunerated by the local enterprise, as visitor status does not permit entry where there is remuneration from a local source or employer.

Business visitors qualifying under the GATS are not permitted to engage in employment for or on behalf of a local employer. Business visitors are entitled to pursue activities that relate to the sale of services including participation in the start-up of a business in the member nation.

The applicant's activities must be limited to business meetings, negotiations, and other types of business contacts. Otherwise, the applicant may not qualify as a business visitor.

2. Intra-Company Transferees

The intra-company provisions under the GATS significantly expand the accessibility to the local labor market of key personnel needed to oversee the operations of foreign service providers. This category is the most generous of the three categories in the GATS.

"Intra-company transferees" are persons of another member nation who have been employed for a period of not less than one year and who seek temporary entry to render services to the same company which is engaged in substantive business operations, or a company constituted locally and engaged in substantive business operations which is owned by or controlled by or affiliated with the aforementioned company. The GATS sets out three specifically defined types of foreign workers who may qualify:

(1) Senior executives;

(2) Senior managers; and

(3) Specialists.

These types of foreign workers may be transferred by a foreign enterprise which is related (parent, subsidiary, or affiliate) to the local transferee enterprise.

"Executives" do not generally perform duties necessary to actual delivery of a service. Rather, executives are responsible for overseeing, directing, and controlling the operation or enterprise. It is not an applicant's title but rather his actual responsibilities that will be considered by immigration officials. That the applicant is an executive is determined by considering whether he or she is an individual who is primarily responsible for:

(1) The direct management of the company, establishing its goals and policies; or

(2) A major component or function of the company, and who has a wide decision-making power subject to minimal additional senior supervision.

"Managers" need not be involved in the actual delivery of service. For example, performing a service, such as an accountant or architect would, will not satisfy the requirement that executive or managerial duties must be undertaken. Moreover, front-line supervisors do not qualify unless the employees supervised by that person are professionals. To determine whether the applicant is a manager, it must be considered if he or she:

(1) Is responsible for directing the enterprise, or department or subdivision of the company, supervising the work of other supervisory, professional, or managerial employees;

(2) Has discretionary control of the daily affairs of the company; and

(3) Has the ability to make personnel decisions.

Admittance under the GATS specialized knowledge provisions does not discharge the applicant or the employer from the responsibility of ensuring that any licensing, registration, or certification requirements are met before commencement of employment. To qualify under the specialized knowledge provisions, the local enterprise must demonstrate that the foreign worker possesses an advanced level of knowledge and expertise of a nature so as to be critical to the well-being of the enterprise. This knowledge need not be readily available locally.

The "business enterprise" is referred to in the text of the GATS as a "juridical person" and is defined as: any legal entity duly constituted or otherwise organized under applicable law, whether for profit or otherwise, and whether privately owned or governmentally owned, including any corporation, trust, partnership, joint venture, sole proprietorship, or association. Both the foreign and the local enterprise must be engaged in a substantive business operation that corresponds to a service sector referred to in the GATS.

The local office must be of real substance having business activities that would require and utilize the executive or management functions of the foreign worker. The local enterprise must be "doing business" defined as providing services on a regular, systematic, and continuous basis. The mere presence of an agent or office in the member nation does not constitute "doing business" within the meaning of the GATS.

The foreign worker may be destined to a "start-up" operation provided that the enterprise is established and can reasonably be expected to grow to a size sufficient to justify the foreign worker's anticipated employment activities at the level required to satisfy the criteria of this provision. The local enterprise may not have been created merely to permit the transfer. There must be employees or the prospects for active growth. The local employer and foreign transferor business must be related either by way of parent, subsidiary, or affiliate relationship.

The definition of "affiliate" includes common ownership of the transferor and transferee company by a third corporation or entity or group of companies. The local operation may also be a branch of the transferor company.

3. Professionals

A "professional" is a person who seeks to engage in an activity at a professional level in a profession set out in the GATS.

The activities to be performed by the applicant must be part of a service contract obtained by an enterprise in another member nation. The list of eligible professions presently includes engineers, agrologists, architects, forestry professionals, geomatic professionals, and land surveyors. It will be expanded to include legal consultants, urban planners, and computer specialists.

The service performed by the foreign professional must be related to a signed contract between the local service consumer and the member nation service provider. The contract cannot be between a service consumer and a foreign personnel placement agency or management consultant. The contract can provide for the payment of remuneration by the foreign service provider or the service consumer. The contract may be between a foreign service provider in a member nation or a locally based company established by the service provider to sell its services.

The applicant must possess the necessary academic credentials and professional qualifications that have been duly recognized, where appropriate, by the local professional association.

With respect to occupations for which licensing is not required, the issuance of the employment authorization can only be granted on presentation of documentation from the appropriate professional association indicating that foreign academic credentials and professional qualifications are recognized. Unlike GATS intra-corporate transferees that possess specialized knowledge, GATS professionals must obtain the necessary accreditation prior to entering a member nation.

C. TEMPORARY ENTRY UNDER THE NORTH AMERICAN FREE TRADE AGREEMENT

The purpose of the North American Free Trade Agreement (NAFTA) is to facilitate trade between the United States, Mexico, and Canada, and gradually abolish trade barriers. The Agreement opens the markets of the three countries and ensures that future legislation will not create barriers to doing business between the signatories.

NAFTA contains special provisions concerning immigration between the three signatory countries. Chapter 16 of NAFTA, entitled "Temporary Entry for Business Persons", provides the mechanisms to facilitate the movement of businesspersons between the three countries.

Chapter 16 eases, on a reciprocal basis, the temporary entry of citizens of the United States, Canada, and Mexico, in specific areas of business activity detailed in the Agreement. However, it must be noted that NAFTA does not replace existing general legislation concerning immigration matters in any of the three countries.

NAFTA grants preferential treatment to certain businesspersons and professionals who are citizens of any of the three countries and who require temporary entry for a purpose recognized by this treaty.

A trilateral Temporary Entry Working Group, which includes representatives from all three countries, has been formed to oversee the implementation and administration of Chapter 16 of NAFTA. The Working Group is also responsible for developing measures to facilitate temporary entry of businesspersons on a reciprocal basis.

NAFTA provides an exemption from the normal requirements set out in the immigration legislation and regulations of the three signatories, which require that no person, other than a citizen or permanent resident, shall engage or continue in employment without a valid and subsisting employment authorization, permit, or visa.

The temporary entry provisions of Chapter 16 are restricted to citizens of the United States, Mexico, and Canada. In the case of the United States, citizens of Puerto Rico are covered by NAFTA, but citizens of Guam, the Northern Mariana Islands, American Samoa, and the United States Virgin Islands are excluded from NAFTA. Permanent residents are not covered, and they continue to be governed by the general provisions concerning temporary entry for foreign workers found in immigration legislation of each country.

1. Business Visitors

Business visitors are business persons who plan to carry on business activity related to research and design, growth, manufacturing, production, marketing, sales, distribution, after-sales service, and general service. The business activities covered by Appendix 1603.A.1 of NAFTA are of a commercial nature and reflect the components of the business cycle.

Applicants who wish to gain entry under the "after-sales service" sub-category of business visitors must comply with a number of additional requirements, and must demonstrate that:

(1) The purpose of entry to a signatory country is to install, repair, service, supervise, or train workers to perform services;

(2) The equipment or machinery (including computer software) is commercial or industrial (not household or personal);

(3) The equipment or machinery was manufactured and purchased outside of the country;

(4) The work is done pursuant to an original sales contract and any warranty or service agreement is incidental to the sale;

(5) The work is carried out during the validity of the warranty or service agreement or any extensions of same; and

(6) The work requires specialized knowledge, and excludes hands-on building or construction work.

"Specialized knowledge" is considered to be a very high degree of knowledge given only to persons who are already skilled in their occupation and have undergone extensive training.

Persons applying under the after-sales service sub-category must possess the level of skill or knowledge necessary to perform the occupation. This level must be at least post-secondary education relevant to the area of service, or the possession of a license, certification, or other accreditation issued by a competent authority or administrative supervisory body. The person seeking entry must also possess the appropriate training, which is viewed as essential to providing the service and may include training and supervising others who will actually perform the activities of the machinery, equipment, or software.

Business visitors must apply for authorizations at the Port of Entry and applications cannot be made in advance at a Consulate or Embassy. The visas are granted for short-term stays and extension can be given if the requirements continue to be met.

2. Professionals

Citizens of the United States, Mexico, or Canada who are professionals identified in Appendix 1603.D.1 of the NAFTA may qualify for temporary entry under the treaty if they:

(1) Have the necessary qualifications to work in their professions;

(2) Have pre-arranged employment with a local employer;

(3) Come for the purpose of providing professional-level services in the same field as their qualification; and

(4) Comply with existing immigration requirements for temporary entry.

Appendix 16.03.D.1 lists more than 60 occupations and is the mechanism by which selected professionals can enter each country to provide their services. It must be noted that the Appendix is a comprehensive list of occupations and cannot be interpreted. An occupation that does not appear in the list is automatically excluded. However, there is some room to allow for different job titles, which may be within the occupations defined in the Appendix.

The Appendix also details Minimum Educational Requirements and Alternative Credentials for each profession. These are the minimum criteria for entry and do not necessarily reflect the educational requirements, accreditation, or licensing necessary to practice a profession. Immigration authorities will not require the necessary provincial licensing to practice the profession. To do so would defeat the purpose of the provisions contained in NAFTA concerning professionals.

Professionals can also be admitted as business visitors under the General Service provisions of Appendix 1603.A.1, when they are not seeking to enter the labor market but will be performing activities such as soliciting business, consulting, providing services, and meeting clients.

Employment in the professionals category must be pre-arranged with an employer, who may be an enterprise or an individual. This includes a relationship of employer-employee, or a contract between a professional and the enterprise.

It must also be noted that the professionals category does not allow self-employment. A person wishing to be self-employed should consider making an application under the trader or investor category, rather than the professional category. However, if a citizen is self-employed, he is not barred from the professional category, provided that the services he renders are pre-arranged with an employer. The employer must be separate from the applicant seeking entry as a professional.

Professionals can apply for NAFTA authorizations at the Port of Entry or make an application at a mission abroad before departing for the country of destination. The temporary authorization issued is initially valid for a maximum of one year, but can be extended, provided that the professional continues to meet entry requirements under that category. Although there is no time limit on extensions, applicants must satisfy Immigration officers that their employment continues to be "temporary" and that they are not using the NAFTA entry provisions as a means to circumvent normal immigration procedures.

3. Intra-Company Transferees

Business persons who are employed in a managerial or executive capacity, or in a position which involves specialized knowledge, may be transferred between NAFTA countries to a firm, corporation, affiliate, or subsidiary of the American, Canadian, or Mexican enterprise.

An executive does not generally perform duties necessary in the production of a product or in the delivery of a service. In smaller businesses, the title of the position may not be sufficient to establish that the position is managerial or executive. To qualify as a manager or executive as described in the intra-company transferee category, the person must be engaging in managerial or executive duties. A first-line supervisor is not considered to be acting in a managerial capacity unless the employees supervised are professional.

A manager does not primarily perform tasks required in production of a product or in the delivery of a service. In smaller businesses, the title of the position may not be sufficient to establish that it is managerial or executive. An applicant seeking to open a new office on behalf of the foreign enterprise may also qualify under this category, if the local enterprise is expected to support a managerial or executive position or, in the case of specialized knowledge, is to be doing business in the country of destination.

Employment authorizations issued under this category can have a maximum validity of three years. However, individuals admitted to open an office or to be employed in a new office are normally issued an initial authorization for a maximum of one year. Extensions can be granted for up to two years, if the person continues to comply with the eligibility requirements of intra-company transferees. It must be noted that the intra-company transferee visa is the only one to have a maximum duration imposed on the total duration of employment. The maximum period of stay for a person employed in an executive or managerial capacity may not exceed seven years. The total period of stay for a person employed in a position requiring specialized knowledge may not exceed five years.

4. Traders

An applicant can be granted trader status if he is a business person who is seeking temporary entry to carry on substantial trade of goods or services principally between the United States, Mexico, and Canada.

The applicant may be trading on his or her own behalf, or as an agent of a person or organization engaged in trade principally between Canada and the United States or Mexico, or he may also be an employee of a person or corporation maintaining trader status in Canada. The individual or corporate persons who own at least a 50 per cent interest (directly or by stock) in the entity established in the country of destination must hold American, Mexican, or Canadian citizenship. Joint ventures and partnerships are limited to two parties only. The applicant who is seeking temporary entry must do so to carry on substantial trade in goods or services, principally between the signatory countries.

When a person is applying under the trader category but will occupy the position of employee, he must be employed in a capacity that is supervisory or executive or involves essential skills. There is an exception to the criterion of essential skills for highly trained technicians. These are persons who are employed by the firm to train or to supervise personnel employed in manufacturing, maintenance, and repair functions, and may be granted trader status even though some manual duties may be performed, provided that the firm cannot obtain the services of qualified local technicians. The emphasis is on "highly trained". For example, a qualified technician coming to Canada to perform warranty repairs on intricate and complex products sold in trade between Canada and the United States or Mexico can be granted trader status if the employing firm establishes that it cannot obtain the services of a qualified Canadian technician.

Traders are issued employment authorizations that can have a maximum duration of one year, but can be extended for up to a maximum of two years, provided that they continue to meet the requirements of the category. Applications must be made at a visa office.

5. Investors

An "investor" is defined as a business person who is seeking temporary entry to develop and direct the operations of an enterprise in which they have invested, or are actively in the process of investing, a substantial amount of capital.

The criteria that must be met include the following:

(1) The applicant must be a citizen of the United States, Canada, or Mexico;

(2) The enterprise or firm to which the applicant is coming has American, Canadian, or Mexican nationality; and

(3) The applicant who is seeking temporary entry must solely "develop and direct" the operations of the enterprise in which he has invested, or is actively in the process of investing, a substantial amount of capital.

Enterprise nationality is determined by means of control or ownership of at least a 50 per cent interest (directly or by stock) in the entity established in the country of destination. Joint ventures are limited to two partners. They may also include parent/subsidiary situations, and the nationality of the corporate entity established must then be considered. The place of incorporation of an enterprise is not an indication of nationality; it is only an indication of ownership and control.

If the applicant is in the process of investing, mere intent to invest or prospective investment arrangements without present commitment will not suffice. The applicant must be close to the start of actual business operations, not merely in the stage of signing contracts or investigating suitable locations and property. The investment funds must be irrevocably committed to the business. Whether an investment has been or will be made, the applicant must demonstrate prior or present possession and control of the funds or other capital assets.

There is no minimum dollar figure established for meeting the requirement of "substantial" investment. Substantiality is normally determined by using a "proportional test" in which the amount invested is weighed against the total value of the particular enterprise in question, or the amount normally considered necessary to establish a viable enterprise of the nature contemplated. Letters from chambers of commerce or statistics from trade associations may be reliable for this purpose. Only the amount already invested or irrevocably committed for investment can be considered in determining substantiality.

The enterprise must be a real and active commercial undertaking that operates to produce some service or commodity for profit. It cannot be a paper organization or a speculative investment. For instance, passive investment in developed or undeveloped real estate or stocks does not qualify.

The objective of investor status is to promote productive investment in the signatory countries. Therefore, an applicant is not entitled to this status if the investment, even when substantial, will return only enough income to provide a living for the applicant and family. If the applicant has substantial income from other sources and does not rely on the investment enterprise to provide a living, the investment may be one of risk and not only marginal.

Where the applicant is an employee, special rules apply. To bring an employee to a signatory country under investor status, the nationality requirements must be met. The prospective employer must be a citizen of the United States, Canada, or Mexico who is maintaining investor status. Alternatively, in the case of a corporation or other business organization employer, the majority ownership must be held by citizens of the United States, Canada, or Mexico who, if not residing in either country, are maintaining investor status in the signatory country.

A citizen of the signatory country who is a permanent resident in another does not qualify to bring an employee under the investor status. Employees must also satisfy Immigration officials that they will be engaged in a supervisory or executive capacity, or that they possess skills essential to the firm's operations in the country of destination. There are two exceptions to the application of the factors concerning essential skills, namely:

(1) Where investor status may be granted to an employee not possessing them when he or she is needed for the start-up of the new enterprise, under certain circumstances; and

(2) In the case of highly trained technicians, who will be brought in to train or supervise other employees.

Employment Authorizations are issued to an investor at the time of entry normally for one year, although they can be extended for up to two years provided that the investor continues to meet the requirements of the category.

NAFTA reflects the already existing preferential trading relationship between the United States and Canada, which has been expanded to include Mexico. Future expansion is possible, and Canada has already negotiated a treaty with Chile, the Canada–Chile Free Trade Agreement (CCFTA), with a view of incorporating Chile into NAFTA. If that happens, CCFTA will be suspended and NAFTA will be modified accordingly to accommodate the new technical requirements. NAFTA has been instrumental in promoting and accelerating the economic integration of North American economies.

D. CONCLUSION

The GATS provisions are in many respects similar in substance to those of the North American Free Trade Agreement (NAFTA), yet because they apply to individuals from more than 122 member nations, they have a much broader application. Like NAFTA, the GATS expands but does not replace the general provisions pertaining to foreign workers. However, in most instances, where United States, Mexican, or Canadian nationals are concerned, the simplest course of action would be to first consider the applicability of NAFTA before turning to the provisions of the GATS.

The use of the intra-company transferee provisions of the GATS should generally be restricted to intra-company transferees whose applications are based on their specialized knowledge. In contrast, the intra-company transferee provisions of NAFTA require that one year of experience must have been obtained within the three-year period immediately preceding the applicant's transfer to the member nation.

The GATS requires that applicants possess "an advanced level of expertise" in certain aspects of the enterprise. In contrast, NAFTA requires advanced expertise only if the transferee's application is based on knowledge of the local enterprise's process and procedures. Under NAFTA, if the application is based on the transferee's knowledge of the local enterprise's product, service, research, equipment, techniques, management, or other interests, the transferee's knowledge need only meet the standard of "specialized knowledge". Given that the GATS threshold of an "advanced level of expertise" is considerably higher than the specialized knowledge requirements of NAFTA, an examination of the applicant's knowledge in relation to the employer's needs is required.

The GATS is widely applicable, as 122 nations are signatories, but NAFTA's provisions are more generous and less restrictive. Both the GATS and NAFTA ease temporary entry for business purposes, but neither replaces existing immigration laws. NAFTA may be expected to include other nations in the near future.

Part IV

Ethical Global Employment — Global Codes of Conduct, Corporate Compliance Programs, Anti-Bribery Policies, and Employment-Crisis Management

CHAPTER 13
THE RISE OF INTERNATIONAL CORPORATE CODES OF CONDUCT AND THE HUMAN RIGHTS CONVENTION

Janet M. Gaymer
Simmons & Simmons
London, England

A. INTRODUCTION

> The courts' decisions will be based on a more overtly principled, indeed moral, basis. The court will look at the positive rights. It will only accept an interference with that right where a justification allowed under the Convention is made out. The scrutiny will not be limited to seeing if the words of an exception can be satisfied. The court will need to be satisfied that the spirit of this exception is made out. It will need to be satisfied that the interference with the protected right is justified in the public interests in a free democratic society . . . the court will need to expand and explain its own view of whether the conduct is legitimate. It will produce in short a decision on the morality of the conduct and not simply its compliance with the bare letter of the law.

These words were the words of the Lord Chancellor, Lord Irvine of Lairg, when commenting on the forthcoming incorporation of the Human Rights Convention into English law through the Human Rights Act 1998.

Although the Human Rights Act is not yet binding in the United Kingdom, it will represent, in the Lord Chancellor's words, a "shift to a rights based system" whereby "a citizen's right" is asserted as a positive entitlement expressed in clear and principled terms. In particular, since the rights set out in the Convention consist of a series of aspirational or moral statements, the English judiciary will have to apply these to particular cases that come before them. They will be required to interpret phrases such as "respect for private life". They will have to make the moral precepts of their judgment explicit and justify them.

They will need to refer to the jurisprudence of other courts and not simply decisions of the European Court of Human Rights. In other words, the judiciary will have to articulate a moral system and ensure that it works in practice. As a consequence, it is arguable that the conduct of parties who appear before courts and tribunals will be tested in a different way. Employment Tribunals, for example, will be required to consider the rights in the Convention, which are stated in general terms. Depending on the rights involved, they may or may not be subject to restrictions to protect other legitimate interests. Such restrictions must be set down in laws and, in the language of the Convention, they must be "necessary in a democratic society".

In the above circumstances, it is not surprising that more and more big United Kingdom companies are issuing to their workforces ethical codes of conduct. However, this rise of the code of conduct is not limited to the United Kingdom.

B. RISE OF INTERNATIONAL CORPORATE CODES OF CONDUCT

A number of comments need to be made about the increased use of corporate codes of conduct internationally.

First, preoccupation with conduct is not a new phenomenon. Since the foundation of the East India Company in 1600 the social responsibilities of multi-national companies have caused comment and a demand for respect for human rights. The East India Company contributed seven to eight per cent of the British state's income and conquered and ruled India until 1858. To pay the Chinese for tea, opium was sold (and bought by the Chinese for silver as counter trade). The desire for sugar to put into tea led to the slave trade. Both slave trade and opium trade were criticized. Robert Clive himself was accused of human rights abuses.

The current picture is of a number of companies using codes of conduct to promote high standards of behavior. The number of companies doing so has more than trebled in the past decade. Global companies have expanded. Of 178 top United Kingdom companies, 18 per cent had implemented codes in 1987 compared with 57 per cent last year. One United Kingdom company distributed a Braille version of its code of conduct to 90,000 employees and translated the code into several European languages. There are a number of reasons why codes of conduct are deemed to be necessary or appropriate. Codes of conduct have been prompted by:

(1) Increased emphasis on corporate governance and standards of behavior generally in the corporate workplace;

(2) An organization's wish to be seen to be socially responsible;

(3) The potential for enhancement of the reputation of a company by demonstrating, for example, integrity and other values which are seen to match the organization's business;

(4) The perception that codes may make plain what conduct is acceptable by employees and others and what is not;

(5) The hope that a code may assist global integration by establishing a global branding or image acceptable across the world;

(6) A belief that a code may be simply good business;

(7) The rise of the not-for-profit sector; and

(8) Incoming legislation which may prompt a re-think about how business is done or may be perceived to have been done.

C. HUMAN RIGHTS AS A BUSINESS ISSUE

When one looks at human rights in a business context it is immediately apparent that it is not a new business issue, as already noted. In 1948 on December 10, the General Assembly of the United Nations adopted and proclaimed the Universal Declaration of Human Rights. This proclaimed the Universal Declaration of Human Rights "as a common standard of achievement for all peoples and all nations to the end that every individual and every organ of society, keeping this Declaration constantly in mind . . .".

Human rights are regulated in many ways and territories.

The Universal Declaration of Human Rights involved economic, social, and cultural rights, as well as civil and political rights. In 1966, International Covenants were adopted by the United Nations General Assembly, one relating to civil and political rights and the other to economic, social, and cultural rights. Regional Human Rights Conventions exist alongside International Covenants and Conventions. The European Convention on Human Rights of 1950 was ratified by some 40 states and the American Convention on Human Rights of 1969 was ratified by some 25 states.

Others cater for particular regional characteristics, such as the more recent African Charter on Human and Peoples' Rights of 1981 ratified by 51 states. International Labor Conventions provide in a more specific and detailed manner for the practical implementation at national level of the principles set out more generally in Covenants.

The Treaty of European Union states that "the Union shall respect fundamental rights as guaranteed by the European Convention on Human Rights and fundamental freedoms . . . and as they derive from the constitutional traditions common to the Member States, the general principles of [community] law". The United Kingdom has no written constitution protecting human rights. However, the European Convention on Human Rights is to be incorporated into United Kingdom law although there are no proposals to incorporate the wider range of economic and social rights contained in the Council of Europe's Social Charter.

D. CODES OF CONDUCT AND HUMAN RIGHTS

When one examines the type of issues which are dealt with in codes of conduct, the codes of large corporations will typically cover:

(1) Political activities;

(2) Health and safety;

(3) Gifts, hospitality, bribes;

(4) Conflicts of interest;

(5) Insider dealing;

(6) Discrimination;

(7) Software copying;

(8) Alcohol and drug abuse;

(9) Harassment;

(10) Use of company information;

(11) Financial transactions;

(12) Fair competition;

(13) Protection of the environment; and

(14) Human rights generally.

In addition, ethical subjects are intruding into the fields of financial reporting and consumer choice. It is reported that the World Bank has told the Big Five accountancy firms not to audit certain Asian economies.[1] The Bank has required that only high-quality international financial reporting standards would suffice. It is important to remember, therefore, that all of the above subjects must be assessed against global and regional backgrounds.

E. DO CODES OF CONDUCT REALLY MAKE A DIFFERENCE?

However, do codes of conduct really make a difference in practice? It is argued that codes of conduct may be culturally specific and lack global impact as a result. Also, codes of conduct may not impress senior executives or shareholders. According to one recent MORI poll, senior executives were far less interested in environmental compliance (24 per cent) and corporate governance than in bottom-line financial information such as earnings (95 per cent) and cashflows (85 per cent). They were simply not interested in social and ethical issues.

In addition, some argue that social and ethical auditing is not widely seen as giving added value. In any event, many codes of conduct are not communicated

---

1 *The Financial Times* (October 19, 1998).

properly to employees or other interested parties. A recent survey by the Institute of Business Ethics found that over half in the survey had a code but the content of the code was unknown to customers, staff, and other stakeholders. Thirty per cent of those surveyed failed to give a copy of the code to employees and only 11 per cent used a staff survey to help revise codes.

It is clear that if a code is to succeed it must become part of the corporate culture and must be backed from the top. Two-thirds of a recent survey said that a code was introduced at the initiative of a chairman or chief executive. As with many issues in business, change must come from the top.

CHAPTER 14

INTERNATIONAL CORPORATE COMPLIANCE PROGRAMS

Carole Basri
Deloitte & Touche LLP
New York, New York, United States

A. INTRODUCTION

In the course of the last few years, international corporate compliance programs have become more and more important. This chapter provides a step-by-step guide for general counsel at multinational corporations to take ownership of their international corporate compliance programs. Companies should have an international corporate compliance program for several reasons:[1]

(1) An effective international compliance program will set an ethical tone and create a global corporate atmosphere that discourages wrongdoing, reducing the likelihood that employees will commit crimes;

(2) An effective international compliance program can detect misconduct at an earlier stage, allowing the organization to act quickly to minimize adverse consequences;

(3) Corporations under government investigation can point to an effective compliance program as a sign of good faith and thus avoid or minimize possible government action against the corporation (this is true not only in the United States but also, for example, the European Union and Australia); and

(4) A convicted corporation with an effective compliance program in operation at the time of the offense will benefit from reduced exposure (this is the case not only in the United States with the federal sentencing guideline penalties, but also in the European Union and Australia, for example).[2]

---

1 Tansey, "Five Common Mistakes in Designing and Implementing a Compliance Program", *PLI Compliance Handbook*, at pp. 581–582 (1996).

2 Tansey, "Five Common Mistakes in Designing and Implementing a Compliance Program", *PLI Compliance Handbook*, at pp. 581–582 (1996).

B. EFFECT

An international compliance program that is thoughtfully designed and carefully enforced can be very influential in creating a more ethical atmosphere and deterring corporate crime globally. Emerging from a corporate climate that does not condone wrongdoing at any level may make potential offenders think twice. As a convicted insider confirms:

> Seeing the policy against insider trading in black and white . . . might have sensitized me to the issue so that when the offer was made, maybe I would have hesitated just long enough for the temptation to pass.[3]

In a multinational corporation, an international compliance program reinforces the idea that ethics is for all employees, not just United States-based employees. This shows the company's sincere commitment to compliance. As Winthrop Swenson stated when he was the legislative counsel for the United States Federal Sentencing Commission:

> It would not be inconceivable for a judge or prosecutor to second-guess the adequacy of a compliance program by examining how well the program was backed, how well it was supported and how well it was valued outside the domestic subsidiaries.[4]

In addition to enforcing international corporate ethics, an effective compliance program can be a cost-saving device. Employee misconduct lays a great financial burden on any organization. It imposes the risk of significant "hard costs", i.e.:

(1) Criminal or administrative fines or penalties resulting from enforcement actions;

(2) Civil damage awards or settlements resulting from private litigation;

(3) Shareholder derivative suits for failure to properly supervise the company's adherence to industry standards in regulated areas;

(4) Lost opportunities to compete due to debarment;

(5) Decreased sales due to damaged reputation; and

(6) Substantial legal fees.[5]

---

3 For a discussion of these benefits, *see* Webb and Molo, "Some Practical Considerations in Developing Effective Compliance Programs: A Framework for Meeting the Requirements of the Sentencing Guidelines", 71 *Washington University Law Quarterly*, (1993), at p. 375; and Webb, Molo, and Hurst, "Understanding and Avoiding Corporate and Executive Criminal Liability", 49 *Bus. Law* 617 (1994).

4 Tansey, "Five Common Mistakes in Designing and Implementing a Compliance Program", *PLI Compliance Handbook*, at p. 582 (1996).

5 Webb and Molo, "Some Practical Considerations in Developing Effective Compliance Programs: A Framework for Meeting the Requirements of the Sentencing Guidelines", 71 *Washington University Law Quarterly*, (1993), at p. 375, citing Pitt and Groskaufmanis, Minimizing Corporate Civil and Criminal Liability: National Joint Conference on White-Collar Crime, at p. 5 (August 31, 1987).

Misconduct also tends to impose "soft costs" — lost employee productivity, often at senior levels, because of the effort expended in addressing a legal problem; disruptions to business operations; damage to employee morale; and future heightened scrutiny by, and accountability to, the Government.[6]

Insofar as the costs of imposing and maintaining an effective compliance program are less than these costs, the company will benefit from creating and maintaining an effective corporate compliance program. In an international setting, these hard and soft costs must be considered.

C. EARLY DETECTION

One of the benefits of a carefully constructed international corporate compliance program is that it promotes early detection globally, similar to the "issue spotting" most in-house counsel regularly do to avoid a major crisis. The difference is that an effective, international corporate compliance program provides for more issue spotting at more levels on a systematic and global basis. This is particularly important for a multinational corporation since one of the biggest issues is how to monitor foreign operations effectively without being intrusive.

Early detection of misconduct can minimize exposure to the severe criminal penalties or civil damages because it allows multinational corporations to deal with problems internally before they are discovered through government investigation. This ability insulates corporations from a variety of unwanted problems and expenses. A company that detects and stops criminal behavior early enough can reduce the costs that would have been incurred had the misconduct continued undetected and may mitigate penalties incurred. Additionally, containment of internal misconduct effectively conveys the message to employees that such behavior will not be tolerated in any part of the company anywhere in the world.

D. KNOWLEDGE

Fortunately, there is a recipe for creating an effective international corporate compliance program including an effective code of conduct. It consists of the following three essential ingredients:

(1) Knowledge of local language and customs;

(2) Knowledge of the industry; and

(3) Knowledge of the local law.

---

6 Webb and Molo, "Some Practical Considerations in Developing Effective Compliance Programs: A Framework for Meeting the Requirements of the Sentencing Guidelines", 71 *Washington University Law Quarterly*, (1993), at pp. 375 and 376.

1. Knowledge of Local Language and Customs

It is necessary to engender enthusiasm at all company locations as well as at all levels of the company. This can be done by involving personnel from all locations in the process of developing the compliance program. While it may take longer to create the compliance program, it will promote an earlier positive response from international personnel at various global locations since their own colleagues helped to create the international compliance program.

If the company does not already have an international code of conduct, a team of directors, executive officers, and business managers from all locations of the company should draft a corporate mission statement and a code of conduct or ethics statement. Then, individual focus groups in each country or location should adapt the language to meet local language requirements while retaining the core principles. Next, enlist the Chief Executive Officer (CEO) to write a letter to all employees and distribute it with the code of conduct explaining why it is important for all employees to make this code of conduct the basis for their work attitude and ethic.

2. Knowledge of the Industry and Company

Knowledge of the company is critical to creating an effective corporate compliance program. Learn about current, past, and recurring problems and issues in the industry and company. Counsel should conduct informational interviews with key employees if they are unfamiliar with certain company business practices and do this at all locations worldwide.

While this is an expensive and time-consuming process, it also means that local needs and customs are considered at an early stage so that ultimately the compliance program will be tailored to the needs of all employees. It may be helpful to conduct focus groups at each location to get employee comments.

3. Knowledge of the Local Law

Effective corporate compliance programs can only be developed when counsel has a firm grasp of the local law in relevant substantive areas. This may require retaining local counsel to assure that local law is being observed.

Finally, in rolling out the corporate compliance plan internationally, make sure that each local plan uses "the seven basic steps", articulated under the Federal Sentencing Guidelines, for establishing an effective corporate compliance program for guidance. These "seven basic steps" provide a good baseline for an effective corporate compliance plan in any circumstances. (However, also consider such international standards as ISO 14,000 for environmental compliance as well as COSO, COCO, and Cadbury for audit compliance standards in the United States, Canada, and England.)

The "seven basic steps" are as follows:

(1) Setting compliance standards/procedures that are reasonably capable of reducing criminal acts;

(2) Assigning specific "high-level personnel" to oversee compliance;

(3) Exercising reasonable care to prevent delegation of substantial discretionary authority to individuals likely to participate in illegal activities;

(4) Effectively communicating standards and procedures to all employees;

(5) Implementing reasonable compliance measures, such as monitoring, auditing, and reporting systems;

(6) Using disciplinary mechanisms to consistently enforce standards and procedures; and

(7) Taking all reasonable steps to respond appropriately after an offense has been detected, including modifying the compliance program.

These seven steps can be interfaced with substantive law for various areas of law. Further, they can be used as the basis for creating corporate compliance programs in other areas where corporate compliance is necessarily based on statutes and/or case law. Indeed, almost any area of law where compliance is necessary to the organization can use the seven steps to create an effective corporate compliance program.

The methodology for antitrust compliance, for example, is to do the following:

(1) Create a baseline of antitrust compliance practices to be adhered to by company personnel;

(2) Designate an antitrust compliance officer;

(3) Create a training program, including a short seminar and a handout or short briefing paper on antitrust compliance practices for applicable personnel;

(4) Monitor and audit personnel on antitrust compliance practices that the company has set forth in the handout and training sessions;

(5) Create a method for personnel to anonymously contact the antitrust compliance officer about antitrust concerns (use a hot line or mail drop);

(6) Create a disciplinary procedure to enforce the required antitrust compliance practices the company has set forth; and

(7) Respond to antitrust offenses with internal investigations and sanctions and by modifying antitrust compliance practices, if necessary.

Some areas in which a United States multinational corporation should consider having an international corporate compliance program are the following:

(1) Customs;

(2) Competition (antitrust);

(3) Foreign Corrupt Practices Act;

(4) Environmental;

(5) Intellectual property; and

(6) Employment practices.

Training, essential in implementing an effective compliance program, requires hard work. As it is not feasible for a central compliance office to train all employees, start with the local managers. A core of trained managers can train others.

Training is the primary method to:

(1) Achieve compliance and avoid risks;

(2) Protect against the "nobody told me" mantra (by obtaining signed statements from training session participants);

(3) Bolster company defenses to liability (by demonstrating that it was not the company's intent to avoid compliance, but an isolated employee's act); and

(4) Instill a sense of responsibility in employees and show that the company cares about compliance.[7]

There are several ways to get your company to support an effective training program in compliance:[8]

(1) Recommend training in an area shortly after the company has experienced a costly problem in that area;

---

[7] Pollan, "Training Managers–Problem Prevention by In-House Counsel", ACCA Docket (Volume 12, 4), at p. 76.

[8] Pollan, "Training Managers–Problem Prevention by In-House Counsel", ACCA Docket (Volume 12, 4), at p. 76.

(2) Recommend training after a new law is enacted or a crisis grabs headlines (sexual harassment, environmental crisis) and has caught senior managers' attention independent of your recommendation;

(3) Volunteer to cover a topic at the next general managers' meeting; or

(4) Build a dynamic, entertaining program and people will want to come.

Once the company is supportive of training programs, how can counsel make them successful. The following are suggested steps:

(1) Choose a corporate compliance topic that is relevant to the audience (every employee does not need a securities or antitrust compliance session);

(2) Know how large an audience you will be addressing, as well as their education level, areas of responsibility, what compliance issues they will need to know to perform their jobs, and length of service to the company;

(3) Stay with the key points and keep it simple;

(4) Break up the training session with some of the following: videotapes, quizzes, role-playing, and breaks;

(5) Motive, then engage the audience using such devices as visuals and prizes;

(6) Prepare a careful outline and learn it (so the presentation can be delivered without notes);

(7) Do not monopolize the programs (get local mangers and other local personnel involved);

(8) Supply handouts even if these are brief, and be sure to include the name and telephone number of the presenter and the local compliance officer in charge in case of future questions or referrals; and

(9) Videotape the session (to use later for absentees, for remote locations, and as evidence of presentation and attendance).[9]

---

[9] Pollan, "Training Managers–Problem Prevention by In-House Counsel", ACCA Docket (Volume 12, 4), at p. 76.

CHAPTER 15

EMPLOYMENT ASPECTS OF EXTRATERRITORIAL ANTI-BRIBERY LAWS

Douglas M. Nabhan
Williams Mullen Christian & Dobbins
Richmond, Virginia, United States

A. INTRODUCTION

The primary responsibility of the human resource function is to administer the bundle of domestic and foreign laws that impact the management of human beings. Probably no set of laws is more difficult to administer than the anti-bribery laws as they apply to foreign operations. The principal reason for this is that the human resource function is generally located thousands of miles away from where the violation of those laws occurs.

It is the responsibility of the human resource staff to prepare managers by helping them to understand the principles of law and codes of conduct so that the company can position itself as an internationally ethical business. As Thomas Donaldson of Wharton Business School in Pennsylvania noted:

> Codes of Conduct must provide clear direction about ethical behavior when the temptation to behave unethically is the strongest. The pronouncement in a code of conduct that bribery is unacceptable is useless unless accompanied by guidelines for gift giving, payments to get goods through customs and "requests" from intermediaries who are hired to ask for bribes. It is only when companies acknowledge the constant reality of bribery in the world marketplace that they can work together to create a methodology to overcome the intolerable and devastating effects of bribery on the world economic order.[1]

This is not an overstatement of the issue. Bribery has more often than not been the rule and not the exception for doing business in foreign countries until recent times.

Recently, Bob Bennett, President Clinton's lawyer in the *Paula Jones* case reminded us that not long ago — and still probably in numerous instances — bribes were common place in America. Many of us believe that you must go to a third world country to be involved in bribery. This is of course not true at all and the

[1] Donaldson, "Values in Tension, Ethics away from Home", *Harvard Business Review* (October 1996).

recent investigation of the International Olympic Committee's actions in Salt Lake City is a recent reminder that bribery is alive and well in the United States.[2]

This illustrates the deficit that exists in corporations in terms of a commitment to a continuing obligation to examine companies practices and policies. Just as we faced the domestic issue of sexual harassment in a vacuum at first, we are now realizing that the elimination of bribery and the implementation of ethical business practices must occur as a part of an ongoing educational and informational program that is deemed an important part of each company's human resource function. No other part of the company is equipped to do the training, teaching, and feedback reviews to make the integration of this issue into corporate training succeed better than the human resource function.

The situation faced with respect to anti-bribery conventions resembles the situation faced in America with the passage of a law called Title VII, which prohibited the discrimination against individuals on the basis of sex. This law was drafted with the intent of giving women equal footing in the workplace. It was not long before courts expanded the definition of discrimination on the basis of sex to a doctrine now known as sexual harassment. From that, the courts expanded the definition further to include two kinds of sexual harassment, *quid pro quo* and sexually hostile work environment harassment.

When this new body of law came along, the courts made it clear that corporations had an obligation to implement policies forbidding this type of harassment and to teach individuals about the prohibitions of the law. Policies were drafted, millions of American workers were taught that the definition of sexual harassment was a difficult and illusory proposition. More should have been done than just explain the law; the United States Supreme Court has taken the definition to the end of the pendulum and simply implemented what can certainly be defined as a strict liability standard holding that the company can only in limited circumstances disprove liability through evidence of training and discipline.

Human resource lawyers face a similar fate in the area of anti-bribery laws unless more is done than to simply develop and administer policies against anti-bribery laws. It is not enough to have accountants and lawyers review payments and make people sign statements that indicate that bribes have not been paid no more than it is tolerable to say that if a woman does not complain of sexual harassment then the company is not at fault.

There is an obligation at the human resource level to implement a plan to insure that education and discussion of these issues is an ongoing dialogue between the

---

2 Salt Lake City would be on most Americans' list as the city in America where this would be least likely to occur. Salt Lake City is one of the most religious cities in America as the headquarters of the Mormon church. If this happened in New York or Chicago few would have been surprised. This demonstrates all the more that we still have much work to do in our own country.

business unit managers, the legal department, the accounting function, top management and the human resource department. The following model maybe useful.

B. MODEL FOR RETIRING FROM THE COMPANY WITHOUT SPENDING TIME IN JAIL

The model involves four interactive components:

(1) Legal staff;

(2) Human resources staff;

(3) Field managers; and

(4) Accounting staff.

Each component has its own responsibilities. Legal staff are responsible for:

(1) Interpretation of laws;

(2) Application of laws to company issues; and

(3) Final arbitration.

Human resources staff are reponsible for:

(1) Promulgation of policies;

(2) Employees training, communications and source; and

(3) Employee advocate and resolution mediator.

Field managers are responsible for:

(1) Establishing relationships;

(2) Providing background information; and

(3) Clearing all payments.

Accounting staff must:

(1) Clear all payments of a questionable nature;

(2) Document all payments and explanations;

(3) Perform audit function; and

(4) Perform reporting function.

C. A CHANGE IN CULTURE — NOT A CHANGE IN POLICY

To have an effective anti-bribery program, there must be a recognition that the company truly must embrace a worldwide policy of rejecting the notion that doing business means paying bribes. Thomas J. Watson, Jr., in his booklet, *A Business and Its Beliefs,* stated:

> If an organization is to meet the challenges of a changing world, it must be prepared to change everything about itself [its basic] beliefs as it moves through corporate life . . . .

> A corporation that moves into the world marketplace must change its cultural norms from a domestic entity to one that is committed to play by the world economic rules.

1. Commitment From the Top

Sales and production managers cannot operate with conflicting goals — greater sales and profit margins with no violation of anti-bribery laws. The company must signal clearly that it will not violate anti-bribery laws no matter what the effect is on sales and profits. This can only come from the top with a statement that is signed off by the top management of the company.

Fortunately, companies have learned in the long run that once people understand that these companies will not pay bribes, they are less likely to be solicited for bribes.

It is, therefore, impossible to implement any kind of effective policy to keep your operation out of criminal trouble unless your operation is committed to that goal. Motorola's Code of Conduct states:

> Funds and assets of Motorola shall not be used directly or indirectly for illegal payments of any kind.

The only leeway in the Motorola's policy is where the refusal to accept a gift would injure Motorola's legitimate business interests.

2. Adoption of Internal Policies and Procedures

In conjunction with a commitment from management to have a zero tolerance policy for bribery, the company should develop policies and guidelines that serve the purpose of educating and training managers to understand the issues, recognize problems and seek solutions to issues that can be very difficult.

While it is the human resource function that will disseminate and train managers on these policies and procedures, they must be drafted in conjunction with the legal and accounting departments. The procedures should include the following functions.

a. Formal Statement of Policy

The company should adopt a succinct policy which clearly states the intent of the company to adhere to the anti-bribery laws.

b. Ethics Guidelines

Just as lawyers have promulgated ethical guidelines, companies should provide their employees with guidelines or ideals that support the formal statement of policy. For example, employees of ABC Company should at all times avoid the appearance of impropriety when dealing with a foreign business transaction.

c. Training

Training should focus on:

(1) Education on the anti-bribery laws;

(2) Examples of prosecutions;

(3) Role playing;

(4) Teaching employees how to properly raise these issues; and

(5) Issues for corporate resolution.

d. Formulation of Intra-Function Committee

A committee comprised of the chief executive officer, a legal officer, accounting officer and a human resource executive, should share joint responsibility for overall supervision of the company's program. While they may delegate certain duties, this committee retains the ultimate responsibility for the corporation.

Where companies have multiple divisions or wholly-owned subsidiaries, each entity should also have a multiple disciplined committee that has ultimate responsibility for compliance with these issues.

e. Resolution, Investigative and Reporting Procedures

It is preferable for a company's own people to raise these issues as oppose to the Department of Justice. Therefore, the company should establish resolution procedures so that employees feel comfortable bringing these issues to management for resolution.

Employees should be encouraged to raise these issues and are entitled to receive assurances that openness in addressing these issues is the preferred course of action. Just as the Department of Justice has a procedure for advisory opinions, the company should make a commitment to respond to an inquiry in writing within a specified amount of time. Lockheed Martin has a website to take complaints about the company's performance within its Code.

Employees, accountants and lawyers should have joint responsibility for formal investigative procedures for several reasons. First, it is less likely that any type of cover-up could be maintained if investigations are monitored by personnel from separate disciplines (i.e., legal, accounting and human resources).

Employees must have continuing education and real life examples concerning the prohibition of providing payments or other benefits to foreign officials, or to third parties who may provide some or all of the payments or benefits to such officials, in exchange for obtaining or retaining business.

Employees should be required to disclose relatives or family members employed by foreign government and should be told in writing that these relationships are not to be used to obtain or retain business from that foreign government to avoid even the appearance of a conflict of interest.

Employees, especially foreign agent representatives, must complete a background check and complete questionnaires before being retained by a United States business. Certainly the first level of inquiry is how the agent was referred to the company. The method of referral which flags a governmental relationship with the customer should result in heightened scrutiny of the agent.

A key component of any investigation is a telephone call and follow up letter to the commercial office of the United States Embassy in the country in question. It is also prudent to contact the appropriate country desk at the United States Department of State and United States Department of Commerce. All conversations and letters should be documented and compiled as a part of the due diligence filings.

Any agreements with representatives/agents should be reviewed in advance and documented with appropriate backup materials indicating due diligence. All agreements should reference the Organization for Economic Cooperation and Development (OECD) Anti-bribery Convention compliance clauses and restate the company's position in support of these conventions. All payments pursuant to the agreement should be fully documented and logged into a separate file so that an investigator does not have to work through numerous accounts.

Accounting is responsible for auditing the company records and should investigate any activity which would typically indicate a questionable payment including:

(1) Payments from petty cash to a particular sales agent;

(2) Numerous payments to the same sales agent in small amounts;

(3) Unusual bonus payments; or

(4) Transfers outside of the company's principle vendors. Payments should be scrutinized to determine is there are any unusual price discounts, payment terms, or political contributions.

Companies have turnover, deaths and terminations. With the stakes as high as they are in these cases, multiple witnesses to a complete and thorough investigation is well worth the extra duplication of personnel.

Finally, corroboration by persons in three separate disciplines provides the basis for a solid defense to a charge of a violation. If three highly trained officials of the company have signed off on a payment or have a record of rejecting payments, this is strong evidence that the company had no intent to violate the law.

f. Internal Investigation

The first source for an internal investigation lies with the Office of the General Counsel where the attorney client privilege applies and can allow the company to correct deficiencies in procedures before the issue rises to the level of a violation of the anti-bribery convention.

Companies should designate a specific individual within the General Counsel's office to monitor OECD Anti-bribery Convention compliance in each major subsidiary or division. Obviously, auditors are essential to the proper administration of internal OECD Anti-bribery Convention compliance. Every company should have outside auditors both domestically and abroad.

g. Retainer of Foreign Counsel

It is virtually impossible to make a determination as to whether there is a violation of the act in some instances unless foreign counsel is retained to render an opinion. Companies are well advised to retain foreign counsel in each jurisdiction where they do business with a firm that is competent to review anti-bribery issues in conjunction with that jurisdictions customs and practices.

h. Entering into Agreement and Partnerships in Foreign Jurisdictions

Foreign sales agents or partners should be chosen on the basis of reputation and merit. The process of choosing a foreign partner should be exhaustive as the time is better spent on the formation of the relationship than later on the dissolution of the relationship which is far more costly. The decision to appoint a particular foreign agent should demonstrate a *bona fide* business reason for the appointment, which should be based on:

(1) The candidate's character and background;

(2) Interview results;

(3) Results from multiple reference checks;

(4) The agent's history;

(5) Potential third party beneficiaries to the appointment;

(6) The number of years in business and successes in the industry;

(7) The qualifications of the agent's staff; and

(8) An analysis of the financial security, resources and other business operations of the agent. No agent should be selected until the entire panel has reviewed and signed off on the business relationship.

i. Disclosure of Business Relationships and Accounting Irregularities

It is essential that before the appointment of the agent that the agent be made aware of the company's policies and procedures concerning the anti-bribery conventions. Agents should be required to certify that they understand and agree to abide by these policies and if possible agree to indemnify the company for their acts in violation of these laws.

j. Drafting Agreements to Comply with the Anti-bribery Convention

Business agreements should be drafted to include representations and warranties that insure compliance with all anti-bribery laws. Joint venture contracts should have affirmative statements that the individual has been trained and understands the applicable laws and agrees to abide by these agreements and laws governing the business relationship.

Sales agents should sign agreements that indicate that their relationship is that of an independent contractor even though investigative entities sometimes ignore that fiction to pursue the investigation and prosecution. It is essential that each business relationship agreement be structured to allow the company to break off the relationship in the event that the company determines that there has been a violation of any domestic or foreign law.

k. Advisory Opinions

In the United States a company which is concerned about a transaction may seek an opinion from the Department of Justice to determine the legitimacy of that transaction. The Department of Justice provides a "safe harbor" for the party who has sought an opinion and is later investigated after having relied on the opinion. Of course, The Attorney General requires that the information furnished be "complete" and "accurate" before the Department of Justice will issue an opinion.

Any request to the Department of Justice must an actual, not a hypothetical, transaction and must be made prior to the requester's commitment to proceed with the transaction. Documents submitted with any request for an opinion are exempt from disclosure under the Freedom of Information Act. Companies would be wise to use this procedure more often in spite of the obvious time delays associated with it.

I. Negotiation Tactics

The following tactics may help United States companies avoid OECD Anti-bribery Convention compliance problems while transacting business:

(1) Make it clear from the beginning that the company does not give bribes. It is more likely that a company will succeed in the avoidance of paying questionable payments by standing firm in its refusal to pay bribes.

(2) Use the OECD Anti-bribery Convention as leverage to rebuff corrupt demands. A company's ability to refuse to submit to demands varies greatly with the nature of the business and the reputation of the company. Those businesses depending on irregular, high-value deals or companies with a less prominent profile may understandably have less leverage.

(3) There are many ways of returning favors to partners without the payment of bribes. For instance, introductions to other business relationships, serving as a reference for that person or entity or the swapping of technologies may allow the company to gain a competitive advantage without running into a violation of the laws.

(4) Foreign trade groups such as chambers of commerce can put forth a united front against bribery, which is a powerful force in many countries. The American Businessman's Group in Riyadh, Saudi Arabia, is a most powerful and persuasive group of responsible businesses who are recognized by the Saudi Arabian government as a force to be reckoned with on certain issues.

D. CONCLUSION

It is only through interactive anti-bribery training, education and feedback administered by the Human Resource function in conjunction with legal, accounting and management that anti-bribery enforcement can be accepted as on ongoing issue.

To overcome the reality of bribery in the world, employees must feel free to discuss these issues and accept strategies with management that overcome the stereotype that bribes must be paid.

A company program that encourages training, education, discussion and resolution of anti-bribery laws and a true corporate commitment is the type of forward thinking team approach that should be adopted to conquer this problem which is as old as the oldest trade routes of the Middle East.

CHAPTER 16
HANDLING CRISES IN INTERNATIONAL EMPLOYMENT OPERATIONS

Carl Bevernage
De Bandt, van Hecke & Lagae
Brussels, Belgium

A. PROPER INTERNATIONAL DECISION-MAKING AND LOCAL IMPLEMENTATION

In the present context of globalization of industrial and commercial investments, decisions regarding the future of an operation generally affect more than one country with sometimes very diverse legal traditions and requirements. Within multi-national corporations, planning, staffing, financing, investment, and dis-investment are done at a variety of levels, not uncommonly without sufficient co-ordination and pooling of knowledge and resources.

Each department has its own rationale and goals, targets, and timing imperatives. They may conflict with the approach that is needed "on the ground". This is especially the case when a plant or office must downsize or close, and also when a business is sold and the buyer has not carefully reviewed manpower issues.

The role of the labor lawyer who is consulted is not confined to advice on local law. He/she must take into account cross-border legal implications, the impact of industrial relations, the role and attitude of the unions, the management associations, and the authorities. In Europe the emerging position of the European works council is a factor which may not be overlooked.

Based on these few preliminary observations, the present chapter seeks to highlight some concerns and formulate certain recommendations which may help corporate headquarters to better prepare a collective dismissal, closing of enterprise, and/or transfer of personnel, seen from Europe and Belgium in particular.

1. Rationale for the Decision

a. Economic and Financial

The economic and financial reasons for a major reorganization are generally worked out at (foreign) headquarters; a level well beyond that of the local affiliate that may be affected by those plans and decisions. Such high-level plans do not always take into account the actual situation on the ground and sometimes fail to incorporate in the executive summary, which will be used both inside the corporation and publicly, factors which are relevant abroad, at the local level. This can undermine the effectiveness of the plan and credibility of management at all levels when it must explain and defend its decision in a foreign environment.

b. Strategic Considerations

The risk of lack of consistency in plans, projects, and (dis-) investments at the local level with visions emerging at the top is even more acute when plant reorganizations are justified by strategic considerations. Not seldomly does a (new) strategy appear to have been improvised.

There has been little or no time for management and staff throughout the corporation to fully comprehend the goal that is set and to translate it into clearly defined action plans or targets. By the time the strategy must be implemented plans may have changed, which leads to major confusion and poor communication.

c. Mergers

When downsizing is a result of a merger and is carried out for the purpose of streamlining production and eliminating manpower overlaps, a very well-defined human resources plan is needed, and there must be a detailed knowledge of the needs and possibilities of local units. Making staff redundant in companies or departments that have performed well before the merger is very difficult to justify and may prove costly to implement.

d. Shareholder Value

For years now, lowering the headcount seems to be an important factor in shareholder confidence. Product innovation, market share, and customer satisfaction often seem less crucial in shoring up stock prices. That the reduction in staff is compensated by growing assistance of independent contractors and consultants and may turn out to be as costly as salaried staff is of no concern.

The quarterly earning reports in the USA (and spreading throughout the rest of the world) have a major impact on the immediate future of companies, employment levels, and job security and override medium- and long-term business prospects. The concept of stakeholder value is only slowly taking root.

2. Involving Local Management in the Preparation

Although decisions are actually taken at the highest level, it is local management that, legally, must take the decision to reorganize and downsize or close operations. In many cases local management is not timely involved in the planning and justification of a re-organization, and little attention is given to applicable legislation. Therefore, local management may not be sufficiently prepared to explain and defend the rationale of a collective dismissal or closing to the authorities, the unions, and the workers. This can cause disruptions and force the company to pay higher severance.

Corporate headquarters sometimes overlook the importance of timely organizing the statutory decision-making by the appropriate shareholder assemblies and/or board(s) of directors that are legally empowered to propose, vote, and enact the reorganization.

3. Roles of Parent Company and Regional Management

The top or regional management which has initiated the decision to re-organize and reduce staff often fails to take responsibility for its decision when local management is challenged by the authorities, the media, the unions or the workers.

They are sometimes hard-pressed to explain their decision in writing and to provide basic data for a good and fair communication.

It is simply crucial that all lines of command live up to the challenge and be available in times of crisis. There can be no conflicting time schedules. Those who are responsible for a major collective dismissal or closing of enterprise must be at the helm and fully accountable when the decision is announced as well as during the first stages of implementation.

4. Informing and Consulting with the Personnel Representatives: European Works Council

Most multinational companies operating in Europe have installed a European Works Council but few have examined whether such EWC must be informed and consulted prior to a mass lay-off or closing of a unit in Europe. They have not studied what interaction is required for (prior/subsequent) information and consultation of the local Works Council or personnel representatives.

5. Local Works Council and /or Union Representatives

It is not uncommon that mass layoffs occur without prior examination of the history of the industrial relations at the plant or sector, and without having studied the records of the information given in the past to the Works Council, the unions, or the personnel regarding the ongoing state of the business and the prospects for employment.

This may lead to inconsistencies in the reasons which are given by management for the reorganization and undermine its credibility. Lack of consistency always results in a higher redundancy cost.

Moreover, data regarding settlements reached by other companies, or in the company itself on a previous occasion, which are essential to start negotiating on a realistic basis, have not always been carefully researched. Such failure causes redundancy plans to be insufficiently focused and helps the unions to take advantage of the ignorance of relevant factors of comparison to extract better compensation.

a. *Informing the Authorities*

If a reorganization is to be successful, it is of vital importance that the authorities not challenge the decision. They can slow down procedures and dismissals. Therefore, the most appropriate level of management must communicate with its counterpart in government and the civil service.

The involvement of foreign management must be carefully considered and weighed. It should only be called in when the reorganization is of a dimension that will attract government attention at a supra-regional or national level.

b. *Informing the Media and the Public*

Co-ordination and timing are the keys. American multinationals communicate with Bloomberg, Reuters, *The Wall Street Journal*, and the like. They should realize that this information is relayed worldwide and that a message that is good for the US market is not always the best for other parts of the globe. Moreover, appropriate concern for the welfare of the redundant staff (and the need for skilled, trained, and experienced manpower) is at present conspicuously lacking in the "corporate speak" which is used in dealing with the financial press. Indeed, very few companies inform the media of the human resources aspects of a reorganization other than to cite the number of workers who are laid off.

The timing of the news release should also be checked against the imperatives (of the law) at local level. In some jurisdictions no decision may be announced before the worker representatives have been informed and consulted on the "intention" of a company to proceed with a mass lay-off.

6. Negotiating the Global Redundancy Package

a. *Negotiation Team*

The negotiating team must be well informed and credible. It must have clearly defined levels and areas of responsibility, especially with regard to the role of the regional and top management in the settlement discussions.

Proper attention must be given to the contents of the communication throughout the company as well as towards the media. The "messengers" must be seen to have authority to speak and decide on behalf of the company.

b. *Costing*

Although essential and self-explanatory, projecting the cost of redundancies is not an easy task. Also, when reserves for layoffs, which are included in the annual accounts, appear to be generous, the unions will not fail to use those numbers to maximize their demands. The price tag must also include the total cost of the closing (spinning off buildings and equipment, environmental cleanup).

The cost of the redundancies, of disposing of the facilities and equipment, and that of the environmental cleanup is not always properly budgeted or correctly allocated. This oversight can make the task of the closing team very awkward and hamper the good outcome of negotiations.

c. *Global Approach*

The negotiators must know what will happen to the personnel in case of a transfer of undertaking and involve the management of the purchaser in the discussions and negotiations with the personnel representatives regarding the numbers of staff that will be transferred and the future conditions of employment. Needless to say, the seller and buyer must speak with one voice.

In case of closing, the members of the negotiation team must know what will happen to the production, the premises, and the equipment. They must have a very good idea of the global situation of the personnel that will be affected and of individual situations which may require special care. Before any announcement is made the negotiators must be thoroughly familiar with their duties towards the Works Council or other personnel representatives.

d. *Planning Contingencies*

Management must decide beforehand how it will deal with strikes, possible plant occupation, picketing, business losses, and whether further production is needed once the decision to close is announced. If some further production is needed, alternative sources must be lined up. Often, demand for a product picks up at the very moment that output is being reduced.

The negotiators must have contacted the law enforcement officers and know whether injunctive relief can be sought or will be pursued in case of industrial action.

e. *Individual Cases*

Collective bargaining does not obviate the need to take care of individual situations. The company must resolve, before starting the process of negotiations, whether to further employ or layoff:

(1) The negotiators;

(2) The personnel that is needed to carry on production during any winding-down period; and

(3) Any members of personnel who are known as "social" cases.

The company cannot overlook the special rights in certain jurisdictions of the "protected" workers, i.e., those who are personnel representatives.

7. Post-Closing Formalities

Once a settlement has been reached, management should not just close the door and leave the premises. It is most appropriate to ensure good communication regarding the contents of the arrangement that has been agreed to and the further plans of the corporation.

Sufficient manpower must be allocated for the purpose of supervising or carrying out obligations which survive the actual closing or layoffs, such as those of social funds, back-to-work schemes, outplacement, and pensions.

B. THEORY AND REALITY

Three recent transactions illustrate the pitfalls in making and implementing international employment decisions.

1. Renault

Renault, a partly state-owned French multinational corporation, posted heavy losses in 1995 and 1996 and decided to streamline production, retire 45,000 workers older than 52 years, and replace them with some 15,000 young workers.

At the end of 1996, Renault decided to close its Belgian Vilvoorde plant with 3,000 workers rather than a plant in Valenciennes, in the north of France, and announced and implemented same in February 1997. The negotiations were finalized in July of that year. Renault faced court battles in France and Belgium as well as political pressure but did not back off. A Brussels criminal court condemned Louis Schweitzer, PDG (president of the management) of the French parent company and the group, to pay a fine of BEF 10 million (about US $270,000) for not having informed the workers' representatives prior to the public announcement of the closing and for not having consulted them on possible alternatives before the decision was taken.

Immediately after the closing, the stock of Renault recovered and Renault posted in 1998 its best year ever. The European Commission did not carry out its threat to withhold subsidies for the amalgamation of two Renault plants in the north of Spain. Renault decided to invest in Russia and Brazil.

The question is whether Renault would have been more successful in closing Vilvoorde if it had informed and consulted the local Works Council in due time. Mr. Schweitzer would certainly have avoided a court condemnation, but it is far from certain that Renault would have been able to close the factory within a period of barely six months.

2. Levi-Strauss

Levi-Strauss, a giant in the jeans business, saw sales declining worldwide whereas the cost of salary escalated in Europe. The corporation decided in 1997 to close three sewing and finishing plants in Belgium (which did not operate at a loss) and one in the north of France. The closure in Belgium affected some 900 workers, mostly female staff. The decision was announced in September 1998. It triggered angry political reactions for the reason that assurances had been given in the beginning of the year that a closure was out of the question.

The unions could not muster a crossborder support in the French and Belgian sites. The female workers who were laid off preferred a relatively generous severance pay. A penal complaint against Levi-Strauss for having provided some of the written technical information in English rather than in Dutch was dismissed and replaced by an administrative fine.

In a more hostile environment, Levi-Strauss would have had to answer difficult questions regarding the apparent lack of consistency in its communication regarding the future of the plants in Belgium. A downturn in business, which was first attributed to a difficult temporary situation, was qualified six months later as a lasting phenomenon.

3. Clark Gum

Clark Gum, the confectionery branch of Warner Lambert, a US pharmaceutical company, has four production sites in Europe: one in the United Kingdom, one in Greece, one in Spain, and one in Belgium. Production is being overseen from the United Kingdom. For years the company intended to close the Belgian site, mainly because consumption of gum is more important in the south of Europe than in the north, but could not bring itself to earmark sufficient funds (only some US $ 10 million) to close the plant. It therefore continued to invest in buildings, machinery, and equipment, leading the workers to believe that the plant had a future.

At the time, early 1998, when money was available on short notice, United States management decided to act. The decision to close the Belgian plant was announced at the very moment local expertise was used and machines were shipped in to train South American staff for a launch of a new product and production on that continent. Personnel representatives insisted that severance be computed on the basis of a very generous package for collective dismissal applied a decade before in another Belgian branch of the company.

In the negotiations, the unions failed to take advantage of the stop-and-go policy of the company and were not able to have the decision to close the Bornem production suspended until it could be ascertained whether Barcelona or Corinth were indeed better and cheaper production centers than the Belgian site.

Part V

Collective Employee Representation in the Era of the Global Employer

CHAPTER 17

THE INTERNATIONAL LABOR ORGANIZATION AND ITS INITIATIVES RELATING TO TRADE UNIONS AND COLLECTIVE BARGAINING

Susanne Borch
Advokat
Charlottenlund, Denmark

A. INTRODUCTION

A discussion on international employment issues such as the topics that we are dealing with in this volume makes it necessary to take a look at the international background of labor law if any such issue exists.

The development of labor law on a national scale took place as early as mid 1890s. One of the first collective agreements between labor and management was entered into in Denmark dealing with issues much like the ones we are still discussing both nationally and internationally. In countries as the United States and the United Kingdom, the need was recognized to deal with such agreements in order not only to improve the living conditions for the employee, but also to improve the competition within industry.

This national development did not result in more international efforts until after World War I, where the international community found that it was of importance to improve the poor living conditions for the worker to make an effort to stop such future disagreements that might cause another war.

This was the beginning of the International Labor Organization and, even though the foundation of this important organization has not meant the cessation of all wars, it has accomplished a huge task in improving the circumstances for the labor law system worldwide.

B. DEVELOPMENT OF THE INTERNATIONAL LABOR ORGANIZATION

The International Labor Organization was founded in 1917 as part of the Peace Treaty of World War I in Versailles. A reason for this was the belief that universal and lasting peace could only be established if it were based on social justice.

The first conference was held in 1919, when the first Constitution and Conventions were adopted and the first governing body was appointed. These conferences have taken place annually ever since and many amendments to the Constitution have taken place, one of the most important being the Declaration of Philadelphia where the important goals, among others, were the following:

(1) Labor is not a commodity;

(2) Freedom of expression and of association are essential to sustain progress; and

(3) Poverty constitutes a danger to property everywhere.

The aims of the Organization were also restated and clarified as a substantial set of rules on equality of all human beings and their right to pursue their well-being, just as the right for the individual to seek full employment was upheld in the amendment.

The annual Conference has been dealing with these problems ever since to create a perspective for the worker.

1. Tripartite System

The International Labor Organization was based in Philadelphia until after World War II, when the office was moved to Geneva, where it is still based.

The International Labor Organization is founded on a tripartite system where the employees, the employers, and the governments are represented in all bodies with one employer, one employee and two government representatives. The Organization itself is based on the same tripartite idea, where the important sections of the Organization consist of the annual Conference, the Governing Body and the Secretariat General. The annual Conference is held once a year in June for three weeks and here the Conventions are dealt with, as the Conference is the legal body of the Organization.

The Conventions presented at the annual Conference have been dealt with in great detail through the years by the Governing Body and by the Secretariat. Not until these bodies have dealt with the Conventions will they be presented to the Conference where, if the vote is two-thirds in favor, the Convention is adopted.

The Governing Body is the executive body of the Organization just as the Secretariat is the office running the day-to-day affairs of the International Labor Organization with a Director-General as the head of office.

2. Conventions, Recommendations and the Supervisory Bodies

The Conventions and Recommendations are examined by the Governing Body and the Secretariat to be presented to the annual Conference. The preparations comprise the presentation of the draft Convention to the representatives of the tripartite system in the various member states through a questionnaire and, after having received the answers from these, reporting on the Convention to be drafted and adopted.

As soon as the Conventions have been passed, they must be implemented into national law 12 to 18 months at the latest after the Conference. If such an implementation has not taken place, a report must be sent to the Secretariat within the time-limit every year until the implementation has taken place.

In case of a member state not complying with the Conventions, the state is violating the international labor standards, and the member state must explain its action to the Secretariat.

These reports are supervised by the Committee of Experts, a group of independent specialists, and these reports are submitted to the Committee on the Application of Conventions and Recommendations.

This short description has shown that the necessity of an international body is still in existence as the way to improve and continue to develop the labor conditions in the future need to be supervised by an internationally recognized body without any specific state influence. It is very important to remember in this context that the individual country — and not, for instance, the European Union — is a member of the International Labor Organization, which probably makes the work of the International Labor Organization more influential as the individual member states' own representatives are participating in the decision-making process.

International labor law development will not only take place through the establishment of an international organization able to deal with the background of the area. It is also necessary to involve the parties in the labor movement in order to have the proper participation and coverage, which is important for the future of the labor movement.

This is done through the establishment of organizations in both management and labor and, when such an establishment has taken place then the development of the collective bargaining system will assist in improving the conditions for the labor market.

C. INTERNATIONAL EMPLOYERS' ORGANIZATIONS

The development of employers' organizations has not been easy, as these organizations normally were established to confront the establishment of unions and were therefore normally kept on a national basis. Still, just before World War I, the first sectoral employers' organizations were developed internationally, for instance, in Scandinavia and in Germany. The development of these organizations continued not as a direct opponents to the unions, but rather to influence the governments as these organizations started out involving themselves more in political and social matters.

Furthermore, these organizations had a huge influence on the election of members who were participate in the tripartite system in the International Labor Organization.

To recognize the various models of the employers organizations and how these are being dealt with, one may distinguish among three systems, namely:

(1) The Nordic model, where global negotiations are dealt with on a national level;

(2) The German model, where the negotiations are dealt with at the level of national branches of industry; and

(3) The model represented in France, Belgium and Italy, where the negotiations are dealt with on several levels.

Apart from participating in negotiations, these organizations normally also partake in training and providing information and advice to the members to improve their threshold of competitiveness and finally dealing with the social aspects.

As to the international organizations, there are the two types, these being:

(1) The International Organization of Employers, which deals primarily with social matters; and

(2) The International Chamber of Commerce, which deals mostly with economic problems.

The International Organization of Employers has 116 members in 118 countries all of them being central employers' federations. This means that the undertakings as such are not able to become a member of this organization even though they might be multinational enterprises. The most important task for the organization is to appoint members to the International Labor Organization just as the International Organization of Employers is acting as consultative member to the International Labor Organization and the executive vice-chairman of the organization will be the employers' vice-chairman in the Governing Body.

The International Organization of Employers has also as a main goal the development of close cooperation with other international bodies such as the World Bank and the World Trade Organization recognizing the importance of influencing other important international bodies to deal with the conditions and problems of the labor market worldwide.

Apart from these two employers' organizations, a number of regional bodies are in existence such as the Council of European Federations (CIFE), originally founded to be able to make direct consultations with the European Economic Cooperation Council. When the OECD replaced that body in 1961, the CIFE was taken over by the Business and Industrial Advisory Committee (BIAC). In the first stages of the European Community, the employers affairs were dealt with by CIFE but eventually that changed when the Union of Industries of the European Community (UNICE) was created in 1958.

This organization, which will be well known to the European Union labor lawyers, consists not only of the member states of the European Union but is also considered as an European employers' organization including other European countries as members such as the Eastern European countries. UNICE is competent to deal in social as well as in economic matters. It maintains an informal but constant contact to the European Union institutions and participates in standing committees for an active participation in the European Union such as in the Standing Committee on Employment and the Tripartite Conferences.

UNICE is governed by a president elected by the Council of Presidents and is dealing in direct contact with the members.

The direct involvement of UNICE in European Union matters and the involvement with the European workers' organizations is also making UNICE the participant in the social dialogue on behalf of the employers and will presumably be the employer representative in the collective agreement on the European level in the future.

UNICE is therefore not only an international organization but also a national federation on an international basis. It is much more complex than other international bodies as we know them and has quite a substantial influence in national matters which are expected to develop in the future when the social dialogue grows into what should become the European Labor Law System in close cooperation with the workers' representatives.

D. INTERNATIONAL TRADE UNION MOVEMENT

The trade unions were also developed nationally to start with and within specific crafts areas to improve the living conditions of the workers, whereas the first international organizations were the International Trade Secretariats based on the identity of the interests of various industries. In 1901, the first international trade organization was founded as a result of international conferences held in Copenhagen, Stuttgart and Dublin, the result of these conferences being the establishment of the International Federation of Trade Unions (IFTU).

This establishment was closely followed by the establishment of two further organizations, i.e., the Red International of Labor Unions (RILU) and the International Federation of Christian Trade Unions (CISC). IFTU was the largest and most representative at the time before World War II. After the cessation of World War II, an opportunity was created for the international trade movement to develop and it was decided in 1945 to disband IFTU and in its place establish the World Federation of Trade Unions (WFTU). The principal founders of the WFTU were the British TUC, the Soviet AUCCTU, and the United States CIO. The founding congress was held in Paris in 1945.

From the development of these federations and up till now the establishment of the International Confederation of Free Trade Unions (ICFTU) has taken place and is by far the most representative of the three existing global trade unions. The ICFTU has as its two important subjects the representation and organization of the members, but it is also involved in all the areas that directly involve labor, including the injustices that might be committed by governments or employers. The Federation deals with the organizational work, for instance, with regard to strengthening weak trade unions that might exist in some countries. The members are the national trade unions centers and as a rule exists only one center per country.

The second federation is the World Federation of Trade Unions (WFTU), which is another federation dealing especially with the living and working conditions of the people, and it has its main objective in the international trade union body of the previous Soviet Union and other countries of Central and Eastern Europe.

The third federation is the World Confederation of Labor (WCL), which has as its main purpose the handling on behalf of the trade unions a humanist, socialist and syndicalist program. The Federation is the successor of the previous Christian Federation CISC.

Finally, the European Trade Union Confederation (ETUC) has been founded in 1973 as an independent body which members includes all the trade unions in the Western European countries and which has 28 countries as members all being from the European countries. The ETUC deals with the trade union policy especially in the European Union and acts as the counterpart to UNICE the employers organization and is the most natural suggestion as the European trade union federation in the European Union's social dialogue and as an opponent to UNICE.

It is considered of huge important that ETUC and UNICE will be participating actively in the discussions on establishing a European collective labor law regime as they will be the logical parties to participate in the development of the social dialogue.

E. COLLECTIVE BARGAINING

To understand the purpose of these organizations and federations we should now consider collective bargaining. Collective bargaining is the main purpose of the employers' and employees' organizations. It is the way to deal with all the conditions within the working environment, living conditions, as well as remuneration and other benefits to be paid out because of the employment, just as problems such as dismissal, sickness, retirement and other areas where the worker might need particular protection are handled by the negotiating parties and where the employer might be under the obligation to participate in some of these areas, either solely or in cooperation with the government.

These negotiations are being handled through the system of collective bargaining, which is the recognized way of dealing with conditions in employment and which has been dealt with both on a national and on an international level. The first recognized steps on an international level were the Conventions Number 87 and 98 of the International Labor Organization.

1. Structure in Collective Bargaining

Collective bargaining is basically undertaken at national level and in this area the various bargaining systems in the world influence the way this is done and the way the agreements are implemented into national law or just respected as the agreement on its own without any legislative measure being taken.

The definition of collective bargaining is the process that will lead to reaching either a collective agreement, as it is called in the United Kingdom, or a labor contract as it is called in the United States. The essence of this is that the bargaining is undertaken by labor and management and on behalf of labor through the trade union in question.

The historical background of the collective bargaining system is that the bargaining started as a way to regulate pay and other conditions of employment and was in the beginning an effort to replace the unilateral decisions of the employer in order for the workers to have a say in the matter. The bargaining took place at enterprise level and often within the craft but eventually this developed into negotiations that took place on industry level, for instance, within the British cotton industry.

In the mid-nineteenth century, the unions were not recognized by governments or by employers and, therefore, the agreements could not be enforced apart from the areas where the agreements were recognized voluntarily by the employers.

It has been a tradition in, for instance, the United Kingdom that the negotiations should be voluntary and therefore very little intervention took place from other parties. Eventually, the Industrial Revolution influenced the way of negotiations worldwide and it was recognized that the agreements that had been negotiated by the parties should have a binding effect.

In this period, the influence from the International Labor Organization became obvious as the foundation of this organization made it clear that it was a duty for the labor parties to come to an understanding that also implemented improved living conditions for workers. This was accompanied by the improvement of pay.

2. Conventions 87 and 98

This became quite clear when the International Labor Organization passed two major Conventions, i.e., the Convention on Freedom of Association Number 87 and the Convention Number 98 on the right to bargain freely and collectively.

These two Conventions deal with the definition of the freedom of association. Just as the worker has been given the right to negotiate freely through representatives in his union with regard to pay and other working conditions, every worker is entitled to meet without hindrance or threat to his employment to discuss his labor conditions.

The Conventions should have been implemented in most member states and even though some states have not ratified the Conventions most of the member states comply with the conditions laid out in these two Conventions, which are dealing with safeguarding of the right for the basic needs of workers.

It might be added, though, as a matter of interest that even though these two Conventions are dealing with the rights of workers in the workplace and in the union to accomplish better living circumstances, no enforcement has been granted in the text. It is very spectacular that the right to strike, which now is considered a fundamental democratic right, is not mentioned in the Conventions. The reason is presumably that the member states were unable to agree on this step at the time of passing at the annual Conference in 1948–1949.

Nevertheless, the right to strike must be considered a fundamental right as a natural consequence of the right to bargain. It is also agreed that some means of enforcement must be possible to get on with the matter at hand as a member state otherwise might result in infinite negotiations without any result and indefinite wild cat strikes.

3. Conduct of Collective Bargaining

The bargaining levels differ from country to country, and it might be said that most European countries have opted for an industry wide-procedure regarding pay, whereas the United States, Canada and Japan generally use enterprise level bargaining, and the Scandinavian system opt for centralized bargaining. Apart from these very general descriptions of the bargaining system, various models are being recognized as, for instance, the areas where the bargaining is carried out at establishment level or even workplace level.

To undertake a collective bargaining, two parties at the minimum must participate and the system opens up for the possibility of more groups of employee participation. Normally, the employee bargaining is being dealt with by the unions or by the works councils on behalf of the union. The bargaining process deals with at least five stages which must be complied with to fulfill the set of rules in this perspective, these being:

(1) Definition of the bargaining unit;

(2) Mutual recognition of the parties;

(3) Preparation and submission of demands and counter demands;

(4) Conduct of negotiations; and

(5) Conclusion of the agreement.

4. Registration

The employers are normally represented by their organization in these matters but are entitled to negotiate themselves on behalf of their business should they want to do so, while the employees normally do not have any influence on the negotiations as these are being dealt with by their union representatives. The employees must be heard before the negotiations, start with regard to approving the list of demands, the election of a team of negotiators just as they are entitled to decide whether they approve of the agreement reached or not.

The union representatives will often be the shop stewards from the companies involved but might also be dealt with by the national trade union if the agreement is to cover this task all industry employees.

The collective agreement will normally touch on the following areas apart from questions of pay and dismissal:

(1) The terms and conditions relevant to the employment, such as retirement, job security, redundancy;

(2) Management questions indirectly affecting the employment relationship;

(3) Social security provisions;

(4) Quality of working life matters, such as health and safety in the workplace;

(5) Regulation of relations between the parties, such as management prerogatives and union security;

(6) Administration of the agreement, relating to grievance procedures and interpretation of the clauses.

The economic development in the country might induce the parties to restrict bargaining. This might occur, for instance, where periods of unemployment are regulating the demands for better pay and other benefits. In such situations, it is recognized that the unions must remove some of the more severe demands to employ as much of the workforce as possible even though it must be the duty of the unions to improve the conditions of the workforce as much as possible without such influence.

5. The Agreement

Another condition that must be looked at regarding the collective bargaining system is the right to strike and lockout and the peace obligation that is enforced as soon as the agreement has come into force.

The peace obligation must be complied with during the period of the agreement but the scope of the peace obligation varies from a relative one, where the parties must refrain from reacting on matters dealt with in the agreement to an absolute one where the parties are under the obligation to refrain from all sorts of industrial action for the period of the agreement. The differences in the interpretation of the peace obligation are closely connected to the interpretation of the right to strike as a fundamental democratic right.

The collective agreement is entered into for a fixed period of time varying from one to five years and most of the more substantial clauses of the agreement will be implemented into the individual employment, often with a reference to the agreement.

When the agreement has come into force there might arise problems which will be classified either as disputes over rights or over interest. Disputes over rights are normally resolved through the ordinary courts, the tribunal system, the labor courts or through arbitration. These disputes are defined as economic or bargaining disputes while the disputes over interest are defined as legal or juridical disputes. The latter disputes must be solved through either political discipline, negotiations, voting or by unilateral action.

F. CONCLUSION

This chapter has considered the International Labor Office, international employers' and employees' organizations, and collective bargaining. One might ask why should this be of importance to an international labor law practitioner dealing with the day-to-day affairs of clients.

This makes it necessary to move one step further and look at how to deal with the interaction between countries, for instance, when seconding an employee to another country, and the problems that might arise in connection with the authorities in this country and with the rights and duties of the person being seconded.

These are mostly dealt with in individual contracts if we are discussing just one person. But in case of a complete labor force being moved from one country to another, how are we going to deal with this particular problem? Will the labor force be included in the host country's collective agreement or will it be possible to continue as a member of the union from the country in origin?

In this perspective, the discussion will arise quite quickly on the rights and duties of workers and especially on the freedom of movement of workers as presented in article 48 of the EEC Treaty within the EU, which is considered a fundamental right. In the European context, the importance of the collective bargaining and the influence of the federations and employers' organizations must be emphasized.

These questions are mentioned to illustrate that an international collective agreement would be extremely useful. Especially in the European Union, the talks on the social dialogue in articles 118 *et seq.* in the Single European Act are considered of extreme importance. This aims to make it possible to deal with an overall general European Collective Agreement which then might be adapted into the individual member states and to the systems applying there. Nevertheless, it would give the general outline of an agreement that would be equivalent for all workers in the EU.

There is, as yet, no experience with what might be called a European Union Collective Agreement but we do have considerable experience with the effects of the European Works Council Directive. It has been working very well with the inter-cooperation between companies in member states and between the European Union and non-member states.

In Denmark, there has been the experience of receiving workers from many member states while the construction of the Big Belt Bridge was underway. There, the discussions on which collective agreement covered whom resulted in wild cat strikes as the unions in Denmark did not accept that the agreements did not cover the foreign workforce. This discussion ended with an agreement on the Danish system covering every worker working in the construction for a certain amount of months, but it would have made the discussions considerably easier if a general European Agreement had applied.

The European Collective Agreement will be negotiated in a not too distant future. It will be based on the discussions and descriptions from the two European organizations, the ETUC and the UNICE. This author believes it necessary that the discussions on the social security aspects be intensified and not only remain a purely national matter. Their development into a more European Union-oriented concern is essential.

With regard to the International Labor Organization, one might want to ask if its existence continues to be of use.

The International Labor Organization is an international body, which deals with matters worldwide. Many countries are less fortunate than the Western ones in dealing in a democratic way in matters regarding the worker. The International Labor Organization is, by its persistent pressure, able to create an influence that is noticed and recognized by most countries.

The International Labor Organization is also developing programs to promote certain projects and to improve the conditions for certain categories of workers, for instance, the project on prevention of child labor which is including the prevention of slavery and prostitution as the two very major aspects in the program. The project has been in force for several years now and is dealt with not only politically on a governmental level but also in legal and financial areas. The influence has turned in the direction of discouraging business with countries that expose children to hard labor and simultaneously encourages businesses to participate actively in instigating programs, for instance, with regard to education, and change of tradition in the families.

The International Labor Organization has not only major importance for the less fortunate but is also an immensely important factor in the industrialized countries where the Conventions are being the important tool in the structure of the labor force and their rights and duties. The International Labor Organization has through its supervisory bodies the possibility to look into the violations of the Conventions in the member states and to point out these violations which might be harmful to the individual. The International Labor Organization does not have any enforcement powers, but no country that is a member of International Labor Organization is keen to be pointed out as not complying with the Conventions.

Being the unique body that it is and being completely neutral with regard to the member states' internal affairs, the International Labor Organization will continue to be of importance to the development of the conditions of workers in the world. Especially with regard to its closer connection to the World Trade Organization, the development of the International Labor Organization will continue in such a way that practitioners will have to acknowledge the importance of this institution.

CHAPTER 18

THE EMERGING ROLE OF LABOR UNIONS AND CROSSBORDER SOLIDARITY EFFORTS

D. Bruce Shine
Shine & Mason
Kingsport, Tennessee, United States

A. INTRODUCTION

During the closing years of the "evil empire", a term coined by Ronald Reagan to describe the Soviet Union and its satellites, corporate America and European undertakings developed with gusto business partnerships with their economic nemesis, the Iron Curtain bloc.

While Pepisco sought outlets in Communist Hungary for its Pizza Hut subsidiary and in turn sold Hungarian bottled wine in the United States, thereby propping up the weakened "evil empire", the American Federation of Labor-Congress of Industrial Organizations (AFL-CIO) used its monies and energies to support Polish workers and others behind the Iron Curtain to shed the Communist political and economic shackles under which they lived.

This stark contrast of placing people over profits still characterizes the difference between crossborder activities of the trade union movement and the motivation behind corporate activity.

Just as corporations may be based in one nation yet crossborders in their search of profits, trade unions are shedding national boundaries to elevate their campaign to raise the living standards of workers in emerging and established markets.

Corporate salaries for top officers have reached almost indecent levels, while at the same time Nike, the United States-based sneaker producer, pays its workers in Indonesia approximately US $30 per month to produce footwear selling for four times the workers' monthly wages. The practice flies in the face of the primary goal of an economic unit to produce goods and services which its workers can purchase.

Following World War II, the non-United States directed activities of the then separate AFL and CIO and the entity they collectively helped create, the International Confederation of Free Trade Unions, were geared to subverting the Communist goal of world domination.[1] Secondarily, unions affiliated with the AFL-CIO engaged in collegial relationships with unions in Europe and Japan representing workers in industries similar to United States based entities. Crossborder activities outside these two areas were the rare occasion.

With American corporations extending production functions outside their home turf, the AFL-CIO recognized the need to exercise its considerable political influence in the United States Congress to halt increasing job exportation. The AFL-CIO proceeded to have written into trade legislation defined worker rights. Whether motivated to increase the cost of producing goods outside the borders of the United States or driven by a desire to elevate worker rights, the result is that goods imported to the United States are required by Congressional mandate to be produced under conditions which recognize:

(1) The right of freedom of association by workers in trade unions;

(2) The right of workers to organize and to bargain collectively;

(3) The absolute prohibition of any form of forced or compulsory labor in the production of imported goods;

(4) A minimum wage for employment of children;

(5) Acceptable conditions for a minimum wage, hours of work and occupational safety and health standards in the production process; and

(6) An acceptable public review process of compliance to assure adherence to items (1)–(5) above.

The Congressional enactments which substantially include the guarantees cited above are incorporated in:

(1) Title V of the Trade Act of 1974;[2]

(2) Caribbean Basin Economic Recovery Act;[3]

(3) Andean Trade Preference Act;[4]

---

1 Morgan, *A Covert Life: Jay Lovestone Communist, Anti-Communist, and Spymaster*, (1999), at pp. 173–176.

2 19 United States Code, section 2462.

3 19 United States Code, section 2701.

4 19 United States Code, section 3201.

(4) Overseas Private Investment Corporation Amendments Act of 1985;[5]

(5) Foreign Operations, Export Financing and Related Programs Appropriations Act of 1995;[6]

(6) Title III of the Trade Act of 1974, as amended;[7]

(7) North American Free Trade Agreement Implementation Act;[8]

(8) Sanders Amendment of 1997 to the Tariff Act of 1930;[9] and

(9) The Uruguay Round Agreements Act.[10]

Isolated examples of earlier crossborder activities by trade unions in the United States include:

(1) The use of the Tariff Act of 1930 by the United Mine Workers to ban the importation of coal from South Africa, where it had been mined by "indentured labor under penal sanctions";

(2) The International Labor Rights Funds formal petition to ban rugs made in India, Nepal, and Pakistan on the basis of pervasive use of child labor in the production of hand-knotted carpets; and

(3) Cooperative efforts by the United States-based International Brotherhood of Teamsters and the CUT, a Brazilian federation of trade unions, to ban the use of child laborers to process orange pulp used in Minute Maid orange juice by Cedrela USA.[11]

Two events during the mid-1990s have necessitated substantive crossborder activities by trade unions based in North America and the European Union. First, the adoption in September 1993 by Canada, Mexico and the United States of the North American Free Trade Agreement and its Side Agreement on Labor Cooperation (NAALC) and, second, the EU's adoption in September 1994 of the European Works Council Directive.[12] Each piece of legislation by its terms contemplates crossborder cooperative efforts to ensure worker information, consultation, and participation.

---

5 22 United States Code, section 2191.

6 22 United States Code, section 262p–264p.

7 19 United States Code, section 2411.

8 19 United States Code, section 3311.

9 19 United States Code, section 1307.

10 19 United States Code, section 3551.

11 The unions and human rights groups contended 15 per cent of the 70,000 fruit pickers in the Brazilian State of San Paolo were under the age of 14.

12 European Community Directive 94/45/EC, *Official Journal,* 1994 L254/64.

B. NORTH AMERICAN EFFORTS

Opposition to NAFTA by American organized labor, while still very much prevalent, has been seen by some trade union leaders to be an unnecessary expenditure of resources on a losing proposition and a closed issue.

The NAFTA Side Agreement neither creates no worker rights nor provides sanctions to remedy violations of workers rights enumerated in the underlying Treaty. Essentially, the Side Agreement establishes a set of substantive labor principles to guide the development of domestic legislation within each signatory nation. Further it sets standards to assess the parties' enforcement practices and erects a framework for extensive trilateral oversight of enforcement practices.[13] Enforcement is limited to each parties' territory and no private right of action under domestic law for violations found to exist.[14] Stripped to its core the Side Agreement possesses twin themes, i.e., deference to the domestic labor law of each signatory and a trilateral oversight on enforcement.

The heart and soul of the Side Agreement lies in the commitment of the signatories to 11 basic Labor Principles or standards. They are:

(1) Protection of workers in association and organization;

(2) Right to engage in collective bargaining;

(3) The right to strike to protect collective interests;

(4) The prohibition on the use of forced labor;

(5) Labor protections for children and young workers;

(6) The adoption by each signatory of minimum employment standards;

(7) The elimination of discrimination in employment practices grounded in race, religion, age, sex and "other" grounds;

(8) Equal pay for both sexes;

(9) The adoption of occupational health and safety standards;

(10) The adoption of a workers' compensation scheme for those injured in the work place; and

(11) The protection of migrant workers.[15]

---

[13] NAALC, Annex 1, 32 ILM at pp. 1499, 1503–1516.

[14] NAALC, Annex 2, 32 ILM at pp. 1499, and 1503.

[15] NAALC, Annex 1, sections 1–11, 32 ILM at pp. 1315–1316.

A adherence to the Labor Principals within the signatory territories necessitates the involvement of private parties. It is this aspect of NAFTA which mandates trade unions in each nation to look beyond their borders to effect compliance with the Treaty's provisions.

The Treaty requires Mexico, Canada, and the United States to create a governmental regulatory body known within the United States as the National Administrative Office (NAO) to monitor compliance with and investigate violations of their domestic labor law.[16] An NAALC secretariat located in Dallas, Texas coordinates compliance with the Side Agreement.

The compliance scheme creates a tripartite review mechanism with three levels of enforcement. The scheme envisages differing levels of review and remedies. The level of review and the remedy implemented is dependent on which of the 11 Labor Principles is alleged to have been violated. The process occurs on three tiers:[17]

(1) NAO Ministerial Consultations;

(2) Evaluation Committee of Expert; and

(3) Arbitration before Arbitral Panels.

In NAO Ministerial Consultations, all 11 Labor Principles, including the right to organize, bargain and strike, are reviewed.

The Evaluation Committee of Experts reviews eight of the eleven Labor Principles, including:

(1) Prohibition of forced labor;

(2) Child labor;

(3) Employment discrimination;

(4) Minimum labor standards (e.g., minimum wages and overtime);

(5) Equal pay for men and women;

(6) Health and safety;

(7) Workers' compensation; and

(8) Protection of migrant workers.

---

16 NAALC, article 3, section 1(a)–(d), 32 ILM at p. 1503.

17 The three-tier description is courtesy of Betty Grdina, Associate General Counsel, International Brotherhood of Teamsters, Washington, D.C.

Arbitration before arbitral panels involves review of three of the Labor Principles:

(1) Health and safety;

(2) Child labor; and

(3) Minimum wages.

Violation of the first two Labor Principles will result only in review and ministerial consultation. When violations are alleged for other Labor Principles, the Evaluation Committee of Experts is brought into play. It has the ability to analyse the effectiveness of the Principles, and issue a report and recommendations relative to a country's labor law adherence to the Treaty.

While a greater discussion is warranted as to the mechanism within NAFTA and its Side Agreement, suffice it to note that the process encourages, as will be explained, crossborder trade union intervention in its implementation. Specifically, any private party, i.e., a labor union or human rights group, may initiate review with their NAO on any matter within the scope of the NAALC. Thus, a United States labor union may initiate the process relative to any alleged violation in Mexico or Canada, with a similar right by a Canadian or Mexican union to lodge with their NAO a complaint over a practice in the United States which they deem to be violative of the 11 Labor Principles.

A contemporary resolved allegation of non-compliance best describes the process. Canada Teamsters Local 973 commenced in 1997 organizing efforts at a McDonald's in St. Hubert's, Quebec. The fast food restaurant closed allegedly for being "unprofitable" shortly after the Teamsters were certified as the employees' bargaining representative.

In Canada, labor law is basically a provincial matter. Quebec and two other provinces are signatories to the Side Agreement in Canada. As a signatory, Quebec is obliged to enforce the 11 Labor Principles within its borders, including the right to engage in collective bargaining.

McDonald's engaged in a lengthy legal battle with the Teamsters over the appropriate grouping of employees constituting the bargaining unit prior to the certification by Quebec labor authorities. Under the Quebec Labor Code, no remedy exists which would require McDonald's to reopen the facility due to remedy the alleged anti-union motivation for its closing.

On October 18, 1998, the International Brotherhood of Teamsters, the AFL-CIO, the CLC and International Labor Rights Fund, a human rights group, petitioned the United States' NAO alleging a violation of the Side Agreement by Quebec in failing to guarantee the principles of freedom of association, right of workers to organize, and right to bargain collectively. Within the mandated 60-day time to act, the United States NAO, on December 18, 1998, accepted the Teamster submission. The "objectives of the review of the submission will be to gather information to assist the NAO to better understand and publically report on the Government of Canada's compliance with the obligations set forth in the NAALC."[18] The NAO was required to complete its review within a period of no less than 120 days, which can be extended to 180 days of the acceptance of the petition.[19] The case, however, was settled by the parties during the review process and no report will be issued, the petition having become moot.

A total of 20 submissions since January 1994 have been filed with NAO offices in Mexico, Canada and the United States. Of that number, 13 have been filed with the United States NAO, 11 involving Mexico and two involving Canada. Five have been filed with Mexico's NAO, all involving allegations against the United States, while only two have been filed with Canada's NAO, one each against the United States and Mexico. It is expected that, as the process develops, a greater number of petitions will be filed. The scope and depth of such activity by trade unions is obvious when the Teamster's Quebec petition and that of other unions filed with Mexico's NAO and against Mexico with the United States NAO are examined.

Activity by trade unions outside NAFTA in North America is best exemplified by the 1998 Trilateral Letter Agreement by railway unions representing 150,000 members in Mexico, Canada and the United States. Meeting in Mexico City in July 1998, three unions "formed a new coalition that will exchange information and coordinate collective bargaining strategies in a bid to bolster organized labor's clout across North American borders".[20] Motivation for United States railway union involvement in the coalition lies in the fact that a number of United States railroads operate in Mexico, Canada, and the United States. The coalition intends to share bargaining strategies and techniques. The alliance, according to United States railway union leader M.A."Mac" Fleming, is to show "unions are willing to work together 'in a way that recognizes no North American border'".[21] Other unions involved in the transportation field, including the Teamsters, have expressed a desire to join in the effort. It is expected the alliance will be a forerunner to other cooperative efforts by trade unions in North America.

C. EUROPEAN UNION EFFORTS

Trade unions within the European Union (EU) have long enjoyed a level of crossborder solidarity, while at the same time limiting their primary activities

---

18 Notice of Determination Regarding Review of Submission, United States No. 9803, United States Department of Labor, at p. 2.

19 For a more in depth discussion of the petitions filed to date, see McGrady, *NAFTA and Workers Rights: A Canadian Perspective*, Vancouver B.C., Nat'l Lawyers Guild 1998 Annual Convention. Copies available from http://laboris.ugam.ca/.

20 *BNA Daily Labor Report*, No. 176, (September 11, 1998), at p. 1.

21 *BNA Daily Labor Report*, No. 176, (September 11, 1998), at p. 2.

within their respective borders. The trade union movement in the EU structurally varies considerably with its counterpart in the United States. Unions in the EU will in many instances trace their historical underpinnings to a specific political, religious, or economic philosophy. Depending on the nation, the trade union may or may not enjoy an exclusive bargaining posture with a particular employer, in some instances multiple unions may share the bargaining role with a given employer.

Today within the EU, while trade unions may not have shed their historical underpinnings, they have, however, seen the necessity to enlarge their crossborder activities, the most obvious example is the European Trade Union Confederation (ETUC). Trade unions in Europe, as in the United States, hold membership in multiple crossborder entities, worldwide in scope, but in most instances directed toward their respective industrial grouping. The International Federation of Chemical, Energy, Mine and General Workers' Unions, International Metal Workers Federation, International Transport Workers Federation and the Postal, Telegraph and Telephone International are but a few of such groupings.

The European Union's adoption of Directive 94/45, calling for the creation of European Works Councils (EWC) where an employer operates in more than one member state and employs at least 1,000 employees, of which 150 or more must exist in each member state, has been the primary catalyst for such crossborder activities. In December 1998 more than 13,000 companies across the EU were legally required to set up an EWC.

Under article 13 of the Directive, undertakings could remove themselves from the Directive's provisions by entering into an agreement with their employees prior to September 22, 1996, the deadline for implementation of the Directive by the member states to set up an EWC or an equivalent procedure covering their entire workforce. Failure to meet the Directive's application by September 22, 1996 put into play one of two options. First, the company's central management could initiate negotiations for the establishment of an EWC[22] or the process would commence at the "written request of at least 100 employees or their representatives in at least two undertakings or establishments in at least two different member states".[23]

On the occurrence of either option, a Special Negotiating Body (SNB) is to be established with a minimum of three and a maximum of 18 members under procedures determined by the member states in which the membership is elected.[24] Additionally, where no employee representatives exist, member states shall provide for the election or appointment of SNB members.[25] Each member state in which the

---

22 European Community Directive 94/45/EC, *Official Journal*, 1994 L254/64, article 5.1.

23 European Community Directive 94/45/EC, *Official Journal*, 1994 L254/64, article 5.1.

24 European Community Directive 94/45/EC, *Official Journal*, 1994 L254/64, article 5.2.(b) and 2.(a).

25 European Community Directive 94/45/EC, *Official Journal*, 1994 L254/64, article 5.2.(a).

undertaking has one or more establishments must have at least one SNB member and representation must otherwise be proportional in terms of the employer's workforce, which scale of representation can be legislated by the member state.[26] Once management has been informed of the SNB's composition,[27] the parties commence negotiating with the view toward concluding an agreement as to the scope, composition, functions, and terms of office of the EWC or implementing a "procedure for the information and consultation of employees".[28] The SNB can utilize "experts of its choice" in conducting negotiations leading to an EWC.[29]

Negotiations leading to an EWC can be terminated by a vote of two-thirds of the SNB and no future action will occur for two years unless the parties negotiate a shorter period.[30] Lastly, the cost relating to the negotiations are to be borne by central management, including the SNB's one expert, often a trade union official.[31]

"[I]n a spirit of co-operation with a view to reaching an agreement", central management and the SNB are to negotiate toward achieving an agreement which will define:

(1) The establishments covered by the EWC;

(2) Composition of the EWC, its number and their term of office;

(3) Functions and procedure for information and consultation of the EWC;

(4) Establish venue, frequency and duration of EWC meetings;

(5) Determine financial and material resources to be allocated to the EWC; and

(6) Set duration of the agreement and procedure for its renegotiation.[32]

While the above defines the scope and structure of EWCs under the Directive, the parties may decide to establish one or more information and consultation procedures to discuss transnational issues affecting workers interests instead of an EWC. In doing so, the agreement must provide a procedure for the employee's

---

26 European Community Directive 94/45/EC, *Official Journal*, 1994 L254/64, article 5.2.(c).

27 European Community Directive 94/45/EC, *Official Journal*, 1994 L254/64, article 5.2.(d).

28 European Community Directive 94/45/EC, *Official Journal*, 1994 L254/64, article 5.3.

29 European Community Directive 94/45/EC, *Official Journal*, 1994 L254/64, article 5.4.

30 European Community Directive 94/45/EC, *Official Journal*, 1994 L254/64, article 5.5.

31 European Community Directive 94/45/EC, *Official Journal*, 1994 L254/64, article 5.6.

32 European Community Directive 94/45/EC, *Official Journal*, 1994 L254/64, article 6.2.(a)–(f).

representatives "to meet and discuss the information conveyed to them".[33] Lastly, the SNB in accomplishing its multiple tasks shall act by majority vote of its members.[34]

Where central management refuses to commence negotiations within six months of a request to do so or after three years of a request, and the parties have not concluded an agreement, the provisions of the Directive's Annex (Subsidiary Requirements) come into play.[35] Member states under the principle of subsidiarity shall provide for the election or appointment of members of EWCs; in accordance with the laws of the member states in which the workers reside, the EWC must be composed of a minimum of three and a maximum of 30 members. The procedure contemplates the Annex EWC will assume those functions provided within the Directive for negotiated EWCs, with near identical rights, duties and prerogatives achieved pursuant to national legislation. Thus, central management is faced with the prospect of either negotiating the parameters of the EWC or having the Annex EWC imposed under terms mandated by its own national legislation.

Recognizing that information shared with the EWC will often contain items confidential to the undertaking, member states are empowered to insure continued confidentially of information among those comprising the EWC, even "after the expiry of their terms of office".[36] Member states are also obligated to insure by national legislation that employees or their representatives are free of retaliation in performing their functions. Employee EWC members are to receive their regular wages and expenses while performing their duties.[37] Lastly, the EWC and central management, as with the SNB, shall perform their function "in a spirit of cooperation".[38]

Consistent throughout the Directive is the recognition of the principle of subsidiary, in that member states are charged with enacting national legislation to implement goals to ensure the workability of the EWC.[39] As with nearly all Directives, a time frame exists for its review and possible need for subsequent amendment by the Commission, gleaned from experience with its provisions.[40]

---

33 European Community Directive 94/45/EC, *Official Journal*, 1994 L254/64, article 6.3.

34 European Community Directive 94/45/EC, *Official Journal*, 1994 L254/64, article 6.5.

35 European Community Directive 94/45/EC, *Official Journal*, 1994 L254/64, article 7.

36 European Community Directive 94/45/EC, *Official Journal*, 1994 L254/64, article 8.

37 European Community Directive 94/45/EC, *Official Journal*, 1994 L254/64, article 10.

38 European Community Directive 94/45/EC, *Official Journal*, 1994 L254/64, article 9.

39 European Community Directive 94/45/EC, *Official Journal*, 1994 L254/64, article 11.

40 European Community Directive 94/45/EC, *Official Journal*, 1994 L254/64, article 15.

The adoption of Directive 94/45 was the culmination of over two decades of activity by the EU Commission to develop worker information, consultation and participation. The initial efforts found their basis in attempts to create new corporate structures which would overlay the existing EU national corporate/undertaking structures. The first attempt by the Commission was the Statute of a European Company[41] (*Societas Europaea,* or "SE") followed with a "Fifth Company Directive",[42] the Verdling Directive[43] and cumulating in the Richard Proposal,[44] none of which were adopted. The philosophical underpinning for each can be traced to the Council's Resolution concerning the Social Action Programme of 1974.[45]

The Works Councils have by necessity compelled trade unions within the EU to crossborders and work collectively, often under the direction of the federation of unions within their respective industries.

While a detailed discussion of the current inner workings of the Works Councils is not possible in this chapter, the goal is to achieve a sharing of information to bridge the gap between transnational corporate decision-making and workers' nationally defined and nationally confined information and consultation rights. The national rights of workers to information concerning their employer at the time of the Directive's adoption varied considerably within the EU member states. The Directive seeks uniformity among the member states for worker information, consultation and participation.

Within the period of their short history, EWCs have consisted of one-day or two-day sessions at a pleasant site where management has played a significant role in the agenda of the session. It is not expected this process will become the dominant scenario for future sessions.

Lord Wedderburn of Charlton, the distinguished professor emeritus of law of the London School of Economics and Political Science, has warned trade unions within the EU to be leery of a process which meets once a year and has the potential to undermine collective bargaining with a menu of "honeyed words".[46] Following Lord Wedderburn's advice, EU trade unions have implemented coordinated efforts to utilize the process as a supplement to collective bargaining. Manuals have been developed. One such manual issued by the European Metal Workers Federation (EMF) advises its affiliates to use the EWC process as an opportunity to enhance

---

41 Statute of a European Company, *Official Journal*, 1970 C 124/1.

42 *Official Journal*, 1972 C 131/49.

43 *Official Journal*,1970 C 297/3.

44 *Official Journal*,1983 C 217/3.

45 Council Resolution of 21 January 1974, *Bulletin of the European Communities*, Supp. 2/74.

46 Wedderburn, "Consultation and Collective Bargaining in Europe: Success or Ideology", (1997) 26 *Industrial Law Journal* 1.

coordination and cooperation for the trade union movement across the EU. The EMF manual contains guidelines for the development of the EWC,the creation of the SNB and the scheduling and agenda-setting of EWC sessions. The process contemplated by the EMF includes monitoring the EWCs from limiting the definition of a business secret up to training and education measures.

Two caveats run through the trade union approach to dealing with the EWC, these being:

(1) An EWC is no replacement for collective bargaining; and

(2) An EWC can be utilized as a vehicle to achieve information and participation to benefit the collective bargaining process.

D. CONCLUSION

Trade unions in the United States and the EU have not in the past moved as fast as the business sector in responding to the changing attitudes of their respective constituencies. A visit to the Internet sites maintained by labor unions evidences a genuine effort to respond to their traditional constituencies and to reach out to those who view the trade union movement as a necessity of the past and an option without relevance to their current needs.

The decline in union membership is best exemplified by the current situation in Germany. Since 1990 union membership in former East Germany has been cut in half. Today three-fourths of the workers in East Germany are outside collective bargaining compared to one-third in West Germany.

In the United States, total union membership grew by more than 100,000 in 1998, but declined from 14.1 per cent of the work force in 1997 to 13.9 per cent in 1998. Yet, at the same time, the AFL-CIO organized 373,600 new members in 1998, with a total membership of 16.2 million.

Trade unions only grow when they are visibly and substantively active for their current and potential members. NAFTA and the EWC Directive have provided trade unions with an opportunity to engage in visible and substantive crossborder activities designed to evidence their ability to meet the current needs of their members and potential members. The initial response to NAFTA and the EWC Directive by trade unions appears well designed and geared to confront the emerging international marketplace.

The demise of the trade union movement has for years been touted by its opponents, yet those who constitute the movement refuse to believe in its ultimate demise. Crossborder union activities mandated by NAFTA and the EWC Directive present a clear opportunity for the revitalization of the trade union movement in Europe and North America.

CHAPTER 19

EUROPEAN WORKS COUNCILS AND OTHER EMERGING CROSSBORDER CONSULTATIVE BODIES

Christopher Seaton
Burges Salmon
Bristol, England

A. INTRODUCTION

The on-going globalization of capital has created a situation whereby more and more employees are employed by organizations and corporations that have a presence in a number of different countries, producing and offering their goods and services across national boundaries.

From a European standpoint, this has led to increasing interest in consultative processes and in raising the level of social dialogue within European companies. For a long time, it seemed that any European directive on employee information and consultation rights in multinational groups of undertakings would never take off, mainly due to the constant opposition of employers. It is therefore perhaps not surprising that when the Council Ministers adopted the European Works Council (EWC) Directive on September 22, 1994, the majority of the trade union movement throughout Europe warmly welcomed it.

The Directive has spawned a significant amount of interest throughout Europe in recent years regarding the improvement of the provision of information to, and consultation with, workers. Indeed, this is the stated objective of the EWC Directive. It seems certain that 1999 will be a year of considerable legislative activity on worker involvement on a number of fronts, such as:

(1) The EWC Directive is to be reviewed by the European Commission before September of this year. It is anticipated that this process will lead to the proposal of amendments to the Directive. Trade unions and employers are currently developing their positions and gearing up for a lobbying task.

(2) In December 1999, the "Extension" Directive will bring the United Kingdom within the scope of the original 1994 EWC Directive.

(3) In November 1998, the European Commission adopted a formal proposal for a new draft Directive on a framework for employee information consultation at a national level. The headline proposal for the new draft Directive was that all undertakings with 50 or more employees will inform and consult employee representatives about a range of business, employment and work organization matters. During 1999, the proposal will start to make its way through what is sure to be a very complex and possibly lengthy legislative procedure.

While agreement was not reached last year, as had been hoped, the Austrian Presidency of the EU drew up compromise proposals for a Directive on employee involvement in European companies. This would be via a European Company Statute, which would allow for a new type of company incorporated in EU rather than national law, which has consistently failed to get adoption by the Council Ministers since the early 1970s.

However, the most recent proposals are regarded by most commentators as creating the best prospect for political agreement for some time. Germany, who have now taken over the Presidency from Austria have reportedly underlined their intention to continue exploring ways of finding an agreement. The failure to reach a political agreement drew heavy criticism from the European Trade Union Confederation (ETUC).

B. EUROPEAN WORKS COUNCILS — OVERVIEW

1. Background

The European Commission had been working on a structure for transnational workers' participation since 1980. The EWC Directive was finally agreed on and adopted on December 22, 1994 by the then 11 member states under the Social Protocol to the Maastricht Treaty.

The EWC Directive requires the establishment of EWCs or a procedure for informing and consulting employees in every "community-scale multi-national enterprise". A community-scale multi-national enterprise is an enterprise with at least 1,000 employees within the member states, including at least 150 employees in each of two member states.

In 1991, when the Maastricht Treaty was agreed, the United Kingdom had been strongly opposed to a Social Chapter within the Treaty and negotiated the right to "opt out". That is why there was a separate Social Protocol to the Maastricht Treaty which did not bind the United Kingdom. The Social Protocol allowed the other member states of the EU to legislate on matters of social policy without binding the United Kingdom. Thus, when the EWC Directive was adopted in 1994 under the Social Protocol, it did not bind the United Kingdom.

At the inter-Governmental conference in Amsterdam on June 16 and 17, 1997, Tony Blair formally reversed John Major's "opt out" of the Social Chapter and asked for a two year transitional period to give companies time to prepare for the two Directives already adopted under the Social Chapter which would bind the United Kingdom as a consequence of the "opt in" — the EWC Directive and the Parental Leave Directive. The terms agreed in Amsterdam formed the Treaty of Amsterdam.

Although the Treaty of Amsterdam was formally signed on October 2, 1997, it was recognized that ratification could take some months. A more rapid means of including the United Kingdom within the scope of the EWC Directive was sought and the solution agreed on by the Council and the Commission consisted of re-adopting the EWC Directive as a whole — in practice this involved the adoption of an "extension" Directive which extends the EWC Directive to the United Kingdom. On December 15, 1997, the Social Affairs Council adopted Directive 97/74/EC, which extended the 1994 EWC Directive to the United Kingdom. The United Kingdom has two years to implement the EWC Directive, i.e. until December 15, 1999.

a. What is the Purpose of the EWC Directive?

The primary aim of the EWC Directive is to improve employees' rights to information and consultation.

The thinking behind the EWC Directive was that existing national procedures for informing and consulting employees (for example, National Works Councils in Germany, France, Belgium and the Netherlands) were not geared to the international structure of businesses and that led to unequal treatment of employees affected by decisions in one or more parts of the businesses.

The idea was that a supra-national structure (such as an EWC) would ensure that all employees affected by management decisions, wherever located, were informed and consulted about business decisions.

b. What is the Scope of the EWC Directive?

The EWC Directive affects any business which:

(1) Employs at least 1000 employees within the member states; and

(2) Has subsidiaries, undertakings or parts of undertakings in two or more different member states each of which employs at least 150 employees.

Before the extension of the EWC Directive to the United Kingdom, there was a popular misconception that United Kingdom companies were not caught by the provisions of the Directive. In fact, the terms of the United Kingdom "opt out" were that companies would be allowed to reach voluntary employee consultation arrangements to suit their own circumstances. In practice, United Kingdom employees were included in the majority of agreements. A number of major United Kingdom headquartered companies (117) were affected by the original Directive because of the size of their non-United Kingdom businesses. A further 511 foreign-owned parent companies which were covered by the Directive had United Kingdom subsidiaries. This meant that almost half of all companies covered by the original Directive (628 out of 1,270) had United Kingdom employees. Of these companies, 230 had already set up EWCs of one sort or another and only three (none of them United Kingdom owned) had excluded the United Kingdom workforce.

The extension of the EWC Directive to the United Kingdom will mean that a much wider range of United Kingdom companies with European trading divisions will be caught. Estimates suggest that more than 1,200 European-wide enterprises and 2,600 subsidiaries will be affected by the time the Directive is fully implemented and that approximately 15-million workers will find themselves involved with EWCs.

The United States, with some 190 companies within the scope of the Directive, is the second most effected business community after Germany.

2. Mechanisms

The Directive provides that to guarantee that the employees of undertakings operating in two or more member states are properly informed and consulted, those undertakings must either create suitable procedures for the "transnational information and consultation of employees" or set up EWCs.

The Directive lays great emphasis on establishing procedures for information and consultation by negotiation. Only if negotiations are unsuccessful or refused do the "fall back" terms for an EWC set down in the Annex to the Directive come into play — these "fall back" terms are known as "the default option". There are three ways in which information and consultation structures can be established which satisfy the EWC Directive:

(1) Article 13 pre-Directive voluntary agreements;

(2) Agreements under articles 5 or 6 of the Directive; and

(3) The default option.

3. Article 13 Pre-Directive Voluntary Agreements

Under the original EWC Directive, a company which had before September 22, 1996 reached an agreement on transnational information and consultation which covered all of its European workforce would not need to implement the EWC Directive. This is permitted by article 13 of the Directive. Quite simply, an employer could establish an EWC on a voluntary basis and thereby escape the rigours of the EWC Directive.

Strictly speaking, the time for initiating voluntary agreements has passed. However, as a result of the "extension" Directive, United Kingdom companies which are caught for the first time will have the opportunity to enter into Voluntary Agreements in the same way as the other qualifying companies had under the original Directive. These voluntary agreements must have been in place by December 15, 1999, or when the United Kingdom actually implements the EWC Directive, if that is earlier. Note however that, if a company qualified under the original Directive, it will not be able to have another bite at the cherry and put a voluntary agreement into place.

4. Agreements Under Articles 5 or 6 of the Directive

The EWC Directive allows the social partners a fair degree of flexibility to negotiate an agreement within the confines of the Directive — this is known as an article 5 or an article 6 Agreement. Under the terms of the original Directive, after September 22, 1996, EWCs could be established by negotiation between a company's central management and an SNB. An SNB is a "special negotiating body". It is the employee side of the negotiating process and comprises a minimum of three and a maximum of 17 members.

There must be one member from each country in which the business exists with additional members where a particular country has a larger number of employees. Member states' implementing legislation sets out how the SNBs are to be elected. In practice, it will usually be the employee representatives who elect the members of the SNBs, but where there are none, the Directive provides that the employees can elect or appoint the SNB.

Essentially, management can initiate the establishment of an EWC or it can await a request by employees to establish one. Any request must be in writing by at least 100 employees (or their representatives) who are in at least two undertakings/establishments in at least two member states. Where such a request is made, central management must arrange for an SNB to be formed with which to have negotiations concerning the scope, composition, functions and terms of office of the EWC.

The SNB and central management have the task of reaching a written agreement covering (but not restricted to) certain headings which are set out in the EWC Directive. The Directive states that they must "negotiate in a spirit of co-operation with a view to reaching an agreement". The subjects that must be covered by the EWC Agreement are:

(1) Scope, being the undertakings or establishments which are covered by the Agreement;

(2) Composition, being the number of members, the allocation of seats and the term of office;

(3) Functions and procedures, being those for information and consultation of the EWC;

(4) Venue, frequency, and duration of meetings of the EWC;

(5) Financial and material resources to be allocated to the EWC;

(6) Duration of the Agreement and the procedure for termination; and

(7) Procedure for renegotiation.

For the purposes of reaching an agreement, the SNB will act by a majority of its members. Any expenses relating to the negotiations between the SNB and central management are to be borne by central management, but member states can lay down budgetary rules regarding the operation of the SNB.

If management does not initiate negotiations and employees do not request an EWC, an employer will not be obliged to establish one. Further, the SNB can decide, by a majority of two-thirds, not to have an EWC but if it does so another request can be made two years after any such decision. If an Agreement cannot be concluded within three years of a request, or if management fails to respond to a request within six months, the default option will apply.

The EWC Directive states that member states can provide sanctions if management remains idle. Enforcement varies in each member state. In some cases it is by way of an injunction; in others it is fines or arbitration.

5. Default Option

The EWC Directive provides a "model form" EWC structure which will apply where:

(1) Central management and the SNB so decides;

(2) Central management refuses to commence negotiations within six months of receipt of the EWC request by employees; and

(3) After three years from the date of the employee request no agreement on an EWC agreement has been reached and the SNB has not taken the decision to stop the process.

The EWC Directive Annex specifies that a "model form" EWC must include the following characteristics:

(1) There should be a minimum of three and a maximum of 30 members. Each member state in which there is an establishment or undertaking is represented by one member with other members in proportion to the number of employees working in the establishment or undertaking.

The members shall be employees appointed by the employee representatives, or if there are none, by the entire body of employees. The form of elections shall be determined by member states.

(2) Where there is a large number of members there should be a select committee of not more than three members.

(3) The scope of the EWC should be limited to information and consultation on matters which concern the establishment or undertakings as a whole or at least two of them in two different member states.

(4) There should be an annual meeting with central management based on a report drawn up by central management setting out matters such as the structure of the undertaking, the probable development of the business, the financial/sales/production performance of the undertaking, investment plans, employment trends, production trends and plans for collective redundancies/closures/relocations/plans for transfers of business.

(5) There should be appropriate feedback to employees without violating any confidentiality obligations (see text, below).

(6) There should be special ad hoc meetings where there is an "extraordinary event affecting employees' interests to a significant extent". For example, transnational collective redundancies, closures or relocations. The meeting should be on the basis of a report drawn up by central management.

(7) The EWC or the select committee can meet on its own before any meeting with management.

(8) Four years after the mandatory requirements apply, the EWC could decide to conclude an Article 5/6 agreement or to continue to apply the mandatory requirement.

(9) Members are entitled to be assisted by an expert of their choice.

(10) The EWC's costs (including those of meetings) are to be borne by central management including those of experts assisting the EWC.

(11) Employee representatives, members of SNBs and members of EWCs are to be protected against adverse treatment for their participation in the EWC.

(12) Employee representatives are to be entitled to paid time off for EWC functions.

6. Issues for Employers

Businesses are understandably concerned about the cost of EWCs. The model form EWC structure provides for costs to be borne by central management. The major expense will usually be the annual meeting. One company held its meeting over two days in the United Kingdom with 30 employee representatives and several from management. The costs of the meeting, including translation facilities for foreign participants, was about £40,000. Companies are also reluctant to deal with increased bureaucracy which they believe could delay important business decisions.

The other area of concern is confidentiality. Although under the Directive management will not be forced to disclose information which could seriously harm the functioning or prejudice the undertaking concerned, the EWC can challenge any such withholding of information.

The EWC Directive provides rules on what is meant by consultation and confidentiality. Consultation under the EWC Directive is defined as "the establishment of a dialogue and exchange of views". It does not provide for collective bargaining or co-determination.

The EWC Directive provides that central management will not be obliged to disclose information which is so confidential that its disclosure would seriously prejudice or harm the interests of the community scale undertaking/group. Nor will members of SNBs or EWCs (or any experts who assist them) be authorized to reveal any information which has expressly been provided to them in confidence.

On a more positive note, businesses have reported improved industrial relations as a direct consequence of employees feeling that they are more involved in the management process of the company.

7. Role of Unions

Trade unions are not mentioned at all in the EWC Directive but employee representatives are mentioned. Because of the requirement in the default option model that there is one member from each of the member states where the community scale undertaking/group has employees, plus additional members where a particular country has a large proportion of employees, there is the real possibility that there may be more non-Trade Union members on an EWC than Trade Union members. Because of this, trade unions see the article 13 Voluntary Agreement process as an opportunity of maximizing their influence in the process.

Despite this, there is no doubt that trade unions consider EWCs to be within their domain. The Trade Union Congress recently published an 88 page guide to its members which, among other things, urges them to be actively involved in the establishment of EWCs. Although some United Kingdom companies have actively encouraged the participation of recognized unions, others have excluded unions from the process.

While trade unions have played an important role in the emergence of voluntary EWCs, they are, of course, not the only means of representing employees. Throughout Europe, statutory employee representation bodies exist alongside unions.

Trade unions are a signatory to 45 per cent of voluntary agreements. However, a quarter of agreements are signed with unspecified employee representatives only, a matter of some concern to trade unions. Research has found that trade unions are more likely to be signatories to agreements in large multinationals than in medium-sized or small multinationals which tend to have employee representatives as signatories. Research has also shown that agreements in United States multinationals were found to be twice as likely to have been concluded with employee representatives than those with European-based multinationals.

One difficulty that has arisen in practice concerns the election process where there is a mixture of unionised employees and unrepresented employees. There has been some friction between employee representatives from different sites within the same undertaking as to who should be on the SNB.

8. The Impact of European Works Councils

There are currently some 600 EWCs. It is anticipated that by September 22, 1999 there will be 2,000 EWCs across Europe.

European Foundation research into voluntary EWC Agreements found that companies headquartered in Germany, France, the United Kingdom and the United States of America account for almost two thirds of the agreements. Around half of the United Kingdom companies meeting the terms of the Directive concluded agreements. The high number of agreements concluded by United Kingdom companies is explained mainly by a concern to avoid negotiating agreements through the SNB procedure and by the preference of voluntary arrangements due to the absence of any tradition of Works Councils in the United Kingdom.

The EWC Directive has been transposed in almost every EEA country concerned. Transposition is still awaited in Luxembourg and Portugal and the European Commission has commenced legal proceedings for non-transposition against both countries. In Italy, the transposition process has not been completed. A collective agreement was reached in November 1996, but back-up legislation is still lacking.

C. FUTURE

1. The 1999 Review of the EWC Directive

As a first step towards reviewing the 1994 EWC Directive, the Commission has commissioned a set of studies from academics, examining the implementation of the Directive in the member states. This process was to be finalised by spring 1999 with the review completed by September of 1999.

2. Trade Union Position

Ever since the Directive was adopted, European trade unions have been urging a number of revisions. The unions' concerns were heightened and focused by the controversy surrounding the announcement of the closure of the Renault's plant in Belgium in 1997, with little or no prior consultation of the workforce and its representatives (including the Renault EWC). Not surprisingly, the Renault EWC brought a court case claiming that the management's announcement of the closure was unlawful in the absence of consultation with the EWC.

The Versailles Appeals Court considered that any decision (having a significant effect on the interests of employees) must lead to information and consultation of the EWC and that information must be provided in "due time". Fines were ultimately ordered against Renault in both France and Belgium. The Renault EWC has been successful in subsequently amending the EWC Agreement and on a wider stage this has led to trade union demands for stricter information and consultation rules.

Proposals include:

(1) Reducing the threshold from 1,000 to 500 and the national-level threshold from 150 employees to 100;

(2) Adding to article 1, which sets out the purpose of the Directive, a statement that "the workers shall be informed and consulted in good time during planning before a decision is taken";

(3) Strengthening the sanctions in the event of non-compliance with the Directive;

(4) The suggestion is that article 9 should be amended to state that relevant management decisions "are valid only if information and consultation was properly carried out"; and

(5) Article 11 should provide that companies not complying with the Directive's information and consultation provisions should be temporarily excluded from the tendering process for the award of public contracts, and from financial support under Community, National or Regional measures (with payments already received to be refunded).

3. Employers' Position

European employers' organizations are some way behind their trade union counterparts in preparing their input into the review process. In general, it appears that employers are not in favor of the September 1999 review, considering that it has come too early, given that relatively little experience has been accumulated to date.

However, there are some issues that employers have indicated that they would like to see addressed, such as:

(1) The particular problems of smaller companies given that smaller firms have fewer resources and have difficulty in coping with the costs for organized meetings; and

(2) The current variations in the national implementing provisions such as the proportional representation of national workforces on SNB and EWCs or the identity of worker representatives.

4. European Company Statute Proposals

Employee involvement is an intrinsic part of these proposals. When existing national companies draw up plans for the formation of a European company, they must take the necessary steps to start negotiations with the representatives of the company's employees on the arrangements for the involvement of employees in the new European Company. For this purpose, an SNB must be set up whose role is to conclude an agreement on the arrangements for "employee involvement". Any agreement on involvement must provide for an EWC like representative body for information on consultation purposes.

Much of the detail of the Austrian proposals is very similar or identical to the provisions of the 1994 EWC Directive although there are some significant differences, particularly in respect of the composition of the SNB which gives stronger emphasis to proportional representation of the national workforce by size in contrast to the EWC Directive, which emphasises the geographical spread of SNB representatives.

Failure to reach a political agreement at the end of 1998 drew heavy criticism from the ETUC who stressed the need for such a statute given the current wave of industrial restructuring and mergers across Europe.

5. National Works Councils

The European Commission has published a draft Directive on National Works Councils (NWC). The draft Directive, which is unlikely to be in force earlier than 2002, will apply to all companies with 50 or more employees, although member states do have the option to raise this threshold to 100 employees.

It seeks to introduce the concept of Works Councils at national level and the Commission sees this initiative as an "essential step in completing the EU's social dimension in achieving the creation of an adaptable, high-skilled and motivated workforce, because of the role of information and consultation in developing adaptability and contributing to increases in productivity".

Member states can permit the social partners to enter into a collective agreement rather than a Works Council, but the general objectives of the draft Directive must be met in such collective agreements. The draft Directive requires employees to inform and consult with the employee representatives in three areas:

(1) The state of the company, i.e., developments on its activities and its economic and financial situation;

(2) Anticipated impact on employment. Employers must inform and consult the NWC on such developments, particularly where it sees employment under threat; and

(3) Substantial changes in a work organization or contractual relation. For example, this would include substantial changes to terms and conditions.

Prime Minister Tony Blair has indicated that he regards the Directive as an unnecessary intrusion and that it would be an excessive burden on smaller businesses. However, the unions within the United Kingdom and Europe are pushing heavily for Governments to keep the Directive on track.

D. CONCLUSION

While it is probably too early to determine the essential influence of EWCs on industrial relations systems, some new tendencies can already be identified:

(1) A form of "cultural change" on the part of trade unions and employee representatives, i.e., increasing awareness of the internationalisation of company strategies which is helping to create a new "European mentality"; and

(2) A creation of networks of employee representatives in different countries allowing for greater coordination and joint action.

The arrival of the Euro has meant that disparities in prices and wages among member states have suddenly become more transparent. A greater flow of information as a result of the EWCs will potentially create tensions in respect of pay bargaining. Some EU trade union federations would wish to see EWC rights extending into collective bargaining and cross-border wage policy matters.

Increasingly, companies with EWCs are being asked to enlarge their geographic scope and turn them into world Works Councils in respect of corporations operating world wide. Aiding these elements are the growth of global companies and mergers between EU based companies and outsiders such as Daimler and Chrysler.

As multinational companies are forced to take on board EWCs, it is probably a logical next step that consultation rights will spread to other areas of the world.

Part VI

National Employment Laws Around the World — An Overview, and Selected Topics in Comparative Employment Law

CHAPTER 20
EMPLOYMENT LAWS AROUND THE GLOBE

Nancy J. Sedmak
Bureau of National Affairs, Inc.
Washington, D.C., United States

A. INTRODUCTION

The following is an overview of employment laws around the world by region, making some observations on specific issues, and some generalizations. Information on employment laws around the world can be very difficult to obtain.[1]

For the non-United States lawyer, it might be interesting to note that the United States has over 20,000 labor and employment lawyers, but not many of these lawyers, yet, have indicated significant interest in handling cases outside the United States. The approach taken by many United States lawyers with clients with overseas labor and employment problems, or the clients themselves, is to "manage the advice" of local lawyers that is to instruct local lawyers how they want the problem handled, sometimes without regard to local requirements. Often, this is because the client wants a uniform policy among all of its branches. Other times this is because of a belief that the method they were taught, or the approach that is taken at headquarters is the way it should be done. Sometimes, it is out of ignorance of the demands and ramifications of the local requirements.

It is becoming more important that not only the United States lawyer and client, as well as the overseas or local lawyer, become familiar with each other's laws and requirements. It will improve communication and make for better decision-making.

1. Homogeneity/Heterogeniety within the Regions

Even though the present chapter approaches the world's employment laws by region, the laws within each region are not necessarily the same. This approach was taken for simplicity's sake, and some mention of differences may be made where possible.

---

1 Keller, ed. *International Labor and Employment Laws* (1997).

2. Legal Protections and Status of Unions

There is a wide variety of approaches to the protections and status of unions. As a rough generalization, there are three basic models — one for the developed, post-industrial countries; one for the industrialized countries; and one for the developing countries. Unions have the strongest status in the industrialized countries, and less in the post-industrial and developing countries.

3. Individual Employment Practices

Legal requirements covering individual employees cannot be so neatly divided as are the status of unions. The distinctions here, however, can be divided based on the efficacy of the laws and the legal systems involved.

Most countries have laws regulating basic employment matters, but the distinctions here are based on how well the laws are enforced. The basic legal requirements in most jurisdictions cover:

(1) Contracts of employment;

(2) Protection from dismissal/layoffs;

(3) Working conditions and working hours; and

(4) Wages, benefits, and social security.

B. TOUR BY REGION

1. United States of America/Canada

Despite geographical and some cultural proximity, the employment laws of these two countries are not very similar. Canada's employment law resembles much more the Western Europe/European Union model, while that of the United States, from the viewpoint of the rest of the world, is an anomaly. Since more time will be spent on Western Europe and the European Union, not many comments about Canada's employment law will be made here.

The United States has weak unions outside the industrial sector, although public employee unions are stronger in that the percentage of employees unionized is much higher, but sometimes the limitation on the right to strike can be viewed as a hindrance on their effectiveness. Of the total United States workforce, only 14 per cent belong to unions, but looking at the private employer workforce, only 10 per cent are unionized.

Individual employment contracts are not required in the United States, and most employees in the United States are "at will". The United States generally provides far fewer benefits than in Western Europe, and very few benefits are required by law. There generally are longer working hours in the United States than Europe, but employees generally receive higher salaries, and have more job mobility.

Multiculturalism, as seen in the United States civil rights laws, is probably the biggest employment issue in the United States. Anti-discrimination laws have become the most vigorously enforced employment laws.

Opportunities for women, generally, are highest in the United States as compared to the rest of the world, but there is also less protectionism, and minimal pregnancy benefits.

There is very little protection from dismissal or layoff (redundancy) for employees in the United States unless the employees are unionized.

2. Western Europe

The countries of Western Europe, and members of the European Union generally, provide generous benefits for employees (some are government provided, some are employer provided). There are strong protections for labor unions (the notable exception being the United Kingdom), and rigid procedures for employee dismissals that effectively provide job security.

"Collective protection" is supported. Works councils, even if unions are present, are required by some countries and by the European Union for employers with operations in multiple European Union countries. Unions generally are strong, and often have industry-wide bargaining and standards.

Advance notice of termination (as much as six or seven months) is the norm in Western Europe, and often severance pay is required in addition to notice of termination. Collective dismissals and layoffs/redundancies place onerous burdens on employers.

There are strong protections for women, often including paid pregnancy leave, both under individual country laws and the European Union. It should be noted that protectionist laws for women are not scorned as they are in the United States. Pregnant women, especially under the European Union Directive, are legally protected from unsafe or hazardous working environments. In the United States, prohibiting women from being able to work in hazardous jobs, if the women so desire, has been ruled to be discriminatory.[2]

There are strict limits on working time under the laws of most countries, as well as the European Union Working Time Directive. Generous vacation/holiday benefits are the norm, usually four to five weeks per year.

---

2 United Auto Workers v. Johnson Controls, 499 U.S. 187, 55 FEP Cases 365 (1991).

3. Eastern Europe/Former Soviet Countries

Many of these countries amended their laws to adapt to a free market economy, but the changes can be uneven and there are pitfalls for the unwary. The underlying policy was that all citizens must be employed, and many of the laws on hours and leave took this in mind. Since the government was the employer the citizens had "entitlements" to their jobs, and the laws are slowly changing to acknowledge or accommodate the concepts of private employment.

Unions still have a strong role, and employees and unions are wary of western investors. There are new and independent unions, and the unions are shedding their identity as government controlled. New businesses often are not unionized, or at least not yet, usually because they are small and entrepreneurial, but they may unionize in the future.

An employer's right to terminate employees is severely restricted, and usually only for serious misconduct.

Collective dismissals or layoffs/redundancies is the one area that has seen the most legal reform, enabling companies attempting to compete in a free market to streamline their operations. The new provisions require advance notice to unions and to a government agency, and unions often have the right to negotiate. An anecdote to show the danger for western investors, especially if not properly sensitized to local requirements, is the attempt by Procter and Gamble to lay off a number of employees in a detergent plant in the Tula region in Russia — it offered generous incentives to employees to voluntary resign. The union challenged the incentives as coercive. Although such incentives can be viewed as a "best practice" in many countries, it was viewed with suspicion in Russia, where western investors are viewed with distrust and layoffs were unknown before.

The employment laws generally provide that individual employment contracts must be in writing, working hours are restricted, employer contributions to state social-security programs are very high, and paid maternity and child-care leaves can be lengthy.

The status of women in the Eastern European and former Soviet countries is very high. It has been claimed that there is no sexual harassment, and women are free to perform almost any and all jobs. How the status of women will fare as these countries move into a free-market economy is yet to be seen, but there is some concern that women will bear the brunt of unemployment.[3]

---

[3] Rimashevskaia, "Changes in Social Policy and Labor Legislation: The Gender Aspect", in Silverman, Vogt, and Yanowitch (eds.), *Double Shift: Transforming Work in Postsocialist and Postindustrial Societies* (1993).

4. Central and South America/Mexico

The laws of Central and South America and Mexico need to be approached with great respect and great skepticism. Foreign investors need to proceed with caution, and local advice is absolutely critical. While on their face the laws appear to give strong protection to employees, how these laws are enforced can depend on who the employer is and who has "taken care" of meeting the basic requirements.

The status of unions in South America is typical of developing countries. While there may or may not be legal protections for unions, and that often depends on the government in power, Chile, supposedly one of the most advanced South American countries, in 1996 had only 2.3 per cent of its workforce engaged in collective bargaining.[4]

Employment laws appear to be extremely protective of employees, with job security a major goal, and labor courts can be sympathetic to employees in dismissals.

Most Latin American countries impose very specific requirements for employment contracts. Working time laws usually specify maximum workweeks, and make overtime voluntary except in special circumstances. Vacation and holiday pay are required by law. Annual bonuses are also mandated. Female workers are covered by protective laws.

Dismissals/terminations are restricted, and severance pay, often one month for each year of employment, is required for discharges without just cause. Advance (generally one to three months) written notice of termination is often required. Notice must contain the date of termination and reasons for the termination.

5. Australia and New Zealand

Australia and New Zealand have been put together because of geographic proximity, but their laws are not very similar.

Australia's laws are similar to Western Europe and the European Union, but with a Common Law aspect, such as the industrial relations commissions awards.

New Zealand recently completely revised its law to be more competitive in the global marketplace. Its approach has been "Thatcherite", weakening unions, and affecting wages, including overtime pay.

---

4 Pier, "Labor Rights in Chile and NAFTA Labor Standards: Questions of Compatibility on the Eve of Free Trade", 19 *Comparative Labor Law Journal* 185, at p. 225 (1998).

6. Asia

Asian employment law is extremely diverse, ranging from advanced capitalist, post-industrial countries to developing countries.

Working time is limited by a maximum workweek (Singapore prohibits mandatory overtime work).

Advance notice of dismissal is required, and severance pay of one month for each year of service is common. In collective dismissals advance notification, consultation with unions, notice to a government agency or even approval from a government agency, and standards for selection of employees for dismissal are required. Inducements to resign voluntarily are a favored option.

Written employment rules and policies are required in some countries, and must be distributed to employees and unions and to a government agency.

However, in some of the developing countries of Asia, child labor is not prohibited or regulated. Also, in some countries, enterprise zones have been established, where special rules, or no rules, apply.

7. Middle East

Religious issues and their interplay and affect on government and the government structure are a significant factor in employment laws in the Middle East.

The employment laws are protective of job security for citizens, and may make distinctions for non-citizens. Advance notice of termination is often required.

The rights of female employees are extremely limited, even in countries with laws that supposedly protect female employees (like Turkey). Pre-employment pregnancy tests assist employers to circumvent the duty to grant pregnancy leave. There are often big differences in the treatment of women in professional jobs compared to women in unskilled jobs.

8. Africa

Employment law in Africa is extremely varied; South Africa is similar to Europe while other countries have no employment laws at all. Some countries offer tax breaks to employers with job-training programs. Many countries have no social security programs or mandated severance pay.

C. ENFORCEMENT OF THE LAW

How the laws are enforced is often more important than what the laws do. Some countries are alleged to have weak or uneven enforcement of their laws (Chile, Italy, Mexico, and Turkey).

Italy, from the United Kingdom's perspective, is said to be willing to sign on to European Union Directives because Italy has little or no intention of doing much to enforce the Directives.

Enterprise zones (EPZ's) and trade and investment treaties between individual countries, on the other hand, can establish geographic areas or special exemptions from employment laws.

In some countries, like Eastern Europe and Russia, the laws can be more rigorously enforced against western investors.

D. WHO THE LAW COVERS

It is fairly typical worldwide that the employment laws often exclude public sector, managerial, domestic, agricultural, temporary, and contract employees. It is also fairly typical that the use of contract and temporary workers is becoming more widely used everywhere.

E. DIFFERENCES IN LEGAL SYSTEMS

The Common Law system as compared to the Civil Law system present some differences that should be noted. For example, in Europe, decisions of the European Court of Justice (ECJ) would be considered precedent by lawyers from Common Law systems.

However, since most countries of the European Union are Civil Law systems, the ECJ does not consider its earlier decisions binding precedent, and does not need to refer to them. However, members of the European Union must abide by decisions of the ECJ. This distinction can be confusing for lawyers from a Common Law legal system.

F. CONTRASTING TRENDS IN POST-INDUSTRIAL COUNTRIES AND IN DEVELOPING COUNTRIES

The status of unions presents an interesting counterpoint between post-industrial countries versus developing countries. Unions are weak and suppressed, in developing countries. Unions are weak, because they are not supported by the workers or by the government in some post-industrial countries. However, this lack of support by the government is different from active suppression (some might disagree). Post-industrial countries have a workforce, and an economy that is dependent on high skills which often coincide with intellectual independence and autonomy.

Western Europe approaches employment rights with a "floor" of protections for individual employees, but joins that with a program of collective protection. The United States has a much more individualized approach, with the barest of "floors", yet a reliance that where there is a union, it is the union and the employer that will negotiate a whole range of issues, much broader than in Europe.

Developing countries attempt to establish a "floor" of rights, but depending on their enthusiasm to create jobs and attract investors the rights may be temporarily ignored, and unions may be somewhat discouraged as impediments to job creation.

G. CONCLUSION

Beyond the scope of this chapter is the interplay of human rights and trade policy. In the view of developing countries, balancing job creation and employment rights can be very tricky. From the perspective of a country with a large number of very poor people, are so-called "sweatshop" conditions that bad compared with the workers' day-to-day existence? On the other hand, unscrupulous employers can take jobs away from higher paid workers in North America and Europe and move them to Asia and Africa where they know they can pay a mere percentage of the earlier salaries.

Another issue beyond the scope of this chapter is the difference between "human rights", as subscribed to in Europe and Canada, and "civil rights", as recognized in the United States. Human rights represents a broader spectrum of rights, and whether the United States will subscribe to that level of rights is yet to be seen.

This chapter has only been able to convey a small amount of information, suitable for those interested in this area to get a start. Often, the law leaves more unsaid than said, so assumptions should be avoided, and more information sought. Above all, readers are warned not to import reactions from home that may be inappropriate in a foreign setting.

CHAPTER 21
COMPENSATION FOR DISMISSAL UNDER ARGENTINE LAW

Mario E. Castro Sammartino
Attorney and Counselor at Law
Buenos Aires, Argentina

A. GENERAL PRINCIPLES

Among other labor guarantees, Argentina's National Constitution protects workers against unfair dismissal.[1] This protection has been achieved through a relatively stabile legal regime. According to this regime, after the expiration of the probation period, the employer is entitled to dismiss an employee without just cause at any time by simply paying compensation.[2]

A breach of duties that prevents the continuation of the relationship because of its seriousness is legally defined as just cause.[3] If the agreement is terminated because of the employee's breach of duties, then the employer need not pay any compensation.

The probation period lasts one month.[4] According to collective bargaining agreements, such period could be extended up to six months. An employer is allowed to take on an employee subject to a probation period only once. During the probation period, the employee shall enjoy the rights and bear the obligations proper to the category covered, union rights included. Any of the parties can terminate the relationship during this period without having to:

(1) Give prior notice;

(2) State just cause; or

(3) Pay any compensation.

---

1 Argentina's National Constitution, section 14 *bis*.

2 Contract of Employment Act, sections 231 *et seq.* Act number 25,013, sections 5–11.

3 Contract of Employment Act, section 242.

4 Contract of Employment Act, section 92 *bis*.

The employer and the employee are bound to make contribution payments to the welfare entities, for family allowances and to the work hazards security systems. They are exempted from the payment of contributions for retirement and pensions, for the National Institute of Social Services and for the National Fund of Employment.

Under Argentina's Labor Law, compensation for dismissal after the probation period depends on the employee's seniority. It amounts to 1/12 of the monthly salary for each month (or fraction exceeding ten days) of service rendered calculated on the highest salary normally and regularly paid during the preceding year or the period of service rendered if this is less than one year.[5]

The salary used to calculate the compensation shall not exceed three times the monthly amount resulting from the average of all the compensations stated in the Collective Bargaining Agreement applied to the worker, excluding seniority benefits. The Ministry of Work and Social Security must set and publicize this limit. For those workers to whom collective bargaining does not apply, the compensation limit shall be that which corresponds to the employer's economic sector.[6]

The compensation may never be inferior to 2/12 of the monthly salary irrespective of the duration of the employee's service.[7]

Whenever the dismissal is carried out without prior notice, compensation for lack of notice must be paid to the employee. This compensation is equal to:

(1) Fifteen days of salary for employees with more than one month and less than three months of seniority;

(2) One month of salary for employees with more than three months and less than five years of seniority; and

(3) Two months of salary for employees with more than five years of seniority.[8]

When the employee has more than one month and less than three months of seniority, the employer must give 15 days' prior notice. When the employee has more than three months and less than five years of seniority, the employer must give one month prior notice. When the employee has more than five years of seniority, the employer must give two months' prior notice. Such notice period commences

---

5 Act Number 25,013, section 7.

6 Act Number 25,013, section 7. In certain cases the compensation limit has been ruled to be unconstitutional (Second Chamber, Court of Appeals on Labor Matters, Tala, Julio C. v. Baker Hughes S.A. *et al*).

7 Act Number 25,013, section 7.

8 Act Number 25,013, section 6.

the day after the receipt of the corresponding notification.[9] During these periods, the rights and obligations arising from the contract of employment will continue between the parties.[10]

Where the employee has not been registered in the company labor books and the employee has previously requested that this be done, a special compensation will be payable. This involves 25 per cent of all salaries not registered and a doubling of the compensation due for seniority and lack of notice.[11]

Any dismissal undertaken on the grounds of race, sex, or religion will be considered discriminatory and will allow the employee to claim for a seniority compensation increased by 30 per cent and no salary limit of any kind will apply to the calculation of the payment.[12]

B. DISMISSAL IN CASE OF FORCE MAJEURE OR LACK OR REDUCTION OF WORK

The employer may dismiss the employee and need only pay reduced compensation equal to 1/18 of the monthly salary if the dismissal is due to:

(1) *Force majeure*; or

(2) Lack or reduction of work not caused by the employer.

The minimum compensation irrespective of time of service is 2/18 of the monthly salary.[13]

Such dismissals must begin with those employees with less seniority within every category of employees. Where workers started employment within the same six-month period, those will be discharged first who have fewer family burdens.[14]

Courts are especially strict when deciding whether *force majeure* or lack of work are in fact the reasons for the dismissals.

C. EMPLOYER'S BANKRUPTCY

When the employer is adjudged to be a bankrupt, labor relationships end within a period that may range from 60 days to four months. In this situation, the

---

9 Act Number 25,013, section 6.

10 Contract of Employment Act, section 238.

11 Act Number 24,013, sections 8–15.

12 Act Number 25,013, section 11, as amended.

13 Act Number 25,013, sections 7 and 10.

14 Act Number 25,013, section 10.

employees are only entitled to half the normal compensation according to seniority. If the employer has gone bankrupt on purpose, the compensation will not be reduced.[15]

D. PROTECTION FOR MATERNITY

Maternity enjoys special protection for the term of seven-and-a-half months before and after giving birth.[16]

To claim the protection, the woman worker must notify the employer of her pregnancy and prove it by means of a certificate issued by a medical doctor wherein as far as possible the anticipated date of delivery should be stated.[17]

To discharge a female worker without just cause during these terms, the employer is obliged to pay for a special compensation equivalent to one year's salary.

In such a case, the employer must also pay for the compensation due on dismissal without notice and for seniority.[18]

E. PROTECTION FOR MARRIAGE

There is also legal protection against dismissal for women who marry.[19] To claim the protection, the female worker must notify the employer in writing of her intention to get married and the prospective date of the marriage.

Marriage will be considered the cause of dismissal whenever it takes place within three months prior to the marriage or six months thereafter. The employer shall pay a compensation equal to that granted in case of dismissal for maternity cause. Case law has extended this protection also to male workers who get married.

F. FIXED TERM AGREEMENTS

A contract of employment may be entered into for a fixed term provided that the term is expressly fixed in writing and the type of tasks and activities normally require a fixed term of employment. This type of contract of employment may not be extended for a total period beyond five years' duration.[20] Upon the expiration of

---

15 Contract of Employment Act, section 251.

16 Contract of Employment Act, section 178.

17 Contract of Employment Act, sections 177 and 178.

18 Contract of Employment Act, sections 178 and 182. Act Number 25,013, sections 6 and 7.

19 Contract of Employment Act, section 180.

20 Contract of Employment Act, sections 90–93.

the term, compensation must be paid to the employee equal to 50 percent of the compensation according to seniority, provided that the period of the contract has not been less than a year.[21]

If wrongful dismissal occurs before expiration of the contract term, the employer must pay the employee not only such compensation but also the damages that the employee has incurred thereby.[22] Judges have considered "damages" to be a sum of money equivalent to the salaries the employee would have earned if he had worked until the expiration of the agreement.

G. SEASONAL AGREEMENTS

A seasonal employment relationship exists when the employee renders services only at certain seasons or portions of the year. During the work season, the employee will have all the rights and duties of a permanent labor relationship. During the recess between one season and another, the relationship is suspended but the labor tie remains.

The employer is obliged to give notice to the employee about his will to renew the relationship at least 30 days before the beginning of the season. Otherwise, the relationship extinguishes. The employee must express his decision to continue the seasonal work or not within five days after his receipt of the employer's notice.[23]

Where seasonal agreements are not renewed the employer must pay compensation equal to 50 per cent of the compensation according to seniority. In the case of wrongful dismissal while rendering services, the employer must pay the employee not only such compensation but also the damages that the employee has incurred thereby.[24]

H. TEMPORARY AGREEMENTS

Whenever a work shall be done or a service rendered due to extraordinary or transitory circumstances of the company or to certain extraordinary services, there shall be temporary contract of employment: the labor relationship begins or finishes with the performance of such work or service.[25]

As long as the work lasts, the employee shall have all the rights and duties of a permanent labor relationship and whether dismissed wrongfully be entitled to the seniority and lack of notice compensations.

---

21 Contract of Employment Act, section 250.

22 Contract of Employment Act, section 95.

23 Contract of Employment Act, section 98.

24 Contract of Employment Act, section 95.

25 Contract of Employment Act, section 99.

I. APPRENTICESHIP AGREEMENT

The apprenticeship agreement must have as its purpose the theoretical and practical training of the apprentice. This training must be proper according to a program under the agreement's term. An apprenticeship contract may be entered into between an employer and a jobless young person between the ages of 15 to 28 years for a minimum period of three months and a maximum period of one year.

The working week shall not exceed 40 hours. Upon the expiration of the agreement's term, the employer must give 30 days' prior notice to the apprentice or otherwise the employer will be obliged to pay half a month's salary as compensation. No seniority compensation is payable upon termination.[26]

J. COMPENSATION UNDER SPECIFIC STATUTES

Certain activities are subject to a specific labor regime through special statutes. When it comes to compensation for dismissal, the Traveling Salesman Statute[27] and the Construction Statute[28] are worth noting.

Apart from the ordinary compensations, the Traveling Salesman Statute provides for an additional compensation equal to 25 per cent of the seniority compensation and of the compensation due on dismissal without notice.[29]

The Construction Statute introduces a particular way of compensating a discharged construction worker. The employer is obliged to deposit, on a monthly basis, a sum of money amounting to 12 per cent of the worker's salary during the first year of the relationship and to eight per cent in the second and subsequent years. This money makes up an "Unemployment Fund" available for the employee at the end of the employment relationship.[30]

K. PROSPECTS

Aiming to lower high unemployment rates and the costs of delivering products and services, the current authorities have focused their concern on giving more flexibility to labor relationships.

Should this tendency continue during the next presidential period, we might expect legal reforms abolishing special statutes, reducing compensation for dismissal and creating new types of labor agreements with minimum or no compensation at the end of the relationship.

---

26 Act Number 25,013, section 1.

27 Act Number 14,546.

28 Act Number 22,250.

29 Act Number 14,546, section 14.

30 Act Number 22,250.

CHAPTER 22

KEY LABOR LAW ISSUES FOR DOING BUSINESS IN MEXICO

Juan Francisco Torres-Landa R. and Octavio Novaro H.
Barrera, Siqueiros y Torres-Landa, S.C.
Mexico, D.F., Mexico

A. INTRODUCTION

One of the key aspects of doing business in Mexico is always related to the question of how our labor environment can be easily explained to companies that are used to engaging in business under a legal framework that is significantly different when compared to the one found in their country of origin.

Although there are different labor topics that always need to be addressed when giving advice to foreign companies that wish to start and/or expand their operations in Mexico, two of the more recurrent topics that foreign companies must understand are:

(1) The consequences of acquiring an already established business from another company; and

(2) The conditions under which the labor relationship between any given employer and employees may be terminated.

Therefore, the following provides an explanation of the key legal aspects in these two topics.

B. EMPLOYER SUBSTITUTION

When an existing business is acquired as part of a normal corporate transaction, one of the main issues to consider has to do with the status of the labor force. Unless the seller expressly terminates all employees and pays them their corresponding severance, the buyer of the operating assets will be deemed to become the new employer of those employees until then working for the seller. Regulation of the employer substitution theory is mainly covered by the Federal Labor Law and to a lesser degree by the Social Security Law.

In the event of a stock acquisition, the target company will continue to have its same obligations as an employer, and the underlying employment conditions, salaries, and benefits cannot be changed by the new management.

It is possible, however, for the seller to agree to terminate all employees previously and give the new administration the flexibility of hiring people from the street under brand new employment conditions. In both cases, however, employees are protected by either safeguarding their existing employment conditions or by the severance payment that is due upon termination without cause.

In the case of an asset deal where the entire operating assets of a business are transferred, then a real employer substitution will take place. In these circumstances there are basically three different alternatives for the new employer to handle the labor obligations associated with the transaction:

(1) Recognition and continuation of existing employment;

(2) Termination with full severance; and

(3) Combined mechanism.

1. Recognition and Continuation of Existing Employment

If the substitute employer (acquiring company) wants to continue with the same operation that the former employer had, the buyer must prepare an individual communication for each of the employees whereby the substitute employer will recognize that the employee will be entitled to the same salary, benefits, and working conditions that he had under the administration of the previous management. The key in this transfer of rights is the recognition by the new employer of the employees' then existing seniority.

Thus, the substitute employer will be responsible for each and any obligation that the former employer had towards its employees. Nonetheless, the former or substituted employer will be jointly and severally liable for said obligations during the six months following the date when the employment substitution communication is delivered to each employee (or from the date the communication is handed to the Union when a Collective Bargaining Agreement exists).[1] Additionally, the joint responsibility will end after two years from the date the employer substitution took place.[2]

This mechanism would be advisable if the new employer has the intention to continue with the operation under the same conditions that were in place with the former or substituted employer. When a Collective Bargaining Agreement exists

---

1 Federal Labor Law, section 41.

2 Social Security Law, section 290.

that is duly registered with the corresponding Conciliation and Arbitration Board ("Board"), the new employer must notify that as of the date of the substitution, and the agreement will be applicable to the new employer.

In this case, the collective labor relationship will not be affected in any way and the Union and/or the unionized workers will still have the same rights and obligations set forth under the respective agreement.

The former employer should also register termination of employment with its employees before the Mexican Social Security System (IMSS) and the Low-Cost Housing Fund Institute (INFONAVIT). Likewise, the substitute employer should give those agencies the respective notice regarding its new employees. Thereafter, the substitute employer will be responsible for the payment of the respective fees to both the Social Security System and Low-Cost Housing Fund Institute.

In these matters, it is advisable to secure a document from both the Social Security System and Low-Cost Housing Fund Institute certifying any outstanding debt of the former employer to determine if there are any amounts that should be claimed from the old employer.

However, even if the document is available, both the Social Security System and Low-Cost Housing Fund Institute always reserve the right to audit the past five calendar year fiscal periods to verify if all applicable fees were timely and fully paid for all employees hired from time to time.

The substitute employer must also give prior notice to the Ministry of Labor regarding any machinery which use has already been approved for the prior employer by said Ministry, causing all registries to be registered under the substitute employer's name. Failing to file this notice could trigger some nominal fines.

Finally, we normally recommend execution of new Employment Agreements (where the same salary, benefits and working conditions that were in place with the former employer would be reflected) between the new employer and the employees, thus complying with section 25 of the Federal Labor Law and avoiding possible fines that can be imposed by the Ministry of Labor for failing to have such documents on file.

2. Termination with Full Severance

Another possibility is for the former employer to terminate the labor relationship with its employees by paying them full severance pursuant to the Federal Labor Law.

In this scenario, the new employer would have the complete liberty to hire any or all of the employees under new and more advantageous working conditions and benefits than those that were granted until then by the former employer.

If this path is followed, it would also be necessary to negotiate the termination of any Collective Bargaining Agreement with the respective Union, as well as to file the respective forms before the Social Security System and Low-Cost Housing Fund Institute giving notice of the termination of the labor employment.

One of the main advantages of this option is that there will be no need to recognize the employees' respective seniority given that a completely new labor relationship would be established. Evidently, the adoption of this alternative will have an automatic consequence on the pricing arrangement between the parties considering the increased closing costs for the seller. The attractiveness of not inheriting employment burdens may nonetheless validate the alternative and may ultimately result in the costs being split in some negotiated percentages.

3. Combined Mechanism

A third option is a combined mechanism whereby the former employee would only pay the employees the amounts due to each of them at the time of termination (such as unused vacations, vacation premium, or Christmas bonus) and would compensate the elimination of other benefits, but without considering any severance payment. As a result, the new employer would have to recognize the respective seniority of each employee, albeit new working conditions, benefits and salary could be established without future negative repercussions for the employer.

Evidently, and in order to secure either of the options contemplated under subsections (2) or (3), the former employer would have to enter into individual negotiations with each of the employees in order for each of them to accept the termination of the labor relationship.

As regards the aforementioned options, we consider that the most appropriate and advisable for any substitute employer would be the one analyzed under subsection (2), since it would enable the new employer to start operations without any of the pitfalls or disadvantages that the former employer may have faced. If this is the case, it would also be advisable to sign a Collective Bargaining Agreement with a friendly Union in order to protect the company from a possible strike claim filed by a hostile Union precisely on the basis of the absence of such agreement (a valid cause under the Federal Labor Law).

C. EMPLOYMENT TERMINATION UNDER MEXICAN LABOR LAW

Another important aspect to consider when any individual or corporation is analyzing the possibility of starting operations in Mexico is the different scenarios under which a labor relationship with any given employee can be terminated and the possible consequences each of the options may have for the employer.

According to the Federal Labor Law, the labor relationship between an employer and any of its employees can be terminated for any of the following causes.

(1) Mutual agreement of both parties;

(2) Termination with cause by the employer;

(3) Termination without cause by the employer;

(4) Termination for the worker's complete disability deriving from non professional risks; and

(5) Termination with cause by the employee.

1. Mutual Agreement of Both Parties

If the worker signs a resignation letter it will be effective on the date it is signed by the employee and delivered to the employer. Employers cannot benefit from post-dated resignation letters or employees who continued to work after tendering those letters.

In addition to the resignation letter, the relevant employee should also sign a full receipt prepared by the employer, establishing that the employee is being paid all amounts due at the time termination takes place, such as unused vacations, vacations premium, the proportion of the Christmas bonus, and due salaries.

In case the employee has been working for the employer for 15 years or more, he would also be entitled to receive payment of a seniority premium equal to 12 days of salary for every year of services rendered. A ceiling of twice the general minimum wage in force at the time this seniority premium is paid applies.[3]

2. Termination with Cause by the Employer

There are a limited number of 15 causes under which an employer can terminate an employee without responsibility.[4] There are no other causes for the employer to terminate an employee without triggering a severance payment obligation.

In this scenario, the employee will also have the right to receive payment of any then due benefits (such as vacation, vacation premium, and Christmas bonus) although, in this case, every worker receives the seniority premium, even if they have been working for less than 15 years for the company. In the case of employees passing away, the benefits should also be paid to their heirs.

---

[3] Federal Labor Law, section 486.

[4] Federal Labor Law, section 47.

In all of these cases of termination for cause, the employer must have all elements to demonstrate in court (if needed) that the termination is valid. If an employee files a claim before the Labor Board arguing having been dismissed without cause, the employer will have the burden of proof to evidence that the termination was justified.

3. Termination without Cause by the Employer

In addition to the payment of the benefits mentioned above with respect to termination by the employer with cause (including the seniority premium for any worker, even if they have been working for less than 15 years for the employer), the employee who is terminated by the employer without cause is also entitled to the payment of three months of integrated salary and 20 days of said salary for every year of services rendered. These amounts together constitute the severance payment mandated by the Federal Labor Law.

The severance payment is based on the integrated salary of the respective employee,[5] which should be calculated in accordance to the Federal Labor Law, section 89. The integrated salary consists of the base salary that the employee has been receiving up to the termination date, plus the *pro rata* share of any benefit, bonus, premium, or any other amount being received for his services.[6]

Additionally, the employer must also pay an amount equal to 20 days of integrated salary for every year of services the employee has rendered.[7] This amount is established by the Federal Labor Law when the relevant employee wishes to be reinstated in his work and the employer refuses to do so.

Even though this payment is not clearly specified in the case the unjustified termination is handled directly by the company and documented in a private manner, it has become customary practice in our country that in order to avoid further litigation, these 20 days of salary are taken into consideration at the time the severance payment is agreed upon and delivered.

An employee being terminated is also entitled to receive the payment of the seniority premium — 12 days of salary for every year of services rendered. Similarly, the employer must also pay any amount that is due to the employee at the time of termination, such as unused vacations, vacation premium, pro-rata sum of Christmas bonus, and earned salaries or any other benefit which may have been established in his favor, such as a savings plan or food coupons.

---

5 Federal Labor Law, section 48.

6 Federal Labor Law, section 84.

7 Federal Labor Law, sections 49 and 50.

Regarding benefits other than the employee's salary, the Federal Labor Law establishes the minimum benefits that should be covered to any given employee rendering services in our country. These minimum benefits are:

(1) The payment of Christmas bonus equal to at least 15 days of salary per complete year of services;[8]

(2) At least a six-day period of paid vacations for his first year of services;[9] and

(3) A vacation premium that should be at least equal to 25 per cent of the salary that should be paid during the vacation period.[10]

Other than the above, the employee will have no right or action to demand an additional payment of any kind, unless the employer has agreed to payment of additional concepts (such as a savings fund, food coupons, and bonuses).

Usually, the severance and other benefits are all paid at the exact moment of termination. A deferred payment will depend on the disposition of the employee and/or the approval of the Conciliation and Arbitration Board.

4. Termination for Worker's Complete Disability Deriving from Non-Professional Risks

In case of termination for worker's complete disability deriving from non-professional risks, the worker will have the right to the benefits entitled to a worker terminated by the employer with cause, plus one month of integrated salary and the grant of a disability pension by the Social Security System, which is regulated by the Social Security Law.

5. Termination with Cause by the Employee

An employee can justifiably terminate his labor employment with an employer if the latter incurs in any of the conducts established in the article (i.e., if the employer fails to timely and/or fully pay the employee's salary and/or benefits).[11]

If the employee decides to terminate his employment with cause, he will have the burden of proof in order to demonstrate that there was a justified cause for this action. If the employee succeeds in demonstrating the situation, he would be entitled to the payments contemplated for termination by the employer without cause; if

---

[8] Federal Labor Law, section 87.

[9] Federal Labor Law, section 76.

[10] Federal Labor Law, section 80.

[11] Federal Labor Law, section 51.

the employee fails to prove this, then payment will only consist of those concepts contemplated in the case of termination by mutual agreement of the parties.

D. CONCLUSIONS

Mexican labor laws differ significantly from rules in other countries governing the relationship between employers and employees. However, the problems usually faced by investors in Mexico do not have to do with unreasonable standards, but rather with the lack of awareness of the applicable standards and compliance with formalities.

All employers must exercise care in the proper management of their labor relations. Employer substitution and employment termination rules are two of the areas where most frequently mistakes are made and where the learning curve for lack of proper preventive advice may be costly.

CHAPTER 23
PROTECTION OF DISABLED EMPLOYEES IN ITALY

Tiziano Membri
Studio Legale
Milan, Italy

A. INTRODUCTION

Knowledge of local law with respect to protection and privileges accorded to certain classes of persons can be important when making international acquisitions and acquiring a local workforce or when setting company employment policies. In many jurisdictions, disabled persons are treated as a protected class for employment purposes. This is the case in Italy.

Besides statutes dealing with the employment of workers who have specific disabilities, Law Number 482 of April 2, 1968, has regulated the employment of disabled workers generally. In 2000, another statutory layer will enter into force and add to the protection afforded to persons with disabilities.

B. DISABLED WORKERS

Law Number 482 of April 2, 1968 (Law Number 482) provided that the Italian companies employing more than 35 employees were obliged to hire disabled workers in a percentage equal to 15 per cent of the workforce. Under Law Number 482, the workforce did not include:

(1) Apprentices;

(2) Young people employed with a *formazione lavoro* contract;

(3) Workers who belong to the so-called "weak categories";

(4) Workers employed with a "reinstatement contract";

(5) *Dirigenti*;

(6) Workers with a fixed-time contract;

(7) Workers belonging to a cooperative of workers to which they are associated; and

(8) Other disabled workers.

Apprenticeship contracts are only for workers under 24 years old whose goal is vocational training. Such contracts may have a duration ranging from 18 months to four years. The *formazione lavoro* contract is a particular kind of contract only for workers under 32 years of age, which may last only up to two years, whose goal is a more sophisticated vocational training.

"Weak categories" include other protected categories of workers, which are rather uncommon and not worth further consideration here. "Reinstatement contract" workers are those that have already been dismissed by other employers and who have a right to be reinstated as soon as possible. *Dirigenti* are executives (qualified by the performance of management functions).

Under Law Number 482, disabled workers were defined as individuals who have some physical disabilities or deficiencies, whether stable or progressive, that reduce by at least 45 per cent their capacity to work. In general, Italian laws protect disabled people who find it difficult to integrate socially and in the workplace and whose disability causes them social disadvantages and to be marginalized. Italian laws also acknowledge that the disabled may have many difficulties to learn skills and their disabilities may diminish their capacity to have full human relations. People with disabilities may face many more problems than "other" workers.

Disabled people were, under Law Number 482 (and, under the new Law, still are), therefore allowed to enroll in special employment registers. These lists differ according to the different kinds and origins of the handicaps. A medical panel appointed by the local prefect (*prefetto*) evaluated the degree of disability.

Certain individuals were not allowed to enlist in the above-cited registers:

(1) Persons who were more than 55 years old;

(2) Persons who were totally unable to work;

(3) Persons who could cause damage to the other workers' health because of their disability; and

(4) Persons who were dangerous to the safety of the equipment and the plant.

If an employer intended to hire a disabled employee, it could make two different types of application:

(1) Numerical application — the only requirement was the specification of the category of worker (blue collar or white collar); or

(2) Nominative application — only for clerks (*personale di concetto*) and more skilled workers, having a position of trust such as supervision or custody duties.

In the event that the disabled employee had worked for another employer for at least one year, his new employer could hire him or her with the so-called "direct passage" from one employer to the other. This entailed fewer bureaucratic obstacles.

The employment agreement for disabled employees could have an undetermined duration or a fixed duration, or even part-time, or *formazione lavoro*.

Under Law Number 482, the employer was obliged to send an official form to the local Labor Office (*Direzione provinciale del lavoro*) every year to notify the percentage of disabled workers hired at that moment. All notifications had to be dispatched before January 31. If the employer failed to notify the percentage of disabled workers, the local Labor Office sent a written warning to the employer, so that it could regularize its position. The local Labor Office also fixed the term by which the employer was obliged to abide in giving the written warning. If the employer did not respect such term, it was sanctioned with a fine ranging from Lit. 5,000 to Lit. 50,000.

The employer had to apply to the local employment office (*ufficio di collocamento*) to hire disabled workers. As soon as the employer notified that it did not meet the percentage of disabled workers required by Law Number 482, it was obliged to file an application with the employment office to hire additional disabled workers. Otherwise, the employer would be sanctioned with a fine linked to the number of workdays and vacant positions according to Law Number 482. The fine ranged only from Lit. 1,500 to Lit. 3,000 per day and per vacant position.

The employer had no possibility of rejecting the disabled employee (i.e. refusing to hire him/her) only on the basis that a suitable position could not be found inside the company. If the employer refused to hire a disabled employee, he was ordered (in the event of litigation) to pay him or her compensation in the form of damages. The employer could be totally or partially exempt in the following particular cases:

(1) Due to the special nature and/or condition of his/her business;

(2) On the basis of a certified situation of crisis:

   (a) Due to restructuring, conversion or reorganization of production;

   (b) During extraordinary administration;

   (c) When the *Cassa Integrazione Guadagni Straordinaria* (special treatment providing unemployment benefits) — intervention was inevitable; and

(3) By virtue of being a maritime or aviation company.

The employer could dismiss the disabled workers for:

(1) Just cause or justified reason (as defined by case law);

(2) Total loss of capacity to work; or

(3) Worsening of the health condition if such condition became dangerous for the other workers' health and for the safety of the equipment and the plant.

When the employer dismissed a disabled employee, that same employer had to inform the local Labor Office within 10 days, so the local Labor Office could possibly send another disabled employee to such employer to be hired. The economic and legal treatment of disabled employees was the same as for all the other workers.

As a matter of fact, the appreciable purposes of such law were neglected. In most cases, the company just refused to hire the disabled worker who, in turn, started litigation. Such litigation was usually settled between the parties by means of the payment of damages to the worker. The sanctions imposed were so minimal that they were not detrimental enough to effect the employers' decision to reject disabled employees.

After many proposals and bills, the Italian Parliament finally enacted a new piece of legislation reducing the number of disabled workers to be hired but at the same time increasing the sanctions for the employers.

C. NEW LAW FOR DISABLED WORKERS

Law Number 68 containing the rules for the so-called "compulsory hiring of disabled workers" (Law Number 68) was enacted on March 12, 1999, and now replaces Law Number 482. Law Number 68 was to come into force on January 17, 2000. Law Number 68 provides that those employers who employ:

(1) A number of workers ranging from 15 to 35, must hire one disabled worker;

(2) A number of workers ranging from 36 to 50, must hire two disabled workers; and

(3) More than 50 workers, must hire disabled workers equal to seven per cent of the workforce.

Law Number 68 establishes general rules and does not abrogate the specific laws governing particular kinds of disabled workers, such as the laws providing the rules for blind switchboard operators,[1] for blind masseurs and massotherapists,[2] blind physiotherapists[3] and blind teachers,[4] which are still in force.

D. HIRING

As soon as the employer reaches the number of employees required by Law Number 68, it will be obliged to file an application with the proper Regional Office (which are yet to be created by means of regional laws) to hire the required number of disabled workers. The application must be sent within 60 days of reaching the above-mentioned numbers of employees.

The employers not fulfilling such filing obligation will be sanctioned with a fine of Lit. 100,000 to be multiplied for the number of workdays and vacant positions. The Italian Labor and Social Security Ministry will adjust such sanction every five years.

The employer is obliged[5] to send an official form to the Regional Office notifying the total number of workers hired in that moment, the number and the names of the workers included in the so-called "reserve quota", the number of vacant positions and the tasks available for disabled workers. Such form is to be considered as an application to hire disabled employees in the event that the required quota is not met.

The Regional Office will then work in connection with the local public, health, educational and formative services to take care of the programming, implementation and verification of the interventions made to favor the placement of disabled employees, and also the hiring, listing, the authorizations and exemptions issuance and the stipulation of conventions.

If the employer fails to notify such data, it will be sanctioned with a fine of Lit. 1-million, and Lit. 100,000 for every day of delay. All the fines will be assigned to the *Fondo per l'occupazione dei disabili* (a special fund that subsidize disabled workers).

---

1 Laws Number 113/1985, Number 594/1957, Number 778/1960, Number 155/1965, Number 231/1967, and Number 397/1971.

2 Laws Number 686/1961 and Number 403/1971.

3 Law Number 29/1994.

4 Law Number 270/1982, article 61.

5 Legislative Decree Number 469 of December 23, 1997, article 4, which grants the regions the powers to implement provisions of Law Number 68.

For the purposes of Law Number 68, the workforce does not include:

(1) *Dirigenti*;

(2) Workers with fixed-term contracts;

(3) Workers belonging to a cooperative of workers to which they are associated;

(4) Workers who became disabled in the course of their employment, but only if their working capacity is lower than 60 per cent; and

(5) Workers who became disabled in the course of their employment and whose disability derives from their employer's fault.

In this case the employer's responsibility for the employee's disability must have been ascertained by a final court judgment assessing the employer's breach of safety and sanitary regulations.

Dirigenti are executives (qualified by the performance of management functions). Workers with fixed-time contracts are only excluded if the term does not exceed nine months.

To calculate the number of workers, part-time workers with no fixed-time contract must be calculated on the basis of the effective hours worked, taking into account the fact that the number of hours is fixed by the collective agreement of each specific sector.[6] According to Law Number 68, disabled workers are:

(1) Individuals of working age (over 15 years old) who have some physical or sensorial disabilities or deficiencies that reduce their capacity to work by more than 45 per cent;

(2) People not fit for work due to previous work accidents who have a diminution of their capacity to work of more than 33 per cent;

(3) Blind people;

(4) Deaf and mute people; and

(5) War-disabled civilians disabled through war and disabled for service with a disability referred to in the first to eighth category on the table enclosed to the act concerning war pensions, approved with President of the Republic's Decree Number 915 of December 23, 1978, as amended.

---

6 Law Number 300 of May 20, 1970, article 18(2).

The degree of disability of persons is evaluated by a medical panel[7] on the basis of a table that contains the various disability percentages[8] approved by the Ministry of Health according to the international classification of disabilities elaborated by the World Health Organization. The unfitness of people to work due to previous work accidents is ascertained by the Italian national institute for work accidents and insurance and professional illness (INAIL) on the basis of the dispositions in force from time to time.

Law Number 68 defines blind people as those who are completely blind and those who have residual eyesight not more than 10 per cent in both eyes in spite of sight correction. Law Number 68 refers to those people who are deaf and mute at birth or who have become mute after their birth but before learning the spoken language.

In the quota reserved to disabled workers, two categories of people may also be included. The first category favors particular kinds of workers who are referred to in special laws, and particularly:

(1) Blind switchboard operators[9] for the employers who have more than five city telephone lines;

(2) Blind masseurs and massotherapists;[10] and

(3) Blind physiotherapists.[11]

The second category concerns only the employers who employ more than 50 workers. They must hire one worker from among the following people:

(1) War orphans and individuals who became orphans by reason of work or service accidents;

(2) Widows or widowers by reason of work or service accidents; or

(3) Italian fugitives returned to Italy.

Disabled people are therefore allowed to enlist in a special employment list kept by the Regional Office. Every Italian region, on the basis of the guidelines adopted by the Italian Prime Minister, fixes the criteria to form such list.

---

7 Law Number 104 of February 5, 1992, article 4.

8 Legislative Decree Number 509 of November 23, 1988.

9 Law Number 113 of March 29, 1985.

10 Law Number 686 of July 21, 1961.

11 Law Number 29 of January 11, 1994.

A nominal request for a specific employee is possible for:

(1) Every hiring when the number of workers ranges from 15 to 35;

(2) Fifty per cent of the hiring when the number of workers ranges from 36 to 50; and

(3) Sixty per cent of the hiring when the number of workers is higher than 50.

It is possible to obtain an exemption from the obligation to hire disabled workers in the following cases:

(1) When the application of *Cassa Integrazione Guadagni Straordinaria* (special treatment providing benefits to the unemployed) is inevitable and the Italian Labor and Social Security Ministry consequently concedes a *Trattamento straordinario di integrazione salariale* (an extraordinary treatment to integrate salaries); and[12]

(2) When the company is subject to *procedura di mobilità* (collective dismissal proceedings after the situation provided for above).[13]

Trattamento straordinario di integrazione salariale is granted:

(1) On the basis of a certified situation of crisis;

(2) On a restructuring, conversion or reorganization of production; and

(3) On bankruptcy, composition with creditors, administrative forced sale and extraordinary administration.

Such exemption persists during the entirety of such extraordinary treatment. The employer may be partially exempt because of the special nature of its business in the following two particular cases:

(1) Public transportation by land, sea and air; but the exemption applies only to traveling staff; and

(2) *Impianti a fune* (telpherage systems), only for staff working in the operative area to fulfill transportation duties.

In all the other cases of partial exemption, usually due to the impossibility for the employer to hire the entire percentage of disabled because of the special nature

---

[12] Law Number 223 of July 23, 1991; and of Law Decree Number 726 of October 30, 1984, articles 1 and 3.

[13] Law Number 223 of July 23, 1991, articles 4 and 24.

of its activity and/or condition of its business, the employer must file an application and must pay Lit. 25,000 for each workday and for each vacant position as a contribution to obtain the exemption.

The Italian Labor and Social Security Ministry will fix the criteria, the principles, and the formalities for the exemption by means of a decree.[14] In any event, the exemption is granted only on the basis of sound justifications.

E. AFTER HIRING

Disabled employees' economic and legal treatment must be the same as that of all the other workers according to the law and the applicable collective bargaining agreement.

When the employer dismisses a disabled employee, it must inform the local Labor Office within 10 days, so that the Regional Office may send another disabled employee to such employer.

It is possible for the employers to enter into particular conventions with the Regional Office so as to agree on particular conditions to hire disabled workers. This convention may include programs to facilitate the integration of the disabled workers in the working environment (for example, training with formative purpose and trial periods longer than those provided for by collective bargaining agreements.

The employer may ask for a verification of the health conditions of a disabled worker in relation to his/her position inside the company only in the presence of:

(1) An apparent aggravation of the disabled worker's health conditions; and

(2) A significant change of the work organization.

A medical panel will evaluate such health conditions[15] on filing of an application by the employer. For the same reasons, a disabled worker may ask for the verification of the compatibility of his/her duties with his/her health conditions.

F. COMMENTS

It is too early to verify whether Law Number 68 will have a more positive impact than Law Number 482 on the actual integration of disabled employees into the

---

[14] The Decree was to be issued within six months of the publication of Law Number 68, i.e., by September 23, 1999, but it has not been issued yet.

[15] Law Number 104 of February 5, 1992, article 4.

Italian labor system. The evident purpose of the new law is to render it easier for a company to hire a disabled worker while at the same time imposing heavier penalties in case of non-compliance.

A problem already arises in respect of those companies whose activities are particularly sophisticated and require extremely skilled workers. In such cases, only experience will give an answer as to the actual application of Law Number 68. Once again Italian labor laws are proof of the attention and carefulness that the Italian legislator pays towards the rights of the disabled with the enactment of *ad hoc* legislation. International employers establishing in Italy will need to pay similar attention to the results of the Italian legislature's concern for disabled workers.

Note: The author thanks Simona Lazzati for her assistance in drafting this chapter.